T0346330

SOLO INTO THE
RISING SUN

THE DANGEROUS MISSIONS OF A
U.S. NAVY BOMBER SQUADRON IN WORLD WAR II

ED KITTRELL

STACKPOLE
BOOKS

Guilford, Connecticut

Published by Stackpole Books
An imprint of The Rowman & Littlefield Publishing Group, Inc.
4501 Forbes Blvd., Ste. 200
Lanham, MD 20706
www.rowman.com

Distributed by NATIONAL BOOK NETWORK

British Library Cataloguing in Publication Information available

Library of Congress Cataloging-in-Publication Data
Names: Kittrell, Ed, 1948– author.
Title: Solo into the Rising Sun : The Dangerous Missions of a U.S. Navy Bomber Squadron in World War II / Ed Kittrell.
Description: Lanham : Rowman & Littlefield Publishing Group, 2020. | Includes bibliographical references and index. | Summary: "The bomber squadron VPB-117—the Blue Raiders—unique not only because its B-24 Liberators flew for the U.S. Navy and not the army, but also because most of the Raiders' missions entailed bombers venturing out over the Pacific, alone, to seek and destroy on long-range missions of a thousand miles out and a thousand back, often at altitudes close enough for sea spray to cloud their windows"— Provided by publisher.
Identifiers: LCCN 2019048510 (print) | LCCN 2019048511 (ebook) | ISBN 9780811739207 (cloth) | ISBN 9780811769129 (epub)
Subjects: LCSH: United States. Navy. Bombing Squadron, 117 | World War, 1939–1945—Aerial operations, American. | World War, 1939–1945—Pacific Ocean. | B-24 (Bomber)
Classification: LCC D790.263 117th .K58 2020 (print) | LCC D790.263 117th (ebook) | DDC 940.54/5973—dc23
LC record available at https://lccn.loc.gov/2019048510
LC ebook record available at https://lccn.loc.gov/2019048511

"Remember them. To think of them in their flesh, not as abstractions. To make no generalizations of war or peace that override their souls. To draw no lessons of history on their behalf. Their history is over. Remember them, just remember them—in their millions—for they were not history, they were only men, women and children. Recall them, if you can, with affection, and recall them, if you can, with love."
—MARK HELPRIN, *A SOLDIER OF THE GREAT WAR*

"There seem to be two quite different needs that produce war writing: the need to report, and the need to remember."
—SAMUEL HYNES

To Jeannie: as always, for everything

And for my sons

And in memory of Lieutenant Edward F. Kittrell, USNR, 1920–1980

Contents

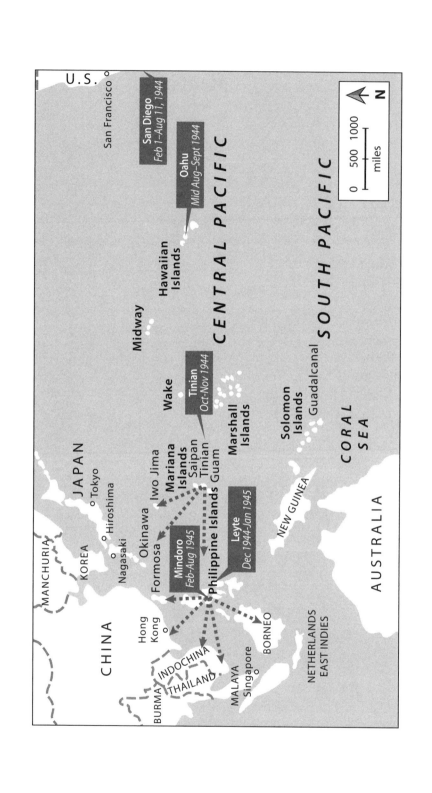

Preface

I had heard the stories. Or, rather, the shards of stories. Fragments broken off from a larger narrative never told. Rarely, and only late at night, with a tumbler of Hiram Walker at his right hand, Dad would suddenly start in the middle: "We get it down into this patch of grass. Everybody's OK. But now it's dark, and it turns out the army air controller told us to land behind the Jap lines."

Sometimes I had heard parts of the story before and could follow the trail as he wandered along. Other times it was new, or at least new to me, and I was lost from the first. Either way, back then it was like pressing a tinny transistor radio to your ear, trying to follow the broadcast of a ballgame through the static of a summer storm. A phrase or a fact, then silence. A sudden change in tone of voice. Gone again. Finally, nothing. What happened? Who won?

This book came about because, as Norman Maclean said, "children . . . like to know how things were before they were born, especially in parts of the world that now seem strange or have even disappeared but were once lived in by their parents."[1] For many of us, that time before we were born was World War II. In school we sat at wooden desks and memorized the names, Anzio to Okinawa. In movies we watched John Wayne and Henry Fonda refight the battles.

But we really wanted to know about the war our parents lived. And that remained mostly curtained off, by our fathers especially. We're not talking about men who had to be hospitalized with what later became the crisply clinical "posttraumatic stress disorder." We're talking about members of the Rotary Club. Ranchers and engineers. Teachers and coaches. They went to college, built businesses, ran for political office.

Part of their silence was a matter of manners. They had been taught it was bad form to talk too much about yourself. It also was bad form to talk about a host of other topics, from sex to mental illness. How much more distasteful was war and killing as a subject?

Especially for those who saw combat, there was something else too. The truth of that time in their lives was hard won. The boredom and bad food. The petty regulations. The moments of yawning, bottomless fear. The elation at finding yourself still alive and the guilt that came with it. You paid a price. Sharing all that too easily was like selling a family heirloom at auction. Only you and a few others knew its real worth. You didn't want to surrender it cheaply. You didn't want to devalue it somehow. Memory wasn't too painful; it was too precious.

Besides, many of the folks back home didn't want you to share too much either. Wives and parents and friends needed reassurance that you were all right. But usually they didn't press—partly from fear of "upsetting" you, partly from fear that the war itself was somehow a contagion and they didn't want to be exposed. That's understandable. In the end, soldiers do our killing for us. For that matter, they do our dying too. Both are subjects about which most people are squeamish. So when the men came home, a kind of quarantine on stories was imposed.

And it applied particularly to their children. Silence would shield us from things we should never have to know. Trying to get past all that years later was like doing archeology, chipping away at decades of accreted secrets, sifting for clues in shrugs or snatches of sentences. Whatever the story and whatever the reason, for me it always ended the same—in silence, Dad staring at the back of his hands resting limply in his lap. So we did as he did and put the war away, or tried to.

My father died a relatively young man, in 1980. Almost two years later, my youngest son, Andrew, was born. He had never known Dad, of course. But as a boy rummaging through the overstuffed attic in my mother's house, he came across the musty briefcase marked "Lt. (j.g.) E. F. Kittrell." It hadn't been opened in many years. Andrew undid the buckled leather straps. He pulled out the survival map of the western Pacific, printed on silk so it would float in the event of a ditching. He opened the flight log, no bigger than a prayer book. First he saw my infant crayon scribblings on the blank pages in the back. Then he began at the beginning. He saw names he'd never heard: Eniwetok, Owi. He saw terse, tense notes written in my father's hand: "Scrap with a Betty, guns jammed. Damn it." "Landed Mindoro, two minutes gas. Too close."

He wanted details, answers. I understood but couldn't help much. More years passed. Andrew went off to study history in college, and when it came time to choose a topic for his senior thesis, he decided to write about a navy squadron his grandfather flew with as a pilot in the Pacific.

A reunion of the squadron, VPB-117, was scheduled for that fall in Pensacola, Florida—the historic cradle of naval aviation. Andrew went, and I went along, mostly out of curiosity. On the first night, for the first time in my life, I spoke with men who had flown in Dad's crew. I met others he had mentioned decades earlier. At the memorial service on the final morning, I heard Dad's name read aloud, one of the many "missing" from the squadron. And I listened while a few dozen survivors, some frail with faltering voices, stood and sang the "Navy Hymn."

I had to know more.

In archives and other documents, in conversations with fliers and their families, in pieces and in time, I learned. VPB-117 was one of the navy's land-based patrol squadrons whose role has been mostly overlooked, even by the experts. They flew four-engine B-24 Liberators on long-range missions, a thousand miles out and a thousand miles back, on search grids that looked like spokes on a wagon wheel. And they flew solo. Unlike bombers in Europe, they had no massive formations or fighter escorts for protection. Each plane was on its own.

At the end of their search sectors, farthest from help and home, they defined the literal limits of American power. Squadron planes regularly flew over Iwo Jima six months before the U.S. invasion. They were still besieging Japanese targets in Borneo, Indochina, and China the day before Tokyo surrendered. Reconnaissance was the priority. But they could and did attack ships and planes, railroads and radar installations, oil storage depots and anything else the enemy owned.

Much of the time they shared the sky with the Japanese. To stay under enemy radar and to keep fighters from diving on them without crashing into the sea themselves, crews often flew a hundred feet or less above the water.[2] It was the same when they attacked enemy ships. There was no secret sight with crosshairs trained on a target miles below. Down on the deck, where ocean spray sometimes clouded cockpit windows, they released their bombs at masthead height with only a pilot's eye to guide them. Often they saw the faces of men manning guns and trying to shoot them out of the sky.

Many missions were routine, even boring. But the margin for error could be as thin as the airplane's skin. Some squadron bombers limped home shot up, short on fuel, or both. Some crashed on takeoff or within sight of the runway. Some ditched in friendly waters where survivors could be picked up. And some planes simply disappeared. They lumbered off into the predawn darkness and never came back. No sightings. No radio contact. No oil slick. Nothing.

Among patrol squadrons, VPB-117's record is especially impressive. One statistic: Pilots who shot down five or more enemy planes were officially designated "aces." In all the navy and all the war, only eight B-24 plane commanders earned that title. Five of the eight flew in VPB-117.[3] They were equally effective at destroying enemy shipping and targets on land. As a result, the squadron received a Presidential Unit Citation, the highest group award the military bestows.[4]

And they did it all despite serious handicaps. VPB-117 often was among the first squadrons to fly from forward positions. That meant taking off and landing overloaded bombers on unpaved, makeshift runways. It meant few spare parts and spotty maintenance, which meant routinely flying unsafe airplanes. It meant frequent encounters with the enemy, sometimes within minutes of taking off. It meant lousy living conditions and no fresh meat for months. To top it all off, for much of its tour the squadron suffered from bad, even bizarre, leadership. The resulting tension and morale problems only made the experience more harrowing. It all took a toll. Some men turned in their wings or feigned illness to avoid missions. Some refused to fly with certain pilots. Some suffered nervous breakdowns. But the missions kept coming. Days after hearing from his wife about the birth of a child he believed was not his own, one distraught pilot tried to dive his bomber into the ocean. Quick thinking by the copilot saved the situation. The pilot wasn't sent home. He wasn't sent to the brig. Before long, he was flying again.[5] There was work to be done.

So there are plenty of reasons to write and to read about this squadron. But the best reason is to learn more about the men themselves. Not just their troubles but their triumphs. And not just their time in the squadron but their lives before and after the war as well. A quick note: This is not a "how I found my father" book. Dad is a relatively minor character in the narrative. To me he was never a minor figure, and the war certainly wasn't a minor experience for him. It was a major event in his life, as it was for all of them. But his story is not the most dramatic.

The focus instead is on a number of men, a number of stories. And it's told as much as possible from their point of view. I have never fought in a war and never been in the military, and my total flying time in a B-24 amounts to thirty minutes. So I can only tell you what I've been told— by what few written records remain or by the men themselves and their families.

People who know say veterans of World War II began to open up more when they reached their sixties. Perhaps by then time and distance had helped put their experiences in perspective. In interviews more than one squadron member said, "I'm telling you things I never told my children."

But some still approached the war as if entering a dark room in their own home. The surroundings were familiar, even comfortable, but they could trip you up if you weren't careful. And by then, of course, these men were very old. From one reunion to the next, a friend's clear eyes turned cloudy, like a window warmed by breath. For many the light was fading fast.

Add to that the fact that war, memory, and truth have a long history of being at odds. Official reports and men's recollections disagree. Different people offer different accounts of the same event. A lifetime later, certainty becomes another casualty. Yet, at some point in time and in our minds, memory *becomes* fact—the shared truth from which we take our lessons and live our lives going forward.

Beyond men's living memories, I learned that the dead speak to us too. In faded letters and diaries. In personal memoirs written decades later.

And in blurry black-and-white, almost always smiling. Pasted together, it all forms a kind of collage.

The result is neither history nor literature nor journalism. Just stories, really. Postcards from a past truly foreign to us, where our parents spent some of the most important days of their lives and about which we know next to nothing.

The book tries to be faithful to that past and to that truth as it was told. War brings out cruelty, yes. It also brings out extraordinary acts of compassion, comradeship, and courage. The men in the squadron found that in each other, and most found it in themselves. They had become members of what we call "the Greatest Generation." The honorific is well earned, but it has the unintended effect of lumping them all together in a class, like the rows of repeating white headstones that symbolize their sacrifice.

Back then, though, they weren't icons. They would say they weren't heroes either. They were husbands and buddies and brothers and sons, like the young pilot writing his mother, reversing the roles, playing the parent, reassuring her that nothing bad would happen:

> Nothing to worry about, so rest easy. . . . This trip is certainly interesting and I wouldn't have missed it for the world. As Dad says the risk is worth the experience. It's rugged and we see some terribly gruesome things every day. We have the advantage and by being smart and <u>always</u> on the ball one has a good chance of beating the deal.[6]

He died two weeks later, before his letter even reached home.

That flier and the rest earned the right to have their stories told. Much has been lost—to regulations, accidents, and indifference. To death and to failing memory. And some was still captive in the hearts and minds of men who chose to stay silent. They earned that right too.

But much remains. And as children of these men, we have a special responsibility to see that it's shared. Because someday soon, we will be the only ones who remember them still young, back home and hopeful, new fathers in a new world they helped create.

When I was five or so, we lived in a beach house on the southern tip of Lake Michigan, in Indiana. Dad managed a Chevy dealership in nearby Gary, and most nights he got home after six. Sometimes before he ate, he asked whether I wanted to take a swim. I never said no.

We walked across the sand and waded in. When the waves reached my chin, he said, "Hop on." I crawled up his back and threw my arms around his neck, and he began a breaststroke. As he swam, he told me about survival drills in the navy, how he'd learned to stay afloat for days if he had to. There was a sandbar beyond the deep water, maybe a quarter mile out, maybe more. Dad took me there and had me stand in the suddenly shallow water.

We turned around. Off to our right, beyond the dunes, flames from the steel mills seethed. West across the water and behind, like a mirage, the lights of Chicago began to shimmer in the sunset. On the shore, our red-brick house looked so small, the distance we'd come so great. Every time we made that trip I was thrilled, but I was never afraid. If he'd asked, I would have gone with him at midnight or in the middle of a shrieking gale. I knew he would always make it. I knew he would never let me go.

War stories are finally not about war but about people. When the last of these fliers dies, the record of their lives will pass on as well, into history. The books will be closed. For a time after that, we, their children, will carry the knowledge of these men in our marrow. But that knowing will not outlive us. And when the last of us dies, the last of their children, a hundred years or more after Hiroshima, the war will finally be over.

There Was a Boy

The stories they tell are polished from handling, familiar as an old scar. And then, one day, they're not.

Late in his long life, it became hard for Bill Swink to squint at that summer sky in 1937. Alzheimer's had bleached the memory, like the sunlight he'd shaded with his hand. But once upon a time there was a boy, walking down a dirt road near his family's farm in Missouri. He had razored airplane pictures from newspapers, built crude models from sticks and scraps, yet never seen a plane in person. That day he heard it before he spotted it, droning in circles like a horsefly, high above a fallow field of grass. Stock still, he watched as the biplane sank to treetop level, the buzz became a bellow, and the pilot made a slow turn at the fence line. He was going to land! Right there!

A few times in a fortunate life we seem to rise from our seat in the shadows and step through the screen and into a movie of our own making, complete with clichés. Bill Swink tore through the tall grass and reached the plane just as the engine stopped and a tall man unhinged himself from the cockpit. He wore a leather helmet, goggles pulled up on his forehead, a leather jacket, silk scarf, jodhpurs, and riding boots. He smiled and asked whether this was the Swink place.

So it wasn't engine trouble. It wasn't a map mistake. This pilot had *meant* to land in Bill's backyard! Turned out his name was Carson Chalk, and, even more amazingly, he was a friend of Bill's father—a classmate and a fellow football player back in high school. He'd gone on to become a naval aviator, and after his time in the service, he'd stayed in Pensacola,

Florida, to open his own flight school. During the sweltering panhandle summers, he closed the school and took off north. He was hoping he could park his plane in the Swinks' field and take people up for rides on Sundays.

It was as if Charles Lindbergh himself had dropped from the sky. Bill became Carson's apprentice, patching holes, tightening wires, even helping tune the engine. And they flew together. Test hops, Carson called them. Lifting off, barely in the air, he would yank back on the stick and corkscrew into the sky. Fields unfurled below them; railroad tracks stitched the countryside. Nearby was the Mississippi, and they flew low over the river, the plane's tail twitching like a carp working its way upstream. Bill was hooked.

Summers never last long enough, and Carson Chalk never returned. But Bill never stopped trying to get back in the air. Two years later, a car pulled into the Swinks' yard. A man in a suit got out and introduced himself as a vice president of Parks Air College in East Saint Louis. He was here to interview William A. Swink, who'd applied for admission on a form in an airplane magazine. Bill's mother informed the man that "William," who'd left his age blank on the application, was a month short of his fourteenth birthday.

Not long after, the family moved into town, Cape Girardeau. And by the time he graduated from high school in 1942, Bill knew exactly what he wanted. The war was six months old, the army was looking for flight crews, and a cadet training program had opened at nearby Harris Field. He took the written tests and showed up for his physical, only to find that his weight was below the minimum required by regulations. He begged. He argued. A young corporal who did the weighing and measuring was sympathetic, but his crusty master sergeant stuck to the book. Bill went home and started eating. A month later, he showed up again. Still too skinny. His grandfather, a doctor, had a scale that also measured height, exactly like the one used at the army camp. Bill weighed himself every week. And once a month for four more months, he showed up at Harris Field, got weighed, and was turned away.

Finally that fall, the doctor's scale showed he'd passed the magic mark. Bill's grandfather said, "I'm not surprised. You've been growing like a weed." Oh, no! The army's weight requirements were tied to height. Bill stood again on the scale to measure how tall he'd become. He saw that because he'd grown, the weight that had been fine for his previous height was once again too low. But it was close. He was now maybe half an inch too tall. So he had an idea. Every day, he practiced standing up straight while bending his knees ever so slightly. He could do it without being noticed; he could do it for a long time without getting cramps in his legs. And it made him seem a half inch shorter. Back to camp. Bill mounted the scale; the corporal looked at the number and smiled. "Hey, Sarge," he said, "our fella has finally made it."

When he first told me the story many years later, Bill Swink stopped here and smiled. Maybe in his mind he was seeing that skinny kid in his skivvies. Maybe he was thinking of his time in VPB-117 or of the Distinguished Flying Cross back home in his bureau. Or maybe he smiled just because he knew what happened next. Because he said he still remembered the sound of boots crossing the plank floor. In his hand the sergeant carried a yard-long pointer, the kind used with wall maps. When he reached Bill, he stepped up, took the pointer, and rapped him across the shins, hard. "Stand up straight," he said. "Now measure him again," he ordered.

The half inch returned. "Aw geez," said the corporal, "how about giving the guy a break?" The sergeant sounded weary, spoke softly: "I'm just trying to save his life."

Bill Swink said nothing. He stepped down, balled his clothes, hugged them to his chest, and turned quickly toward the door. He did not want them to see him cry.[7]

Caught in the Current

They grew up in another time—another country, almost. As boys they played for hours without an adult ever interfering or even knowing exactly where they were. They had the run of their immediate world—barns and back alleys, ponds and fields and hideouts by the train tracks where you had to beware of the bums.

The Depression was their common denominator. Whether, or how much, their own families suffered was not what bound them. It was the bone-certain knowledge, as children, that bad things could happen to anyone. Events could swoop down like a dust storm and leave your life in splinters.

It was an in-between era. Locomotives steamed as they had for a hundred years, and horses still sometimes delivered the morning milk. But so much was so new. Almost all of them were born before Hollywood made its first talking picture. Yet by the time they were old enough to go themselves, movies were the way of American life. Fifteen cents got you inside the darkened doors, just in time for the newsreels. Politicians and athletes ten feet tall. And aviators!

Theirs was the first full generation for whom flight had always been a fact. One of their number would later break the sound barrier.[8] Another would be the first American to orbit Earth.[9] But back then flying was, like them, in its adolescence. The stories and images were larger than life: heroic, like Charles Lindbergh; mysterious, like Amelia Earhart. And every week, it seemed, there were new records. Farther, higher, and always faster. Often, the movies took up the narrative. David Niven and Errol Flynn in *The Dawn Patrol*: dashing and doomed British pilots in the Great War, back at base with whiskies in hand, singing the squadron song: "Here's a toast to the dead alreeeeady ... and hurraaaah for the next man who dieees." Clink![10]

That earlier war, in fact, never seemed quite finished. Not for their fathers, some of whom had been gassed or gutted by the slaughter they saw.[11] And not for those they fought either. The boys had watched that at the movies too. Newsreels showing the parades of banners in Berlin, Japan's rising sun eclipsing Movietone maps of Asia.[12] Politicians waved papers, promising peace. But few felt so sure. Despite the twists and turns, it seemed history was a river obeying its own gravity, falling always into the inevitable ocean. And sooner or later, everyone would be caught in the current.

Before the squadron, two stories: one of an enlisted man and one of a pilot.

When I became seventeen years old, I was a junior in the Brinkley, Arkansas, high school and working in Renick's Drug Store as a soda jerk.

In the spring of 1943, Gene Kern was the oldest of five brothers, his father's helper and his mother's pride. Art Kern had an eighth-grade education but was smart, strong, a hard worker. He'd been a mechanic, farmed, bought and sold scrap metal. His wife, Hazel, was beautiful, with auburn hair and an easy smile. She was a schoolteacher, with a college degree. They raised their sons first on a farm and then in small towns in Arkansas. Gene went barefoot all summer, wore bib overalls to school, and, on Sundays, put on corduroy pants to sing in the Methodist choir.[13]

The biggest event in his life so far had come when he was thirteen. Barnstormers brought one of the early passenger planes to town—a Ford Trimotor, sheathed in shiny aluminum. Gene and his dad drove out to see it and watched while people lined up to pay $5 for a ride. Gene asked whether he could go, and Art said no—it was a foolish amount of money to waste. Customers began boarding. Gene asked again. Still no. The pilot started the engines. Gene pleaded. His father put a $5 bill in his palm and said, "Go." He sprinted to the door beneath the broad wing. The seats were all taken, so Gene was told he could stand between the pilot and the copilot. He walked down the middle of the six rows, one seat on each side, straight to the cockpit.[14] The pilots threw the throttles forward; the tail wheel lifted. The engines belched blue flame from the exhaust; bright sunlight bounced off flooded rice fields. The whole thing lasted less than fifteen minutes.[15]

Pearl Harbor happened in the middle of Gene's sophomore year in high school. His shop class immediately began carving wooden models of planes for use in aircraft identification training for pilots. That year his dad also started a business selling steam boilers to lumber mills, and Gene found himself hanging from a chair, a hundred feet in the air, riveting a smokestack together.[16] In the fall the family moved to the nearby town of Brinkley, halfway between Little Rock and Memphis on Highway 70. Gene started his junior year as the new kid in school, tried out for the football team and didn't like it, and then got the job at the pharmacy.

Sometimes we only see a crossroads in the rearview mirror. If Gene had stayed in high school, he would have graduated in June 1944. Even if he had enlisted or been drafted right away, he would have been in training well into 1945; there is a good chance he would never have gone overseas or seen combat. But he wasn't thinking about that behind the counter at Renick's. He'd dated a little at his new school and made a few friends, but he wasn't fitting in. Plus, things weren't going well at home. Money was scarce, and his parents were arguing. Gene was restless, and anyway, boys his age don't really need reasons. One day he hitchhiked to Memphis and talked to a navy recruiter.

He had to get a parent's signature, and his father refused. Asking to go out and get killed was the stupidest idea he'd ever heard. It took a lot longer than getting the ride in the plane, but after two weeks of wheedling, Art Kern relented. Then he took Gene to a friend who had served in World War I. The veteran gave him three pieces of advice: don't make close friends, don't loan money, and watch out for crooked gamblers.

Art and Hazel drove Gene back to Memphis, all three in the front seat of the family flatbed truck, his mother in the middle. Not much was said. When they came to the intersection near the recruiting office, Gene said, "This is where I get off." His mother cried, leaned over, and kissed him. He opened the door and walked around to his father's side, where the window was rolled down. His dad took three $5 bills from his pocket. "I wish it could be more," he said, "but it's all I have." They shook hands, he started the truck, and Gene turned away.

After being sworn in, Gene spent the next two days in a hotel room: "There were six or eight of us headed for the San Diego Naval Training Station. I was green as grass. Most of the men with me were older. There were crap games going already in the hotel."

Gene kept to himself. The train trip to California took three days and nights, first through flatlands and then across the desert. Memphis was as far from home as he had ever been, so he got his first good look at America out the window. Mostly it was empty space speckled with sagebrush or back porches with peeling paint, as the train sat on sidings for hours at a time to let others pass. And, always, more crap games.[17]

When they passed through the boot camp gate, they were met by catcalls from sailors ("You'll be sooooorry"), followed by hours standing naked in line in front of doctors before they were issued sea bags and uniforms. Gene was assigned to Company 43-92, which meant his was the ninety-second company of 180 men to start boot camp in 1943—and it was only March. The place was a factory, and the foremen were chief petty officers. For the first three weeks they made recruits wear leggings, left over from the eighteenth century. No reason, navy tradition. They gave you a wooden board on which were written the Thirteen General Orders, arcane and complicated rules for standing watch that had to be memorized. They showed you which knots to use when you hung your clothes out to dry, and if you tied the wrong ones, they threw your uniform on the ground while the entire company marched over it.[18]

They marched everywhere, in fact. To the rifle range, to classes on firefighting or semaphore signaling, to the shower. They learned to stay in step on "The Grinder," a ten-acre blacktop square in the center of camp. One day the company was issued full field packs and marched five miles up a shifting, sandy beach to an amusement park with a big swimming pool and a twenty-foot tower. Gene and the others were told to jump fully clothed from the tower, tread water for ten minutes minimum, and swim the length of the pool four times. Then, while still treading water, they had to take off their pants, tie knots in each leg down by the cuff, put the pants behind their backs, bring them forward over heads, and fill them with air to make an emergency flotation device.

For three months they learned the rules, passed the tests, and endured the drudgery—or they didn't. Some walked out; some washed out. Most got by. And some, like Gene, jumped in with both feet. At one base he heard the record for sit-ups was three thousand. He tried to break it and was past two thousand when his buddy doing the counting got bored and left. It was the same in the classroom. A week or two before the end of boot camp, everyone took aptitude tests. Gene did well and was told to fill out a form listing his top choices for further training. He remembered the ride in the Trimotor and asked for Aviation Ordnance School in Oklahoma.

This was a twelve-week course, arranged by subject. One week on electricity, one week on hydraulics, with a written test every Friday. On Saturday at noon, everyone lined up on the parade ground for marching and inspection. If you passed, you were at liberty until Monday morning. Most weekends Gene stayed on base, but other times he took the bus to town and left his boyhood behind. There were beer binges, three or four guys going out together, one designated to stay sober and get everyone home while the others usually drank themselves sick.

Then there were girls—lots of them. Growing up, parents and preachers had drilled the rules of sex into their heads like multiplication tables or spelling lessons. But with the war on it seemed like everyone had been let out for recess, boys and girls alike. Because servicemen were not allowed on the streets after midnight, sailors rented hotel rooms and hoped for the best. One evening Gene and a buddy were approached by two women about their age who asked whether they would take them to dinner. At the restaurant the girls said they were from a country town about an hour away and had come to the city to earn money. One put her hand on Gene's leg and asked, "Have you ever been with a woman who sells herself?" He said no, he didn't believe in that. "You will," she said. Afterward, at the hotel, the women demanded $5 each. Gene and his buddy refused. The girls threatened to call the cops. The guys told them to go ahead. The next night they saw them again, with two other sailors.

The meetings were always random. Gene was on his way to church one Sunday morning when a blonde in her thirties stopped him on the street, pulled a bottle out of her purse, and asked where he was going. When he told her, she asked whether she could come along. After church they went to a movie, where she made her intentions plain. But she didn't have a place of her own, and Gene had to get back to base. They parted with a gentle kiss.[19]

About this time Gene was chosen to be an air crewman. It meant that instead of loading bombs onto a carrier or at a field somewhere, he would be in a dive bomber or torpedo bomber, maybe even a flying boat. It meant he would get flight pay. It meant he would get wings. It also meant he would get intimately acquainted with the Caliber .50 Browning Machine Gun M2 Aircraft, Basic. He was given a gunnery manual that told him the gun fired fourteen shots a second. The bullets left the barrel at almost two thousand miles per hour and could kill a man four miles away.[20]

The manual also showed him how to aim, using drawings of a news-boy on a moving bike throwing papers onto a porch:

> The first time he tosses a newspaper he discovers a simple fact: if he aims directly at a front porch, he misses, and the paper lands next door. The forward motion of his bicycle carries the newspaper forward too.

The trick, then, was to aim behind your target and let momentum take the bullets where you wanted them to go. Easy enough to understand on paper but harder to learn in practice. Out on the firing range, a small armor-plated locomotive ran endlessly around an oval track. Each side of the engine was covered with white sheets stretched on a frame. A half mile away, with petty officers pacing behind them, young men fingered the controls of the Browning for the first time. The trigger was on the right-hand grip, making things harder for left-handers like Gene. The slightest touch sent bullets by the dozens flying out the barrel. The first try was always a shock; ears rang, shoulders shook. Rounds arced high into the sky and spit dirt far in front of the target. It was frightening and, let's face it, fun. Gradually most learned how to focus on the white sheets circling the track. Rounds pinged off the little engine; bullets dipped in different-colored paint for each shooter helped instructors keep score. The next step was to squeeze into a bomber turret bolted to a flatbed truck that circled the track, sometimes in tandem with the little engine, sometimes moving in the opposite direction.

The final test came in South Carolina, when Gene finally got into the air. It was his first flight since the Trimotor four years earlier. Again they shot at sheets with different-colored bullets, but this time the targets were towed by airplanes. They flew Venturas, fast twin-engine bombers with top turrets and .50-caliber guns. Heading out over the ocean for the first time, Gene started feeling airsick. But he kept it in check and took his turn on the guns. His fellow recruit wasn't so lucky. When he announced he was going to be sick, the instructor told him if he got any vomit on the airplane, he would be grounded for good. So the sailor threw up in his hat and held it in his lap all the way home.[21] At the end of the course in South Carolina, ten months after he stepped out of the truck in Memphis, Gene took an oath:

> I am a United States Naval Aircrewman, member of a combat team. My pilot and shipmates place their trust in me and my guns. I will care for my plane and guns as I care for my life. In them I hold the power of life and death—life for my countrymen, death for the enemy. I will uphold my trust by protecting my pilot and plane to the absolute limit of my ability. So help me God.[22]

The navy then gave him his wings, a brand-new leather flight jacket, a seven-day leave, and orders to report to North Island Naval Air Station in San Diego.

He headed home to Brinkley and called up Margie Baker, the prettiest girl in school. They had dated a few times before. Gene drove to a secluded spot in the country, but Margie said she wasn't comfortable. The next day he heard that many in his class, now seniors, were meeting at a bar out near the airport that night. Gene shined his shoes and put on his dress blues. When he got there, Margie was dancing with a football player. Other boys were talking about ways to avoid the draft. The girls were mostly indifferent. He fit in even less than he had before. After fifteen minutes, he left quietly.[23]

A few days later, he boarded a train for another long ride to San Diego. The cars were crowded, just like before. He saw a couple stretched out in the aisle, making love under a blanket. No one paid any attention. Again, there were long hours spent on sidings. The scenery was familiar, but Gene was different. He wasn't a boy. He wasn't a virgin. He'd traveled from one end of the country to the other. And now he was on his way to war.[24]

Growing up, my big goal was to be the first in my family to graduate from high school.

Galen Bull did better than that, eventually becoming a college professor of physics. But first he grew up on a farm that had been in his father's family almost since the Civil War, walking to a country school with all eight grades in a single room.[25] He flew and fought in history's biggest conflict. Later, on a remote Pacific island, he watched the rainbow plume and felt the heat and the wind from a hydrogen bomb blast. Like so many in his time, he survived history's shock wave and succeeded beyond anything he might have hoped.

The first big step was high school in Wellman, Iowa, which seemed huge after his one-room schoolhouse. Galen played six-man football and graduated with thirty others in the class of 1938. He was just sixteen and wanted to go to the University of Iowa in nearby Iowa City, but corn was selling for five cents a bushel, and the money wasn't there. He settled instead for a nearby junior college. The summer after his first year, the school decided to offer Civilian Pilot Training (CPT), a government program to create a corps of trained pilots by helping students get their licenses. The classroom portion was taught by the dean of the college, who was getting a stipend for every student he enrolled. But the fun part came at the airfield just outside of town.

When old pilots say they "loved to fly," the romance was real. Airliners today can weigh more than four hundred tons; every landing is more like a controlled crash.[26] The two-seat Taylorcraft Galen learned on weighed seven hundred pounds. Light and limber, like a girl on a dance floor, it let you lead even when you didn't know how.[27] And when it landed, the plane hung barely in the air—a sigh, almost—before the wheels finally kissed the grass.

Galen's instructor, in fact, turned out to be a woman. Virginia Snodgrass was a member of the Ninety-Nines, the first licensed women pilots in America, and she had trophies from the prestigious Bendix Air Races across the country.[28] Her husband, Jack, was a pilot too, and even their six-year-old daughter could fly. But Virginia was the boss. Redheaded, freckle faced, and in her thirties, she brooked no nonsense.

Student and instructor sat side by side in the enclosed cockpit. On his first flight, Galen was in the air before he knew it, and then, one hundred feet above the field, Virginia cut the engine. Startled, he turned the control wheel to the left, hoping to point the nose back toward the field for a landing. "Don't ever do that," Virginia snapped. "You turn the plane without power, you'll spiral in." Trial and error was how she taught everything. There were stalls, the plane climbing an invisible rope straight up, gasping and wheezing, finally losing its grip and falling, only to catch itself on the way down. Galen learned to slip like a canoe through crosswind currents and over invisible rapids of turbulence. He navigated by compass and dead reckoning, a map showing rivers, railroads, and highways unfurled in his lap. Gradually he realized that if he relaxed and let the plane fly itself a bit, he actually had more control. Soon he began to see himself and the plane, not the ground or the sky, as the fixed spot around which everything revolved. When he banked, the horizon tilted, not the plane. He pointed the nose and the earth shrank or rose up. But he stayed still, in charge, the center of the universe.

Before his first solo, Virginia told him to "bring the plane back unharmed." When he did, two hours later, Galen was a qualified pilot, age seventeen. He went back to junior college and commuted from the farm, driving an old Model A past fields bearded with corn stubble. To help pay for school, he got a job on the midnight shift at a cement plant in Iowa City, stacking one-hundred-pound blocks as they came off an assembly line. And it was on the Iowa campus that he first saw posters with the slogan "Earn Your Navy Wings of Gold." The university had become part of the V-5 program, which offered flight officer training to men with two years of college. As a cadet you got a salary, clothing, room, and board. If you made the grade, you would be a commissioned officer and earn flight pay. In the summer of 1941, Galen signed up. He passed the physical, went back to school for the fall semester, and waited.[29] On December 7 he was washing a truck when he heard the radio broadcast. The letter from the navy arrived soon after, telling him to report for duty—on Christmas Eve.

Cadets lived in a dorm on the Iowa campus, four to a room. They came from all over the country and were called "ninety-day wonders" because the navy basically gave them three months to shape up or ship out. This was "preflight" school—no time in airplanes. Instead, the program had two areas of emphasis.

One was physical training. Swimming first thing every morning. Outdoor calisthenics in the snow wearing nothing more than gym shorts and shirts, teams pushing a four-foot-high ball back and forth through the drifts. Everything, in fact, seemed a competition—close-order drill, two-mile runs, the obstacle course. You never knew what was designed to weed you out, what was supposed to prepare you for the life-and-death challenges you could face in combat, or whether the whole thing was just an elaborate hazing before you were sworn into the fraternity of fliers.[30]

And then there was football. Some admiral had the bright idea that the Naval Training Centers around the country should field football teams of their own, playing a full schedule against established college programs. The players would be cadets, and there were rules prohibiting "concentration of personnel for the express purpose of building up a team rather than for the purpose of specific naval duties." But more than a few college and even pro players found their way into the programs and onto the rosters. The team in Iowa City was called the Seahawks, and the cadets were cannon fodder for the pros at practice. They managed to make it through, even sometimes to hold their own. But they also left more than a little blood on the snow.[31]

Besides conditioning and competition, the other big priority at preflight school was "learning the navy way." A thousand miles from the

nearest ocean, you couldn't say, "I'm going upstairs to the second floor."
You had to say, "I'm taking the ladder to the second deck." Every time you
saw an officer, you had to "brace the bulkhead"—stand at attention, back
against the wall, and salute. "By your leave, sir!" Many of the officers were
"factory boys" from Annapolis, and they treated everyone in the program
like plebes. You jumped to your feet whenever an instructor entered a
classroom. When you answered a question, you began by shouting "Sir!"
like a barking dog. You studied semaphore signaling, aircraft identification, Morse code. But you also attended entire lectures on the proper
way to salute. You learned there was even a "navy way" to shave. Some
resented the regimentation. They weren't draftees; they were volunteers.
They'd been to college and were going to be aviators. Cream of the crop,
they'd been told on enlisting. But the war at that point was only months
old, the shock of Pearl Harbor still as sharp as the smell of cordite. So as
winter wound down and March turned the fields to mud, some cadets
were culled. Some opted out. But most shouldered their sea bags and
moved on.

Galen's next stop was Hutchison, Kansas. The base was brand new,
the runway not yet paved, with mud, sand, and snow everywhere and
wind blowing across an ocean of prairie. Discipline was still stressed, but
it wasn't spit and polish like preflight. This was "E-base," the *E* standing for elimination. In the classroom they studied tactics, aircraft performance, and recognition.

The rest of the time they were in the air. The trainer here was an open-
cockpit biplane called the Stearman, also known as the "Yellow Peril."
If flying the Taylorcraft was like paddling a canoe, flying the Stearman
was more like swimming in the stream itself. You were immersed in the
air; stick a hand out, and you felt its force immediately. Before long you
could gauge your speed just by listening to the pitch of the wind as it
moved over the wings. The Stearman was faster and far more acrobatic,
but Galen's CPT training made it easier for him than for some others.
His instructor was a French Canadian named La Porte. Communication
inside the plane was through a device called the Gosport tube, nothing
more than a glorified garden hose with a funnel at one end. The tube
connected to holes in the student's leather helmet; the funnel was for

the instructor, who sat in front. The instructor could speak through the tube, but the student couldn't talk back. On many early-spring flights over Kansas, La Porte would shout into the tube, "I'm cold, how about you?" Galen would shake his head. La Porte would cut the flight short anyway, writing in his report, "Cadet was cold."

Galen got the hang of things quickly. They practiced touch-and-go landings in a circle painted on the ground to simulate conditions on a carrier. There were aerobatics, loops, crossovers, formation flights. If you failed twice at any task, you got a "down check" and went back for more training. This went on for months, and in the end maybe half the class, including several of Galen's friends, didn't make it. Morse code got some of them. Or swimming tests. Or airsickness. But mostly it was the flying they couldn't master. Failure was handled discreetly; usually the guy was gone before his friends even knew.

In the fall Galen was sent to Corpus Christi, Texas, for advanced training, the last stop before you got your wings. The routine was a half day of classroom work on subjects like navigation and a half day in the air. Most of the time they flew a single wing, open-cockpit plane, the SNV, known to students as the "Vultee Vibrator." Another step up from the Stearman, with twice the horsepower, it had full flight controls for students as well as instructors, plus an intercom so they could talk to each other. That was especially useful since the training included instrument flying. You began indoors on a Link trainer, learning how to use the artificial horizon on the gauges, how to turn and descend without a visual reference. Then you tried it in the real world, flying from Corpus to tiny Beeville with curtains over the windows in the cockpit. As before, this went on until you mastered the skills, mustered out—or crashed. In the year before Galen arrived, more than 550 aircraft accidents at the base had killed ninety-one cadets and instructors. In only two cases were the crashes caused by mechanical failure. All the rest were due to pilot error.[32]

Cadets were given a choice about what planes they wanted to fly. Galen picked carrier planes, but those slots were all full, so he was assigned to the flying boats. Soon he was hearing the tick-tick-tick as the hull of the PBY sliced through the wave tops before getting airborne. The P-boats were slow, but they could soar like a frigate bird and stay in the air more than twenty hours. Training flights covered the Gulf of Mexico, looking for patrolling American submarines but usually finding whales and fishing boats instead. They learned to search not by staring but by seeing from the corners of their eyes—movement, an unusual reflection on the water that shouldn't be there. Anything that broke the monotony of waves and wide horizons.

Finally, graduation day came. The navy said you "earned" your wings, but you actually had to buy them, just like every other part of your uniform.

They had all kinds, even some that were already tarnished to look like you'd been out in combat. The solid gold ones cost $70. Mine were gold plated and I paid $7, which was a third of one month's salary. I still have them, and they still shine.

The ceremony was held outdoors, and instead of listening to the speeches, Galen watched the seagulls whirl overhead, back from gorging themselves on gulf shrimp, dropping indelible crimson dung on the dress whites of one hundred or so new naval aviators.

From there he went for more months of operational training in Jacksonville, Florida. Instrument work, classroom time, practice dropping depth charges, bombing. Best were the overnight flights to the Bahamas. Landing their seaplane in the dark, phosphorescent plankton trailing their wake like the tail of a comet. They went deep-sea fishing and watched the familiar constellations turn over in the night sky like pages from a boyhood book.

At last word came: He was being sent across the country. A week later, Galen stepped off a train in San Diego, walked to the foot of Broadway, and reported to Combined Fleet Air, Western Pacific. A bored officer opened his file, looked through his records, and said, "You're going to Camp Kearny, outside of town."

"What's out there?" he asked.

"Bombers," the officer said. "Your new squadron."[33]

Pop

Ambition is both a sail and an anchor. It pulls you forward, helping reach goals you might otherwise not have set or met. But it also weighs you down with expectations, your own and others'. And in the end, you either sink or you swim.

Everett Olin Rigsbee Jr. was raised on the plains of West Texas, in Fort Stockton, where his father was an agent for the Santa Fe railroad. The second youngest of six children, three girls and three boys, "Ebb" was four hundred miles from the nearest ocean and had no known navy connections among family or friends. Yet he had a burning desire to attend the U.S. Naval Academy in Annapolis, Maryland.

His first application failed. Brains were not a problem. He and his siblings were all smart; during World War II his older brother would work as a code breaker. What Everett lacked was clout. So after high school he left for Texas A&M University, while his father prevailed on the local congressman. And the following fall, in 1926, he enrolled as a first-year student at the academy—a "youngster," in Annapolis parlance.[34]

The academy was a storied place with established norms and traditions, and the young Rigsbee loved it all. He played football for four years—but on the B team, not the varsity. Like his classmates of that era, he took summer "cruises" aboard navy warships—to Panama and the West Coast, to the East Coast and Cuba, across the Atlantic to Barcelona, Naples, and London.[35] He was a good, but not top, student—graduating 167th out of 405 in his class.[36] The Annapolis yearbook of 1930 featured profiles of each graduate, written by classmates in a sometimes cryptic, in-crowd style. Rigsbee's was fairly typical:

> In days of old, God created this tiny sphere, and then, to season the unleavened mass, He created Texas, the land of mighty oil wells, hardy sagebrush and wild cowboys. Out of this savage wilderness emerged a lad destined to enter the service of Neptune. He was exposed to the usual grade and high schools, finally matriculating at A. & M. Tiring of dear old A. & M. he turned his face towards the Navy. The requisites of his pre-destination being amply attained, he became one of our chosen few.
>
> Sunny, roguish, spankable at times, Pop is an excellent companion. He has the priceless faculty of making friends in the truest sense of the word. He possesses the unusual ability of combining with this happy-go-lucky disposition a real determination to accomplish the job at hand, whether it be a juice P-work, or a letter to the O.A.O. He is a true southerner, however, and has made a real study of picking these occasions and rarely expends his energy uselessly. . . .
>
> But let this be as it may, the fact remains that Pop was born a gentleman; the Naval Academy made him an officer. Thus the age-old aspiration of the service has been attained: an "Officer and a Gentleman."[37]

To partially translate, "juice P-work" was a course in radio given by the Electrical Engineering Department.[38] And "O.A.O." was shorthand for the "one and only." In Rigsbee's case, her name was Mary Alice Briggs, a native of East Saint Louis, Illinois. Nobody now alive knows how they met. But a *New York Times* story on graduation exercises for the 1930 class noted that ten midshipmen and their fiancées—including Rigsbee and Miss Briggs— were married in the academy chapel following the commencement ceremony.[39] And the only Rigsbee family history, written in 1934 by his uncle Edward, said Everett "then went with the Navy for a two-year cruise around the world. His bride and her mother followed on another vessel and joined him occasionally. To them a daughter was born, Barbara Jean."[40]

His uncle's account failed to mention that Rigsbee's daughter was born within months of the wedding, and the marriage did not last long. At some point there was a divorce, and Rigsbee saw little of his daughter thereafter. But the sardonic nickname given by his classmates stuck, and he was "Pop" to his friends ever after.[41]

He spent several years at sea, eventually as senior engineering watch officer on the USS *California*, flagship of the Pacific Fleet. But by then his ambition and attention were focused on becoming a naval aviator. In part, he may have been drawn to the glamour of flying. But it likely also seemed a good opportunity—an up-and-coming branch where a young man could make a name for himself. So in January 1934 Rigsbee set off for Pensacola Naval Air Station in Florida.[42]

He came at the tail end of an era. The "Annapolis of the Air" had been training pilots for twenty years by then, most of them academy graduates. But their numbers had fallen off after World War I; the year Rigsbee arrived only thirty-five officers earned their Wings of Gold.[43] That would change dramatically as the buildup to the next war began. But when he first saw the airplane hangars on the waterfront and the officers club at the Octagon, Pensacola was still a little sleepy, a little clubby.

You began with an instructor on a single-engine floatplane, learning to taxi, take off, and make a simple climb before going on to spirals and landings, slips and wingovers. Next up were landplanes, mastering stunts and flying in formation, making carrier landings in a small space. The third stage included instrument flying and gunnery. Then you learned to fly torpedo planes and PBYs, the twin-engine patrol planes. Finally, you graduated to fighters—flying in formation, night flying, gunnery, and bombing.

Meanwhile, afternoon work in the classroom covered everything from navigation, to power plants, to gunnery, to packing a parachute. In the end, about three in every ten students at Pensacola didn't make the grade.[44] But Rigsbee received his Wings of Gold as Naval Aviator Number 4101 and officially graduated on April 5, 1935.[45]

His next posting took him to San Diego and a dive bomber squadron on the USS *Lexington*, one of the navy's first aircraft carriers. The ship participated in war games and, in the summer of 1937, helped search for Amelia Earhart after she had gone missing in the Pacific during her attempted around-the-world flight.[46]

A few months later, Rigsbee was sent back across the country to become assistant operations officer at the Anacostia Naval Air Station in Washington, DC.[47] And there, his career really began to take off. He was assigned to fly top navy officers, as well as government officials and others, on inspection tours throughout the United States, Mexico, the Caribbean, and South America. Thanks to his Texas boyhood, he spoke fluent Spanish, which meant he often served as translator as well as pilot. His natural ability to get along with almost anyone also helped. And the experience led him to set a lofty goal—one day he would be like those he flew, an admiral himself.[48]

Around this time, Rigsbee also made a dramatic change in his personal life. Her name was Helen McLaren Broadfoot. She had grown up in Marin County, north of San Francisco. While in college, she had majored in theater and starred in plays. And after graduating, she continued to act locally while also helping run a nursery school. Beautiful and talented, for her stage name she became simply "Helen McLaren." One of the productions she starred in was a solid melodrama called *The Drunkard*.[49] It did so well locally that it was staged in San Francisco and then went on tour to Los Angeles and, finally, to San Diego in the summer of 1939.[50]

For some reason—almost surely having to do with navy business—Rigsbee was in San Diego as well and decided to take in the play at the Old Globe Theater in Balboa Park. It was literally love at first sight. He became a stage-door Johnny, hanging around after performances and waiting for Helen to appear. They were married less than three months later, at Coronado Naval Air Station in San Diego.

She went back with him to Anacostia, but he was gone a lot, flying the brass. So Helen returned to Marin and to the nursery school.[51] It wasn't long before Rigsbee was back in California as well. He did a six-month stint as materiel officer for Patrol Squadron 44 and then, in January 1941, was assigned as aide and flag lieutenant to Rear Admiral John S. McCain, who would later command the navy's Fast Carrier Task Force in World War II and be on the deck of the USS *Missouri* for the surrender in Tokyo

Bay. He and McCain may have met earlier, during his time at Anacostia. At the sprawling navy base on North Island in San Diego, Rigsbee's new job involved being a jack-of-all-trades for whatever the admiral needed. And once the war broke out, that included dealing with personnel issues for replacement aircraft squadrons in the Pacific. Rigsbee must have done it all well, because he similarly served three other admirals in succession: Charles Pownall, William Keene-Harrell, and Mark Mitscher.[52]

But by then, the war had been going on for some time, and an ambitious officer like Rigsbee had to know that a combat command would be important to his own career. He may have been lobbying for just such an assignment, but problems experienced by one of his mentors may also have inadvertently helped his cause.

In 1943, Rear Admiral Charles "Baldy" Pownall had been tapped to head a new strategy that grouped aircraft carriers together to lead assaults on Japanese-held islands. First came an attack in September on Marcus Island in the central Pacific, doing great damage to the Japanese base. But Pownall, worried about retaliation from enemy submarines or planes based several hours away, wanted to retire from the area without searching for several downed American airmen. Rising star Captain J. J. "Jocko" Clark, commanding the USS *Yorktown* as part of the task force, angrily confronted Pownall. "You've got the widest yellow streak of any admiral I've ever seen in my life," he told him. "I don't care if when I return to Pearl Harbor, I don't have a ship and I don't have any command. You can make me a Seaman Second (Class) tomorrow. But this is my ship and those are my boys out there, and I'm going to send out a search for them." Pownall relented. The search didn't find the American fliers, but an enemy ship did; they spent the rest of the war in a Japanese prison camp.

Two later strikes in the Gilbert and Marshall Islands raised similar doubts, and when Admiral Chester Nimitz, commander of the Pacific Fleet, asked his air chief to appraise several admirals for important potential commands, the report on Pownall was succinct: "Over-cautious in plans and operations. He worries intensely before and during operations. Lack of aggressiveness resented by subordinates." Just before Christmas, Pownall was relieved of his carrier command and became Commander, Air Force, Pacific Fleet—a desk job.

Sometime that same month, Rigsbee was chosen to head a new patrol plane squadron. The timing may have been coincidental. Maybe Pownall, before or after his transfer, had a hand in the move. Or maybe another of the admirals Rigsbee had served put in a good word. However it happened, Pop got what he wanted.[53]

His second-in-command was Harold McDonald, a 1935 Annapolis grad who was manager of the football team there and had gotten his wings at Pensacola in 1941. For his first three pilots Rigsbee chose men with no combat experience and not much navy background but who had ferried warplanes from West Coast factories to destinations across the country, racking up thousands of flight hours.

Two of them were well into their thirties. Tom Mulvihill was from Montana, where his family owned a large ranch. But he had always been much more interested in flying, including teaching students in the Civilian Pilot Training program.[54] Harold McGaughey, whom everyone knew as "Mac," had been involved with airplanes for decades. His logbook showed more than sixteen thousand hours in the air, including service as a test pilot for both the army and the navy.[55] The third pilot was much younger. Dan Moore had finished two years of law school before joining the navy, earning his wings, and being assigned to the ferrying flights. Rigsbee made Mulvihill the squadron's chief pilot, responsible for checking out the skills of everyone who would eventually fly for VPB-117. Mac became engineering officer, developing and testing special modifications that made the squadron's planes more effective and efficient. Dan Moore was given the often difficult job of making sure VPB-117 had all the supplies and equipment it needed.[56]

The rest of the squadron's plane commanders came from the ranks of current navy pilots. Some had earned their wings early in the war at either Pensacola or Corpus Christi, which had opened in 1941. Many had been copilots on previous combat tours in places like the Aleutian Islands and Guadalcanal, which made them the only squadron members with actual experience fighting the enemy.

They would fly the B-24 Liberator—or, as the navy called it, the PB4Y-1. It was the workhorse of the war; more had been built than any other bomber. Navy modifications included replacing the plexiglass "greenhouse" for the bow machine gunner with a rotating turret. Because they would usually be flying long patrols over open water, camouflage paint was light blue on top, light gray on the bottom. The only elegant thing about the plane was its Davis wing, 110 feet tip to tip, thin and tapered, built to lift and flex with a heavy load. It flexed so well, in fact, that it unnerved most fliers the first time they saw it in action.[57] But as they would learn (sometimes the hard way), it was a tough airplane that could take a lot of punishment and still manage to make it back.

Home was Camp Kearny, on a mesa outside San Diego. The navy had been using it for a decade, mainly as a base for dirigibles. But it had now become a training center for crews and squadrons flying Liberators—most of which were built, conveniently, at a Consolidated Aircraft plant nearby.[58] VPB-117's official commissioning ceremony was held at the base on February 1, 1944. A dozen or more officers and crew assembled on the shady side of a small administration building, where Rigsbee briefly spoke about how "each of us is going to be dependent upon the loyalty, alertness and teamwork of every other man in the organization."[59] He gave the squadron a nickname, the "Exterminators," borrowed from a racehorse. Then Helen broke a bottle of champagne over VPB-117's as-yet only airplane—a two-seater Taylor Cub.[60]

It was a low-key affair, but Rigsbee clearly had high hopes. He wrote his brother Hub about the event, "I have a grand bunch of boys and I think I got them off to a good start. And all of us think we have the best darn outfit in the whole Navy!"[61]

The squadron's ranks soon would swell to more than two hundred enlisted men and officers. They spent the first two months mostly sorting out roles for the officers and enlisted men, bringing in prospective pilots from other bases and squadrons, getting and testing new planes, and battling the bureaucracy for the hundreds of mundane items and authorizations they would need. One extra wrinkle: The squadron would be the first equipped with new low-altitude radar bombing gear. The plan was to scour the ocean at night, finding Japanese ships and sinking them under cover of darkness. The new equipment would also require an extra crewman and special training.[62]

Rigsbee himself focused mostly on the duties of a commanding officer, and he clearly didn't intend to be called a coward like his mentor Admiral Pownall. So in one of the early meetings with an assembled group of pilots, he launched into an animated pep talk about how VPB-117 would go on the warpath in the Pacific, exterminating the Japanese wherever they were found. To many in the room, it was an over-the-top performance—unsettling, especially coming from a leader who had never been in combat himself. At the end of his speech, he told anyone not with him on this mission to raise his hand. Four who had already served combat tours did. Rigsbee was surprised and angry. So he continued his harangue, at the end of which he again asked the pilots for a show of hands. The original four still dissented. And this time they were joined by a fifth, also a combat veteran.[63]

Rigsbee was incensed. He immediately left, got into his Taylor Cub, and flew to the Fleet Air Wing's headquarters on North Island. He told the admiral about the meeting and asked to have the five pilots sent to another squadron. The admiral refused, saying, "What makes you think somebody else is going to want VPB-117's dirty linen? Handle this yourself." Somehow the story of the meeting got out, and the squadron grapevine quickly gave the five a sardonic nickname: the "Dirty Linen Boys." The following day Rigsbee brought the pilots into his office and read them the navy articles of mutiny. There was more discussion and, in the end, one of the five decided to leave the squadron. The other four stayed, flew, and fought.[64]

Meanwhile, the winnowing process for potential pilots continued. They practiced bombing and navigation, instrument flying, gunnery, and night flying. Some didn't measure up; a few opted out.[65] And then, on the morning of June 4, VPB-117 suffered its first casualties.

John Golden, who'd been a copilot in VB-102 on Guadalcanal and a good friend of my dad's, was taking off on a training flight. He rose into heavy fog, made a left turn, broke out on top of the overcast, and then went back into the clouds. You could hear the engines racing before the plane came out below the clouds again, this time at less than one hundred feet. Golden pulled back on the yoke, and the nose rose one more time, the wings rocking from side to side in a power stall before the left wing tip hit the ground.

The squadron's enlisted men had just finished morning muster and gotten their instructions for the day. Walking across an open area, they suddenly saw Golden's plane coming straight at them. For some, there was no time to run and no place to hide. The Liberator crashed and burned. In all, seventeen men in the plane and on the ground were killed.[66]

Besides running the squadron, Rigsbee also flew occasional training missions. And, as with the "Dirty Linen Boys," there were sometimes troubling incidents. He chose some men who had served under him during his North Island command to be part of Crew 1, filled in with others, and tapped O'Neill Osborne, who had been running a navy navigation school, as his navigator. But he still needed a copilot. So he took an alphabetical list of potential pilots for the squadron and started at the top, with Bill Allsopp.

He didn't have to look further. Allsopp's first flight with Rigsbee was a long-haul navigation hop, from San Diego to Texas and back. On the homeward leg, Rigsbee took them up to twenty-five thousand feet; shortly thereafter, he said he had to answer nature's call. He told Bill to take the pilot's seat and keep the plane on the same course and altitude. Bill did as ordered, but Rigsbee never came back. Time passed. The wings began to ice up, and crew members were fainting from lack of oxygen at that altitude. Allsopp, who'd put on an oxygen mask so he could keep flying, started to descend and sent the head enlisted man to look for the commander. He found him passed out in the bomb bay. When they reached nine thousand feet, Rigsbee and the others began to wake up, whereupon the commander returned to the cockpit and calmly asked Allsopp, "Are we coming into San Diego?" Bill told him no, they were descending and heading back toward Texas so they could melt the ice and get more fuel. Rigsbee said nothing, but within a few days he named Bill his copilot.

On another, later training flight to Texas, their number four engine quit, out of gas. Bill quickly cross-fed fuel to it, said they'd have to land and refuel, and began checking maps for a likely spot. Again Rigsbee said nothing but continued to fly due west toward California. This went on for a while until Allsopp reached under his seat and pulled out a three-cell battery flashlight. He was afraid he would have to knock Rigsbee out or they would crash. Finally, without a word, Rigsbee turned and began to descend. Allsopp spotted a dirt airfield with a little café attached and stayed with the plane while it was being refueled. Rigsbee and the rest of the crew went inside. Later, the navigator came and told Bill that Rigsbee would like to see him. The café had a lunch counter with a dozen or so stools. Allsopp came in, and the crew, who had been chatting, fell completely silent. Only one stool, next to Rigsbee, was unoccupied. Bill sat down. Rigsbee waited for a moment; then he said, "Bill, they have a meat sandwich that I think is pretty good. You ought to try it." The entire room exhaled, and the crew went back to talking among themselves. That's when Rigsbee leaned over and said, very quietly, "I want to thank you for this morning, Bill."

That's how it was with them. There were other incidents. But each time, Rigsbee later thanked Bill privately. And they formed a bond. Allsopp went on to have a storied career in aviation, but in the squadron and afterward, he never publicly disparaged the man he called "the Skipper."[67]

As for others in the crew, even a lifetime later they had trouble pinning down Rigsbee's personality. One remembered him as "a good leader, but not a good pilot."[68] Another said, "I loved him. He was kind of my father figure out there."[69] But others talked about him often yelling at the crew or veering back and forth from friendly to aloof. Another said he frequently "seemed depressed."[70] Within the squadron as a whole, memories of Rigsbee were similarly mixed. One pilot said he behaved "erratically" at times: "he could be charming, then turn around and bite everyone's head off."[71] On one thing almost everyone agreed: Rigsbee felt pressure to succeed. The squadron was his one big chance.

As the weeks wore on, the winnowing process found most pilots and crews settling into their roles. July was a busy month for everyone, as they prepared to leave in August for final training in Hawaii. Rigsbee threw a big going-away party for officers and their wives, at which he formally announced all the crews. The entertainment was singer Peggy Lee, who'd had several number one hits and sung on nationwide radio broadcasts.[72]

Meanwhile, unmarried enlisted men set out to enjoy their final taste of freedom. Some likely headed one last time to the Consolidated Aircraft plant on Pacific Highway—where the shifts changed at midnight, four in ten workers were women, there were plenty of nearby places to dance the night away with big bands like those of Tommy Dorsey and Harry James, and a guy could truthfully say he was about to fly into battle in one of the planes built at the factory, maybe even by the young lady herself. As pickup lines went, it was about as good as you could get.[73]

But in the back of their minds those last few weeks and days, there must also have been questions. More than half the plane commanders had previously been in combat. But the rest of the men—including their commanding officer and probably nine out of ten crew members—had never seen what a .50-caliber slug could do to a human body or faced the possibility that their own lives could easily end in the next five minutes. So the fourteen-hour flight from San Diego to Hawaii—longer than from New York to Los Angeles, all of it over empty ocean and done at night so they could navigate by the stars—was their first giant step into the unknown.

Meanwhile, in the wider world of the Pacific war, America had been on the offensive for nearly two years. To the north, the Japanese had been pushed out of the Aleutian Islands. To the south, battles on "Bloody Tarawa" and a yearlong struggle to take Guadalcanal had driven the enemy from the Gilbert and Solomon Islands. Then war planners turned their attention to the Mariana Islands in the central Pacific.

From mid-June to early August 1944, marines fought and defeated Japanese troops on Saipan, Tinian, and Guam. Offshore, on a single day, fighters from American carriers shot down 429 Japanese planes while losing only 29 of their own.[74] And as the ground troops were mopping up in the Marianas, VPB-117 learned that it would be one of the first squadrons to fly from Tinian.

That gave extra incentive and attention to their final six weeks of training. Flying out of the naval air station at Kaneohe Bay on Oahu, they practiced sleeve gunnery and low-altitude bombing, tactics for intercepting fighters.[75] They flew over to Hilo on the big island of Hawaii, sometimes at night, for practice and a little bit of leave. Some took bus rides into Honolulu, but the pace kept everyone pretty busy.

And then, on September 27, 1944, they left everything behind. Getting to the real war took three days. The first leg was from Kaneohe to Johnston

Island, where six Seabees had recently died from bad moonshine they'd cooked up.[76] The second was from Johnston to Eniwetok, where all the palm trees on the island had been beheaded during the navy bombardment in February.[77] The final day brought them to Tinian, but it wasn't really what they had pictured when they thought of the South Pacific. There were almost no palm trees—just evergreens, mostly pine. Not much jungle, but huge fields of sugarcane. Hardly any beaches, just rocky coastline and cliffs full of caves. The island was fairly flat though—and, most important, just within range of Tokyo for the new B-29s. So construction crews had taken over two captured Japanese airfields and started building more runways.[78]

But the army's campaign to bomb the heart of Japan wouldn't even begin for nearly two months. In the meantime, Rigsbee's squadron would use the island as a base for patrols and potential strikes against the Japanese—which is why, on one of their first nights on Tinian, VPB-117 became the star of the show during Tokyo Rose's radio broadcast.[79] She knew the name of their commanding officer. She knew how many planes they had. She knew about their super-secret radar. She even read them the serial numbers of several radar units in the planes. She told them they would all soon be hanging by their heels in a square in Tokyo. And she called them the "Blue Raiders of the Sky" because of their camouflage paint. It was a little eerie to hear, but they did like the nickname. So, instead of the "Exterminators," they became the "Blue Raiders."[80]

Living conditions were marginal. Construction workers brought crushed coral to an old sugarcane field, dumped it out along with some used, soggy tents, and told the men, "Welcome home." The crews leveled out the coral as best they could, put up the tents, and set up their cots. There was mud everywhere, so they broke up old wooden ammo boxes and built floors in the tents. They slogged to the mess tent; they slogged to preflight briefings in the dark; they slogged to the showers—which were nothing more than oil drums filled with water and set up high above on a wooden platform. Open air, not even a curtain. There was no electricity or running water anywhere. Drinking water was whatever tank trucks could pump from surface ponds, treated with so much chlorine it made your throat sore.

And they quickly learned they were not alone. The army said hundreds of Japanese soldiers were still hiding on the island. They came into the mess area at night; you could hear the cans rattle as they raided the garbage. The cooks had carbines and captured or shot quite a few, more than the marine patrols. Then there were the raids by Japanese pilots from other bases. The men had been told to dig foxholes by their tents, but the soil went down only a foot or so before they reached solid coral. So they gave up and hoped for the best.[81] One night four bombers flew over the field and dropped antipersonnel bombs, putting a few shrapnel holes in one of the squadron's planes. Japanese radio later said the attack caused "great devastation," which the guys took as a compliment.[82] In the middle of the melee, someone jumped into the top turret of a parked American plane and shot down one of the Japanese raiders, which crashed into the sea off the end of the runway. But the enemy crew apparently got out and swam back to the island—because a few nights later someone noticed the running lights flickering on an American twin-engine bomber parked near the runway. The Japanese were trying to start the engines and make their escape when a group of fliers came running with pistols and rifles. Someone started shooting, everyone else joined in, and, predictably, the plane's gas tanks went up. Next morning the area was cordoned off. All that remained were the skeletons of the plane and the three Japanese.[83]

Because he was the senior naval aviator at the base, Rigsbee commanded what was known as Task Unit 30.5.3, which included not only the newly named Blue Raiders but also four other squadrons. Together they set up patrols that searched west toward the Philippines, northwest toward Okinawa, and north toward Iwo Jima—three island groups that U.S. troops would invade over the next six months. The flights took them one thousand miles out, across one hundred miles or so, and one thousand miles back across open water, most of the time blank as a blackboard on the first day of school. The job involved looking for the Japanese fleet and merchant shipping, as well as spying on Japanese-held islands. They were also allowed to attack "targets of opportunity"—enemy ships, planes, and bases. It was an important enough mission to rate coverage by the *New York Times*. War correspondent Robert Trumbull quoted Rigsbee as saying, "We can do a thousand miles all right, but I won't guarantee very much more. That's how close we cut it, and sometimes we come back with a cupful of gas."[84]

There were other problems. A serious lack of spare parts kept too many planes down for repairs. The runway was a little short and at the end dropped off a cliff two hundred feet above the ocean. It was also pitted, which meant that only the most experienced pilots were allowed to take off with the extra weight of bombs. To top it all off, their super-secret night-bombing radar could hardly be used. Turned out many American submarines were in the area, surfacing under the cover of darkness, and the radar couldn't distinguish them from Japanese ships. So pilots wouldn't know whether they were attacking the enemy or the good guys.[85]

Still, they managed to do some damage. In October, squadron planes sank seven Japanese cargo ships, shot down two planes, and destroyed an enemy weather and radio station.[86] By the end of the month, Rigsbee himself got in on the action. On one flight, he and Graham Squires strafed and sank a cargo ship. A photo of the attack is still on file in the National Archives and Records Administration.[87] Ten days later, Rigsbee and Dan Moore did the same.[88]

And then, on November 11, "Pop" had his most important mission yet. He and the commander of another squadron were picked to protect and spot for navy ships that would bombard Iwo Jima at night. Both planes carried extra ammunition and bombs, as well as a navy spotter in contact with the ships by radio. The other plane left first and, when it got to the target, was attacked by Japanese fighters, Zeros. The pilot led them away beyond their point of no return but, because of the encounter, was low on fuel and had to head back to Tinian. That left the rest of the job to Rigsbee.

They arrived a half hour before midnight. At the first target, an airfield, cloud cover went down to five hundred feet above the water, so they flew low and slow. Antiaircraft fire from the island sent white bursts flashing in front of and behind them. Then the American ships opened up, shells and tracers arcing over the plane, falling on the field.[89] The enemy guns went silent. Then they crossed over to the other side of the island, where the cloud cover had lifted, and spotted for another bombardment. After that, Rigsbee decided to get in on the action himself. So he made three passes at the second airfield, dropping one-hundred-pound bombs that exploded in the area where Japanese planes were parked.[90] All in all, an exciting and successful night. Elated, after the long trip home Rigsbee buzzed the field at Tinian before almost stalling in a sharp turn.[91] They landed safely just before 6 a.m.

But there were still troubling signs. On one flight, as they took off from the runway that dropped off to the ocean, Rigsbee didn't apply enough power, and when they reached the end, they fell like a rock toward the water. He reacted by pulling on the wheel to get the nose up, which would have stalled the plane and doomed them. Allsopp quickly pushed the throttles to the stops and then held them and the wheel in place against Rigsbee's pressure. They were having a tug-of-war, but Bill was younger and stronger, and Rigsbee gradually relented. They flew literally around the wave tops for five miles before anyone on the island could see whether they were still in the air. Neither said anything about it during the eleven-hour mission. But when they got back that night, a jeep was there to pick up Rigsbee. He waited until the driver started the engine—again, so no one could hear—then called Bill over and said quietly, "Thanks for this morning."[92]

But soon the Blue Raiders would be on the move again. When the Japanese drove the Americans from the Philippines in the spring of 1942, General Douglas MacArthur had vowed to come back. At a secret meeting in Hawaii more than two years later, he convinced President Franklin Roosevelt and a reluctant Admiral Chester Nimitz, commander in chief of the Pacific Fleet, to make good on that pledge. And so, on October 20, 1944, MacArthur walked ashore from a landing craft near the airfield at Tacloban on the island of Leyte and proclaimed, "I have returned." Less than a month later, while still on Tinian, VPB-117 learned it would be the first bomber squadron to fly from Tacloban. And it wouldn't be easy.[93]

The men arrived the first week of December at a makeshift base that was, at the time, called the world's busiest airport. It almost certainly was the most dangerous. The presence of more than a dozen army and marine fighter squadrons meant takeoffs and landings were more or less constant. The traffic pattern was frequently full, and not just with Americans. Sometimes, especially at dusk, Japanese pilots would try to sneak into the line, hoping to hide from radar long enough to make an attack.

The runway ran right along the ocean. At high tide, the eastern edge was only three or four feet above the water. Because so many squadrons were based in such a small space, the strip itself was literally lined with planes—parked wingtip to wingtip the full length of the runway, noses almost edging out onto the landing surface. The navy's B-24 had the widest wingspan of any plane at the base. That left squadron pilots little clearance—nerve-racking enough in good weather, but much tougher in a storm, in the dark, or when trying to nurse a crippled plane home on its last, lurching legs.

In many ways, worse than the landings were the takeoffs. The runway was made of Marston matting, interlocking steel plates rolled out on top of coral and sand. The navy Liberators were not only the widest airplanes at the base but also the heaviest. With extra fuel tanks in the bomb bay to extend their range, they were routinely and seriously overloaded. So as they groaned to gather speed on takeoff, the flexible matting would roll up in front of the wheels the way bread dough buckles when pushed by a rolling pin. It was like trying to take off uphill. At the end of the runway (and the Liberators were always near the end of the runway before getting airborne), the metal links snapped like the tip of a whip, breaking off the steel plates at the end. The result was a runway that lost more precious feet of surface every day.[94]

The steel itself was also slick as ice when wet. And, of course, it was monsoon season, the worst in years.[95] Many days the conditions were "zero-zero"—zero visibility, zero ceiling. Taking off and landing with clouds down on the deck, lightning and pelting rain, and wind shear was routine. The bad weather, the overcrowded airstrip, the enemy attacks meant that the army almost always kept bulldozers stationed at the end of the runway, engines running. When a crash happened, the men were pulled from the plane and the carcass quickly shoved into the water. At low tide the ocean side looked like a giant junkyard.[96]

In short, Tacloban was a harrowing hell of a place to be a bomber pilot. And it didn't seem much safer on the ground. Americans controlled only the area immediately around the field. Nearby the enemy was still a serious threat. Too serious for VPB-117 to set up tents, headquarters, a camp of any kind.

So for the first two weeks they were quartered offshore on ships, including a seaplane tender, the USS *Currituck*. It was the flagship of Rear Admiral Frank D. Wagner, head of the Fleet Air Wing that included the Blue Raiders. Crews were ferried back and forth to the strip in LCVPs—landing craft like those used in storming the beaches of Normandy. The men ate in the ship's mess, which meant the food was marginally better than K rations. But officers shared very cramped quarters, and the only sleeping space for enlisted men was on deck. Again, it was monsoon season, meaning there were driving rains almost every night. Men wrapped themselves in blankets and jostled for shelter under the wing of a seaplane or an overhang of any kind. To make matters worse, while crews were off on missions, sailors sometimes stole their bedding and sold it to the Filipinos.[97]

For entertainment most nights, squadron crews watched the air raids. The Japanese hadn't given up on recapturing the field, or at least rendering it inoperable, so they kept up a steady stream of attacks. On the outgoing leg of its patrol, one VPB-117 crew reported sighting a formation of about thirty transport planes escorted by twelve Zeros. Returning to Tacloban at dusk, the same plane waited in a landing pattern while a Liberator with a blown tire was cleared from the runway. Suddenly at sunset, the air-raid siren blew. Tracers and searchlights slashed the sky. A bulldozer quickly shoved the disabled plane off the runway and into the bay, and the Blue Raiders got the go-ahead to land. On final approach, they realized that the plane behind them was one of the Japanese transports they'd seen earlier. Later they learned it was full of suicide troops who hoped to land on the strip, jump out, and blow up as many planes as possible. A marine antiaircraft battery at the end of the runway waited until the American plane passed over and then opened up on the transport.[98] On the *Currituck* they watched it explode in a throb of white light.[99] Days later, Japanese bodies were still washing up on the beach. After wading ashore around the same dead soldier for almost a week, a disgusted crew chief finally found a shovel and buried him on the spot, in the sand.[100]

The air raids continued even after the squadron moved onto land. And there they had other problems. When you ran to a foxhole during a raid, you had to first check for cobras before diving in. And if there were no handy holes, you simply ran into the water. During one air raid, a crewman was chatting with someone nearby in the dark, until he realized his companion was a dead Japanese soldier.[101] Often the enemy would attack when the Blue Raiders were heading to their planes at 4 a.m. During one such raid, the fliers chatted with an antiaircraft crew in its emplacement. The gunners said they had been out in the war zone for almost four years, moving up with the troops and planes as they went. When a pilot said they should be relieved soon, they said it was more likely they'd be killed first. Several days later, they were.[102]

So it had been an eventful first week in the Philippines. And it ended with the loss of VPB-117's commanding officer.

On December 6, Rigsbee's first mission at the new base took them north, where they strafed one ship and sighted six Japanese fighters who stayed just out of firing range. Coming back to Tacloban, he lined up too low on the runway. As had happened at other times, Bill Allsopp took control, brought the plane up, and dropped it onto the matting. Once on the ground, he said, "You've got it," and Rigsbee began taxiing the plane. Turning around at the end of the runway, the wingtip of the Liberator sliced through the nose of an army fighter parked alongside the strip. With its radar dome hanging from a few wires, Allsopp thought the P-39 looked like a beheaded bird.

Rigsbee said nothing, but when the plane was safely parked, he quickly headed off to see about the damaged fighter. The crew went to wait by the LCVP that would take them to the *Currituck*. Two hours later, there was still no sign of "the Skipper." Allsopp finally told the coxswain at the helm to shove off. Just as he did, Rigsbee came running up the beach and jumped on board. He immediately assumed command and ordered the coxswain to steer two points off the starboard bow. The coxswain said he couldn't go that way. Rigsbee repeated the order, and the coxswain again said he couldn't. Rigsbee told him he was his superior officer, the commander of a squadron, and was ordering him to steer two points off the starboard bow. The sailor shrugged and complied. In minutes the launch shuddered and stopped.

The coxswain said, "Sir, I was trying to say there's a reef down there. We just knocked the prop off." Rigsbee was silent for a second and then told the crew to strip down to their skivvies. They would go over the side, he said, dive down, and recover the prop. The water was black; it was 11 p.m. There was no chance of finding anything. The crew froze. Rigsbee stood in the bow, Allsopp in the stern. The men slowly looked toward Bill. The only sound was water lapping against the LCVP. Allsopp shook his head slightly. No one moved; no one spoke. As in the plane, he may have been trying to protect "the Skipper"—keep him from making a big mistake. But this time they weren't alone, and Bill wasn't at the controls.

So suddenly, like a line tied too loosely around a cleat, everything came undone.

His voice rising, Rigsbee called them bastards and told them they would be charged with willfully disobeying an order. Then he began to cry, very quietly. He sat down, took off his shoes and socks, stripped off his shirt, and jumped over the side. He floated for a moment, dove into the darkness, and disappeared. Time passed. Rigsbee surfaced nearby and went down a second time. Again he rose; again he dove. The third time he came up sobbing, "I can't find it." Bill Allsopp quietly leaned over the gunwale and said, "Skipper, why don't you come back in the boat?"

It's not clear how they got back to the *Currituck*. But by the time they did, Rigsbee's anger had returned. He charged past the crew, up the gangway. At the top, the officer of the deck took one look at him—barefoot and bare chested, soaking wet, wearing nothing but his khaki pants—and stopped him from boarding. By the time Allsopp and the rest arrived, Rigsbee was shouting that he was a squadron commander and wanted to see the admiral. The officer was threatening to put him in the brig.

What happened next no one knew. The story circulated in the squadron later that Rigsbee eventually did see the admiral, argued with him vociferously, and was led away. Some kind of confrontation clearly took place. The crew never reported the incident, and no officers ever asked them about it. But an hour after boarding the ship, as Allsopp was drinking coffee in the wardroom, he felt a hand on his shoulder.

It was Rigsbee, who asked whether they could speak privately in the passageway.

"They think I need a rest, Bill, so they're sending me to Sydney," he said.

"That's terrible, Skipper," Allsopp replied.

Rigsbee said he had left orders that Bill was to take over his crew. Allsopp thanked him. They shook hands. Rigsbee turned and walked away.[103]

He returned three weeks later. Galen Bull was sent to fly him back, and on the way home he said Rigsbee seemed "very quiet, very uncertain."[104] On Christmas Day 1944, they assembled the squadron around a large mudhole in an area near some tents. They had finally gotten onto land, but it was far from dry. A photo shows Rigsbee standing next to a jeep, a piece of paper rolled up in his hand. He looks a little thinner but still handsome. Nearby is Harold McDonald, now VPB-117's commander. On the other side of the puddle, the rest of the men are arranged in a large semicircle, with Tom Mulvihill, now second in command, in front of them. Some of the men look bored, or unsure, or a little sad.[105]

In the picture, Rigsbee is speaking. A lifetime later, I asked those who were there what he said. No one remembered. And then he was gone.

The World We Face

How does a soldier make peace with war?

James Jones, who fought on Guadalcanal and wrote *From Here to Eternity* and *The Thin Red Line*, said the only way was to accept that your life was no longer your own—it was just on loan to you for the duration.[106] And it's a good analogy. Some men paid the ultimate price and lost everything. Some redeemed the note later and closed the books. And some paid in installments, for the rest of their lives.

Bill Pedretti was a bona fide California golden boy. Not that he was born into a cushy life. He grew up in a one-bedroom house made entirely of river stones dredged from a dry creek bed in California's San Fernando Valley. In 1932, it was still mostly open country, and Bill lived with his mother, a typist, and his father, who painted houses. Like lots of young boys, he loved being around animals. So he became a budding nine-year-old rabbit farmer. Around that time he also rescued an abandoned puppy from under the house of a neighbor, who let Bill keep the dog. Puzzling for weeks to come up with just the right name, he finally settled on what the little German Shepherd responded to when called: "Here, Boy!"[107]

As he grew, so did Bill's goals and hopes. By the time he reached high school, he wanted more than anything to go to the Naval Academy and become a pilot. In his senior year, he took the admission exam for Annapolis. His score ranked him third in the state, but the family story said the academy was accepting only two applicants from California.[108] He swallowed his disappointment and finished as valedictorian at San

Fernando High, Class of 1941. His graduation address was titled "The World We Face":

> Thus far, we in America have been able to keep out of the war. Today, however, the oceans are no barriers, and we are vitally affected by whatever happens to the rest of the world. What the future holds for us, no one can accurately foretell. But it requires no great insight to see that the next few years will, in all likelihood, be very important ones in the history of our nation. The things to be done immediately, the legislation to be adopted, the leaders to be developed, and the reaction and response of the American people to the events which lie ahead in the struggle between democracy and dictatorship, will irrevocably fashion the pattern of our future life.[109]

A few months later, he was at the University of California, Los Angeles (UCLA), in the Reserve Officer Training Corp, studying engineering and working on his civilian pilot's license when, as he had predicted, war broke out. Bill applied to become a navy pilot and, after preflight school, was sent for flight training in Oakland. Day after day he climbed into the back seat of a Stearman biplane, spending half the time practicing takeoffs and landings, basic turns and stalls, and the other half as a passenger while his instructor showed him what the plane could really do. He tried to describe the sensation in a letter to his parents:

> I spend most of the time hanging out in the breeze by my safety belt. Your knees get up around your neck and it seems about ten men are trying to pull you out of the cockpit in some of the maneuvers. Sometimes your eyes feel like they are being pulled out of your head. I sort of get a kick out of it all, though—it is a lot of fun.[110]

He was over six feet tall, handsome, with hazel eyes. So there was a girl too: Marilyn. They had met in high school, at the local swimming pool.[111] She was a year younger, now at UCLA herself, and she sometimes took the train up to Oakland to see Bill.[112] After a few months, he left for Corpus Christi, Texas, and final training.

Here, the flying was more serious and more dangerous. In those days, in an average group of twenty cadets, one would be killed and another five or more would "wash out."[113] Maybe Bill worried he might be one of them, but on September 4, 1943, he received his wings and his commission as a naval officer. He had achieved his life's ambition. He was twenty years old.

Glen Box had wanted to go to Annapolis and become a navy pilot too. Older than Bill Pedretti by more than nine years, he grew up on his family's dairy farm in Missouri. But his eyes were always on the sky. As a young boy, he would straighten up whenever he heard the distant drone of an airplane and follow it all the way across the sky until it disappeared. His father humored him; after all, what young boy in the 1920s wasn't in love with airplanes? But his plans for his oldest son were clear—he would inherit the farm, work it, and keep it in the family. He refused to sign consent papers for Glen's Naval Academy application.

Still, Glen wouldn't be denied. As soon as he was twenty-one and able to enlist on his own, he joined the navy. He started as an ordinary seaman, his first duty on the carrier *Lexington* bringing him closer to airplanes and to his goal. He was bright, he worked hard, and within a few years he was accepted into training as a naval aviation pilot—an enlisted man with wings.

Flying took him to Hawaii where, on an observation flight with an officer in 1937, Glen looked down at Pearl Harbor crowded with warships and said it would be easy for an enemy to disable most of the fleet with one attack.[114] Four years later, on a Sunday morning, he was shaving in his barracks on Ford Island next to Battleship Row when an explosion knocked him off his feet and shattered the mirror. He thought one of the squadron's planes must have crashed nearby until he ran outside and saw the USS *Arizona* burning and sinking.[115]

Things began happening very quickly after that. He met and married a girl from Illinois before being shipped to Australia with a PBY squadron. While he was overseas, his new wife started living with a marine captain who didn't know she was married. In early 1943, Glen returned home, divorced his wife, and was commissioned an officer and ordered to Norfolk, Virginia, as a test pilot and instructor. He had one other occasional duty: because he was very handsome, the navy sometimes used him for publicity photos and recruitment posters.[116]

But it was Glen's experience as an instructor that got him transferred to VPB-117. The plan was to have him check out and prepare the young pilots for combat. He would then stay with the squadron as a spare pilot when it went into the war. Meanwhile, Bill Pedretti, after more training, had also been assigned to the squadron. He was picked for a plane crew commanded by Ensign Homer Heard, who had flown PBYs during a previous combat tour. They trained for months before, finally, word came they were leaving for the combat zone.

Just a few days from departure, Ensign Heard was checking out a brand-new plane with a skeleton crew. Bringing it in for a landing, the Liberator didn't stop and ran off the end of the runway into a ditch. No one was hurt, but the plane was damaged, and Heard was relieved as plane commander.[117] Glen was ordered to replace him.

Nine years older, Glen took Bill under his wing as they trained during August and September in Hawaii. Serious and soft-spoken, Bill listened closely. Finally, in early October they left for the front.

On Tinian, like other crews, they found that many of the search sectors were "blue water" patrols, never spotting any land to speak of. But the Bonin Islands to the north were Japanese strongholds and heavily fortified. Within the first week, a plane from a sister squadron at the base reported itself under attack by Zeros based on Iwo Jima and was never heard from again. The next day two Liberators went in looking for survivors. They were attacked by eight Zeros and shot six of them down. From then on, searches near Iwo Jima always included two planes rather than one. The Zeros stayed out of the Liberators' machine-gun range and sometimes dropped phosphorous bombs that fell harmlessly into the water.[118] Even so, Iwo and the nearby islands were still known as a "hot" sector. Scuttlebutt said some crewmen actually scheduled voluntary circumcisions on the day they were listed for Iwo.[119]

Not long after arriving, Glen's crew became the first in the squadron to contact the enemy. They found two large Japanese landing ships and tried to bomb them from ten thousand feet. The closest hit was one hundred feet away from one of the ships, doing no damage.[120] Then, a few weeks later, passing over Muko Jima, they spotted a small building on the island's highest spot, with three antennas outside. Glen went into a gliding attack on what he assumed was some kind of radio station, roaring to within 150 feet and dropping bombs that destroyed the building. There was no antiaircraft fire from the island—only one soldier with a machine gun whose tracers fell like fireworks, well short of the plane.[121]

Four days later, again on their homeward leg, the right waist gunner glimpsed a plane flying just beneath the cloud cover, heading in the opposite direction. Glen changed course to follow, telling Bill to take the controls while he studied the plane through his binoculars. It was an Emily, a four-engine Japanese flying boat with a crew of ten. And even though it was heading away from Tinian, Glen decided to chase. He lightened the Liberator by dropping its bombs, and for the next half hour they slowly gained on the Emily, which was using full power trying to get away. They closed in from above and behind, with the Emily less than five hundred feet off the water.

When they got within range, Glen pushed the throttles forward, diving toward the target. Shells from the Emily's cannons chewed off a piece of the Liberator's left wingtip. At the same moment, Glen's bow and top turrets opened up, shaking the flight deck and spilling cartridge casings onto the floor. First one and then two of the flying boat's engines bloomed with flame. Losing altitude and airspeed, the Emily started a shallow turn to the right. Glen tried to follow, but the Liberator was going too fast and passed just above the flying boat.

At that moment Bill looked out his window and saw the Japanese pilot in his cockpit below. Their eyes locked. It was a face he would never forget.[122] An instant later, the Liberator's tail gunner splintered the Emily's canopy. Out of control and falling fast, it nosed into the water and exploded. There were no life rafts, no survivors. It all took less than five minutes.[123] The next day the squadron learned that the Emily was almost certainly searching for a battle-damaged American submarine nearby that could not submerge. It was a sitting duck, desperately trying to get

SOLO INTO THE RISING SUN

back home. Glen and Bill were told their attack probably saved the sub, its men, and seven downed fliers they had rescued.[124]

A week or so later, the crew again drew the sector that included Muko Jima, where they earlier bombed the radio installation. Glen decided to see whether the Japanese had repaired anything, maybe make a strafing run. He didn't know that the enemy had since brought in antiaircraft guns. He was still a mile or two from the target when he saw a single flash from the island. On instinct, he pulled up and away, but the shell scored a direct hit on the port side outboard engine. Out his window, Glen saw it streaming fire.

He immediately told Bill to feather the prop—rotate the now still blades so they were parallel, rather than perpendicular, to the airflow. Bill hit the switch above the windshield. Nothing happened, and he knew that things had immediately gone from bad to worse. The frozen propeller blades would now act as a drag, slowing the plane and forcing it to use more fuel on the long trip back to base. But the more immediate problem was the fire that could spread to the fuel tanks in the wing. The only way to put it out was to cut off the gas to the crippled engine.

Minus one engine, the Liberator kept losing altitude. Glen told the crew to jettison the bombs and "drop them safe," unarmed, so they wouldn't explode beneath them. Finally, only four hundred feet above the water, Glen and Bill got control and leveled off. Because the power was now much stronger on one side than the other, the plane wanted to pull off center. The two pilots had to brace themselves in their seats and put their full weight on the rudder pedals to keep the Liberator more or less on course. And they'd have to do it for hours, all the way home.

Tinian was more than eight hundred miles away, with nothing but ocean between. Radioman John Summers sent a message to base about what had happened. The rest of the crew began lightening the ship, throwing out machine guns, ammo, anything they could pick up or tear out of its moorings. Glen asked for help on the radio, and a squadron plane one sector over was diverted. It had been midday when they were hit, and Graham Squires reached them at about 5 p.m. to join up for the rest of the trip home. Maybe two hours to go. Things were starting to look up.

Foot still jammed on the rudder pedal, Bill watched the sun sink outside his window. The crew kept radioing their position and checking fuel levels. Darkness was falling fast, but every minute brought them closer. Then, sixty miles out, the lights of Tinian glittered. Fuel gauges showed 240 gallons, and Glen felt sure they had enough left. For the first time, the crew unclenched. Someone cracked a joke over the intercom. Graham Squires called on the radio. An earlier run-in with fighters near Iwo Jima had used up extra fuel, and now he was getting low. He wanted to know whether it was OK for him to go on ahead, since they were within sight of home. Glen and the tower both agreed.[125]

Glen told Bill, plus the navigator, head mechanic, and radioman John Summers, to stay at their posts; then he sent the rest of the crew to their ditching stations. Just a precaution, he said. So the men put on their Mae Wests, lay with their feet up against the bulkhead behind the bomb bay, and waited. It was pitch dark, but now they were only thirty miles from the field, less than fifteen minutes flying time. They were five hundred feet off the water, landing lights on. Everything under control.

Then, without warning, the number two engine quit. Ten seconds later, number four. What happened? Were the gauges wrong? It didn't matter: the plane was falling; they had maybe less than a minute. Glen ordered everyone but Bill to join the others at the ditching station. On his way, Summers sent a two-word message over the radio: "Going down." He got a "roger" back from base before he and the rest put on their life vests, lay down on top of the men already there, and locked arms. Summers pictured his mother getting a telegram. Glen swung the plane left, to head into the wind.[126] Together, he and Bill pulled back on the yoke to bring the nose up into a stall. As they did, the last engine died. For a final few seconds, the only sound was the wind over the wings.

The next thing anyone remembered was black water. The plane had broken into three pieces—the nose and cockpit, the bomb bay, and the tail section. No one knew exactly how he got clear of the wreckage. The left wing, the one with the damaged engine, was still floating and partially attached to the fuselage. Bill came up first, seemingly unhurt but fighting off shock. He saw Glen and swam toward him. Glen's right leg was broken, and he was in serious pain. Together, they began to make out crewmen in the water nearby and shouted to them to gather around the wing. Some were in even worse shape. Ken Henry, the navigator, couldn't stay afloat. He'd lost his life jacket and had a broken back and two broken legs. Glen swam to him and held him up. Bill saw waist gunner John Craig in the water without a life jacket. He grabbed him and put him on the wing while he went to look for a life raft and more survivors. There was no raft, but he found radarman Jim Carlin struggling weakly in the water, semiconscious, with a torn and useless life jacket. Bill dragged him back to the group. But when he got there, he saw that John Craig had somehow slipped off the wing and under the waves. It was a moment, Bill's daughter told me decades later, that he never forgot.

They had been in the water less than five minutes. Bill and Glen compared notes about the missing. No one saw two of the crewmen, Basil Martin and Bill Pierson, ever clear the wreckage. Someone had spotted head mechanic Wayne Kellogg right after the crash, without a life jacket and clinging to an oxygen bottle. Gunner Sam Bagwell had been seen too, but now neither could be found. Meanwhile, the fuselage began to sink. Glen and Bill pulled Henry and Carlin away from the wreck as it went under. They called out to see whether anyone else could hear. No reply.[127]

But in the pitch dark, several house-high waves away, John Summers was floating alone. He had no life jacket, something was clearly wrong with his leg, and he was having trouble staying afloat. He saw a curl of white water, like waves breaking on a reef, and swam toward it. It was another piece of the plane's wing, afloat on the surface. He climbed aboard and was washed off by a wave. Again he pulled himself up, and again he was swept away. When he got back a third time, he heard a gurgling noise and realized the wing was about to sink. He swam away so as not to be pulled under. He began treading water, but his clothes were weighing him down, so he stripped them off. Every so often he called out but never heard an answer.

In the darkness he lost track of time, but at some point Summers turned around and saw bow gunner John Presley and tail gunner Bob Lamar. He wasn't alone after all! Presley and Lamar both had on life jackets, half inflated. They also had a head rest from the pilot's seat cushion, which they gave to Summers. They compared notes about the crash. All had called out and heard nothing, so they decided they were the only survivors. Several times through the night, they drifted apart and lost sight of each other, but waves or the current or just plain luck brought them back together.

Despite the darkness, the squadron sent out a search plane. Summers, Lamar, and Presley heard the motors. Lamar, who still had his .38 pistol strapped to his waist, fired off a few tracer rounds. The crew of the plane saw the tracers and dropped a smoke light. They kept circling but couldn't see the survivors. The plane radioed its position to a nearby destroyer, which headed for the scene. The men could see the ship's searchlight split the dark nearby, but the destroyer never spotted them either.[128]

Meanwhile, men in the other group were holding on to each other and to the hope that they could somehow survive until daylight. In the dark, they could feel big fish nosing around, bumping them. One poked his snout between Bill's legs and lifted him out of the water. He kicked back at the fish.

Glen Box continued to hold up Ken Henry, who was so badly hurt he couldn't help himself at all. Henry was in tremendous pain, but he stayed calm. Jim Carlin, who had a fractured skull, was a bigger problem. The official aircraft action report in the National Archives reads,

Most of the time Carlin was out of his head. His struggles kept Ensign Pedretti constantly battling him as well as the waters. Once Ensign Pedretti was almost at the point of utter exhaustion. His tongue was swollen. He could hardly see. He was sick and vomiting nothing but salt water. Carlin broke away from him.

Pedretti just lay in the water. He couldn't even kick at a curious fish. He said that he thought his heart would either beat his insides to a pulp or else beat a hole through his chest. But all he could do was hang in his [life] jacket, thinking that he would not be able to come up from the next breaking swell to get air. However, he held onto his will to survive in a numb sort of way.

Presently he came out of his stupor just enough to hear Carlin calling. Somehow, he doesn't know the method, he got to

Carlin. Carlin was so far gone that he was not even struggling. Ensign Pedretti just reached out and laid hold of Carlin, and they remained afloat.

Toward daybreak, Carlin began to struggle again. Bill didn't have the strength to hold him but wouldn't let go. Glen suggested they switch; he took Carlin, and Bill stayed with Ken Henry—who told him to let go if he became too exhausted himself. Bill kept Henry afloat.[129]

In the first light of dawn, between tall waves, Summers, Lamar, and Presley spotted the other four in the water. They slowly swam in their direction, lost sight, and found them again.[130] Then everyone heard the sound of airplane engines, four of them, a Liberator. With the last of their strength, the men thrashed in the water, hoping that would help someone see them. The search plane banked, circled, dropped low for a closer look, and waggled its wings. At last.

The plane dropped a life raft about seventy-five yards away. Bill and another survivor swam to it. When they got there, they found that the inflation bottle was broken, but the raft itself was partially buoyant. They towed it back to the group, put Carlin and Henry in the raft, and had the others hang on to the sides. A second plane came in, dropping smoke lights and another raft. Again, Bill swam to it. It inflated perfectly. Carlin and Henry went in the inflated raft, the rest of the men held onto the outside, Glen got into the other raft, and Bill held the two together. The search plane guided a destroyer to the site, and the men were pulled aboard—several unconscious, the rest completely spent.[131]

For two days and nights, ranging as far away as two hundred miles, ships and planes searched for the others. They found only bits of floating debris. Between them, the seven survivors had three broken legs, one broken back, a fractured skull, two broken ankles, bite wounds from fish, and too many cuts and bruises to count. All suffered from exposure and exhaustion.[132]

Some would spend many months recuperating. John Summers, for instance, underwent half a dozen operations on his feet and wasn't discharged from the hospital until the spring of 1946. Others would take only a few days to recover. They had fought together; had survived a life-threatening, life-changing event; had saved each other against all odds. Yet once they were separated on board the destroyer that morning, most never saw each other again.[133]

A *New York Times* article on the squadron later recounted the story of the ditching in dramatic fashion:

> Struggling in the sable swells, Lieutenant Box counted noses by the faint light of the stars and found five of his men missing. He and his co-pilot, Ensign Albert W. Pedretti of Roscoe, Calif., kept the others alive in a battle against odds that will be a bright chapter in the history of naval aviation.[134]

Glen Box spent the next eight months in military hospitals recovering. He received the Distinguished Flying Cross and the Navy and Marine Corps Medal.[135] Bill Pedretti asked to stay with the squadron, but the navy sent him home, where he spent some time in a hospital. He and Marilyn married almost two months to the day after the crash, at the Little Country Church of Hollywood, a favorite place for celebrities to tie the knot. Bill was promoted to lieutenant junior grade and stationed in San Diego. With Marilyn proudly looking on, in early June—like Glen—he received the Distinguished Flying Cross and the Navy and Marine Corps Medal in a public ceremony at North Island.[136]

If this were the script of a 1940s movie, now the music would swell, and the credits would roll. But true stories sometimes end differently.

Glen Box was finally released from the hospital in the summer of 1945 and assigned to the naval air station in Jacksonville, Florida. One day he went with a friend to pick up some tailoring done at the on-base officers' uniform shop. The woman in charge there was named Miriam, a former teacher who had moved to Florida with her parents. She was an avid football fan, and for their first date Glen took her to a game. But he'd never played the sport or followed it much, so before they went, he bought and read a book, a sort of layman's guide to the game. That way, he figured, he could at least follow what was happening and converse with Miriam.[137] He needn't have worried. They were soon in love and married in 1946. Glen wore dress whites with his medals attached, and everyone remembered the sight of the war hero so nervous his knees knocked. That same year they moved to California and Glen enrolled at UCLA under a navy program that paid for his undergraduate degree.

For the next fifteen years the navy life took them and their four children to Alaska, Hawaii, California, Texas, Maryland, and Newfoundland. Glen retired in 1961 as a lieutenant commander, after twenty-six years of service.[138] He and Miriam moved to Jacksonville, where they had met. Because his navy pension wasn't enough to support the family, he tried selling insurance for a couple of years. But for the first time in his life, he was a failure, because he wouldn't sell people policies they couldn't afford.

The family finances went from bad to worse. A day of reckoning came in a diner where Glen had stopped for lunch. He felt a piece of paper on the floor of the booth where he sat alone. Thinking it was a fallen napkin, he slid it under his shoe and looked down. It turned out to be a $20 bill. Glen sat still and then quietly cried. His family needed the money, so he swallowed his pride and pocketed the bill before anyone noticed.[139]

He quit selling insurance the next day, went back to school, got a master's degree from Jacksonville University, and taught high school history and geography for more than a decade. His obituary noted that he had been elected president of the Duval County Teachers Association as well as president of the Silver Eagles Association, a national group of enlisted naval aviation pilots.

And every Christmas before he died in 1983, Glen sent a card to Bill Pedretti.[140]

So what about Bill? He settled at first into married life and his duties as a pilot, testing and ferrying planes from his base in San Diego. He loved flying. He was smart and a decorated war hero. He saw a bright future for himself in the navy. But Marilyn wasn't so sure. So he struggled with questions about the future.

A couple of weeks after V-J Day, he wrote to his parents,

> I know that if I get out of the Navy I'm a damned fool. If I stay in I'll make damned good money, I'll be able to get everything we

need, and by the time I'm forty-five I'll be able to retire. It looks awfully good to me. By staying in I'd have lots of fun and not a worry in the world.

Then there is Marilyn. She doesn't have much to say, but she definitely wants me out. She thinks I should go back to school. I'm going to look funny going to school and trying to make a living too.

Less than a month later, the decision was made:

I guess I'm going to get out of the Navy. That way everyone will be happy. Of course I don't know when, or what I'm going to do outside. I hate like hell to go back to school.

He postponed his separation until the end of the year so he could collect his maximum pay. In November, around the first anniversary of the crash, he got a letter from the mother of crewman Basil Martin:

If I could hear from you . . . just how my boy was wounded and if he spoke any words before the plane went down. Oh, how I would love to talk to someone that could tell me about the last day. Please if you will write and let me know how bad my son was wounded and if he spoke anything to tell his parents. He was our only child and we do miss him.

Bill wrote back and tried to comfort her. The week before Christmas, she replied,

I know how you would feel over such a disaster, as most of the ones that went through such horrible times do not care to recall it. That is why I am more than thankful to you for telling what happened.

A few weeks later, Bill resigned his commission. But he never really left the navy and that night in the water behind. All his life, he kept a framed picture of his Liberator in his bedroom. Years later, his younger brother said Bill's hopes and aspirations went down with the wreck.

But, at first, it didn't really seem that way. He took college courses at night for several years but never earned his degree. Following in his father's footsteps, he went into the painting business and within a decade was vice president of a large commercial painting company. He and Marilyn had two daughters and a son, the last born in 1963. He joined the Los Angeles Athletic Club and Brentwood Country Club. They often entertained at home. He loved opera, playing it at full volume on the stereo.

In his spare time, Bill enjoyed sports of all kinds. Waterskiing, sailing, fishing, darts, tennis, badminton, archery—he took up each challenge and then moved on once he'd mastered it. The exception was golf, which he never quite conquered. That's probably why he continued to play for the rest of his life.[141]

He also insisted that all his children be good swimmers, able to handle themselves in the ocean.[142]

But there were troubles too. He and Marilyn were both strong willed, sometimes hotheaded. They lived in an elegant house, and once he refused her request for new drapes. She sold the diamond from her engagement ring and bought them anyway. But there was no doubt that they loved each other. And the storms usually passed.

What finally broke them up was Bill's drinking. It's hard to say why or when it became a real problem. But he got in the habit of stopping off somewhere on the way home from work. Hours later he would call Marilyn, who would pick him up and bring him home. As his daughters became older, they took over the chauffeuring duties. When they got to the tavern or club, he would greet them happily, introduce his new friends, and order another round for everyone. He was a boon companion and the center of attention. His girls often sat at the end of the bar sipping tea, waiting until the party wound down and he decided it was time to leave.

Less often, Bill drank at family gatherings. But when he did, he sometimes recounted the story of his crash. And when he got to the part about John Craig slipping off the wing, he cried. As if something in Bill had died that night too. As if, ever since, he'd been living on borrowed time. And the price he'd paid was never quite enough.[143]

In 1970, Bill's daughters threw a twenty-fifth anniversary party for their parents. But within a year, Marilyn left him. When his lawyer showed Bill the divorce papers, he saw that Marilyn would get less than half his earnings. He asked the court to increase his payments to her.

After the decree was final, Bill still referred to Marilyn as his wife. He never took off his wedding ring, even having it resized as his fingers got fatter. His work suffered. He lost jobs but always found another. His last home was a trailer in San Bernardino.

Bill died in 1987. He never remarried. Neither did Marilyn.[144]

The only nonfiction book James Jones wrote about the war was titled simply *WWII*. In its final paragraph, he tried to sum up what that time had meant to him and so many others. They were, he said, "a whole generation of men who would walk into history looking backwards, peering forever over their shoulders behind them. . . . None of them would ever really get over it."[145]

I'll Be Seeing You

At first all I had was a photocopy, the ghost of a since-lost snapshot taken outside a tent on Tinian. It showed Harold Stang and Bill Benn, pilot and copilot of VPB-117's Crew 14 and, everyone said, best friends. Harold stood in rumpled khakis, right hand on hip, left hand resting on a rope tied to the tent pole. Next to him Bill wore combat boots, white athletic socks, shorts, and what looked like a fatigue jacket, hand in his pocket. Harold had stevedore shoulders and a shock of dark hair standing straight up. Bill was rangy and balding. Both were looking at the camera. Both were grinning. A hand-lettered caption read,

> Benn was a man of varied talents. He ran the high hurdles in the Olympic games, a sharp wit, a connoisseur of jive music, and a graduate aeronautical engineer.[146]

Which, it turns out, was mostly true.

"He was born smiling." That's what his mother said, and that's what you remembered most—the smile. But what you noticed first about Bill Benn were the long legs. He grew up in Minneapolis, gangly but graceful, loose limbs, light feet. He had a light touch with people too. Lots of friends, lots of fun, popular without seeming to try. A good kid with just enough mischief to make things interesting.

Like many boys back then, his interests ran to sports, girls, music—and flying. As an athlete he was a born runner. By the time he reached Washburn High, Bill was over six feet, gobbling up ground with oversized strides. He became a champion hurdler and high jumper and captain of the track team. A newspaper picture shows his left leg already over a hurdle, his right trailing perfectly parallel to the ground, arms spread wide like a bird. Even in the photo's foreshortened perspective, it's clear the rest of the runners are hopelessly behind. In his senior year Bill set state records in both the high and the low hurdles.[147] That summer, in an exhibition race against 1936 Olympic hopefuls, he finished a close second to Fritz Pollard Jr., who went on to win a bronze medal in Berlin.[148]

Away from the track and the classroom, where he did well but didn't set any records, Bill spent most of his time on music. Swing, jazz, jive—he couldn't get enough. Once he saw his kid sister Patty pocket a Baby Ruth candy bar at the corner store. He made her return it and apologize to the owner. Outside, Patty begged him not to tell their mother. Bill agreed, but only if she stopped listening to *Jack Armstrong, the All-American Boy* on the radio every afternoon at five. He wanted that time to hear broadcasts of his favorite bands.

Bill had a paper route all through high school to pay for his records— Dorsey, Krupa, Goodman. And what he didn't spend on music he spent on clothes.[149] He liked to look sharp, especially on Saturday nights when he'd lead cars full of friends to the downtown hotels where the big orchestras played. Because they were underage, and because Bill was the tallest and the best talker, he was the one who wheedled their way in. Almost every time, it worked. And almost every Sunday, after a night full of foxtrots, he fell asleep in the family pew at eleven o'clock Mass.[150]

So let's see: Jazz buff, good dresser, great dancer. Strong student, star athlete. That took care of the music, the sports—and the girls. Which left flying. As boys, Bill and his buddies rode bikes out of town to Wold-Chamberlain Field, named for two Minneapolis fliers killed over Château-Thierry during World War I.[151] Often the boys were the only ones around, wandering through a wooden hangar quiet as an empty church. They ran their hands over the wings of the parked planes and tested the guy wires that held the frames together.

Then one summer, while Bill was still in his teens, the Benns rented a cottage on the Virginia shore. He immediately fell in love with beach life. They had picnics, built bonfires. He swam and ran to stay in shape. But he liked best rowing out from shore in a dinghy while navy fliers from nearby Norfolk buzzed the boat. The speed, the noise, the joy on their faces as they flashed by only feet above—he wanted all of that. He didn't even mind getting seasick every time.

His father was often away on business, so Bill handled many "man of the house" duties. He also became very close to his mother. She wasn't Mom; she became "Nellie."[152] In the fall of 1936 Bill enrolled at the University of Minnesota. It had a track team; it also was one of the few schools that offered a degree in aeronautical engineering. Bill starred again as a hurdler. He joined a jock fraternity, Phi Delta Theta (1940 Minnesota yearbook: "They work hard . . . study[?] . . . hard[?]"). He kept dating and dancing. He even enjoyed his engineering courses. And he got his first taste of flying through the Civilian Pilot Training program at the university.[153]

After graduating in 1941, Bill went to work in Philadelphia at the Naval Aircraft Factory, established during World War I to design and produce combat and experimental planes. The job came with a permanent draft deferment, and it was very interesting.[154] So was his social life. He had a rich friend who owned his own plane, "a deluxe job." Weekends they'd fly to Washington or New York. He wrote Nellie about a typical trip:

> Del and I had a swell time in Washington. I'm certainly crazy about that town. We arrived there about noon on Saturday and Del checked into the Annapolis and we met his girl there (very choice). Dave came and he and I went to a Minnesota reunion at the Hotel 2400. I met a swell gal from Duluth. We toured the town, dancing, etc. We went through the zoo on Sunday and she invited me over to the club she stays at for Sunday dinner. We flew home about seven o'clock Sunday night. I saw lots of people I knew at the reunion. Much fun, we drank beer, etc.[155]

"Touring the town" with "a swell gal." You can almost see him swirling her around a hotel ballroom and later lighting her cigarette as they linger at a table. Maybe the next day, after Sunday dinner, she goes with him to the airport. He smiles, says he hopes they'll meet again. She watches as he and Del climb into the plane and close the doors. Evening shadows stretch; an engine coughs, then roars. It was the stuff of Hollywood scripts. But reality intruded. Less than a month after he wrote that note, the Japanese bombed Pearl Harbor. Everything changed, including Bill. To his family he seemed older, more serious. His job would have kept him out of the service, but he began to talk about enlisting. By summer he was a naval aviation cadet, on his way to basic training.[156]

In peacetime, it's unlikely that Harold Stang would have met Bill Benn, much less become his boss and friend. They came from different worlds. But war not only tears people apart but also throws them together. And sometimes they stick.

Harold's father was a railroad worker from Germany who immigrated to America before World War I. Peter Stang had it in his head to be a farmer, so he settled in Colorado. He and his wife, Sophie, had a bumper crop of children—four girls and, finally, a boy born on Halloween 1917. It was World War I, and anti-German feeling ran high. Restaurants relabeled sauerkraut "liberty cabbage."[157] German immigrants were legally imprisoned simply for saying the kaiser would win.[158] But the family's biggest problem wasn't prejudice; it was Peter's failure as a farmer. Everything he planted withered. So they moved to Cheyenne, Wyoming, a major hub for the Union Pacific. Peter was once again a railroad man.[159] Young Harold grew up fishing the Jackson Hole, reveling in rodeos and anything western. He finished his formal education in the sixth grade; that was as much as the public school offered. Then the Depression hit. He collected bottles for cash. He borrowed a truck, went up into the mountains, dug coal by hand, and sold it back in town.

And Harold helped his father take one last stab at farming. Peter had heard that sugar beets were a practically foolproof crop, so he found some land and planted them. The field was on a terraced hillside, with water for irrigation held in at the top by an earthen berm. Harold would leave a warm bed well before sunrise, hike to the top of the hill, and shovel a small opening in the dam. As the water began to trickle, he would walk to the bottom, lay in the last row, and go back to sleep under a wide Wyoming sky. The water dribbled down, back and forth between the beets, until it finally splashed on his forehead, waking him in time for other chores.

Harold was baptized this way every day. Then one morning he awoke to a strange sound. Not a tractor, not a truck on the highway. He wiped the water from his face and sat up. It was a biplane. Someone had rented the neighboring field to barnstormers, pilots who flew around the country selling airplane rides and doing stunts. He watched them the rest of the day and the days after. Here was a way off the prairie and over the mountains. Before long he left home to join the navy and become a pilot. He was sixteen.[160]

Naturally, he lied about his age on the application. The navy found out and shipped him home. He spent the next three years working for the Civilian Conservation Corps and helping his father farm. Throwing fifty pounds of sugar beets over his shoulder with a pitchfork made him very strong—and very determined never to be landlocked or earthbound again. At age nineteen he joined the navy once more.[161]

The recruiter had told him he could become a pilot. And they did put him in a squadron aboard the USS *Ranger*, the first navy ship built from the keel up as an aircraft carrier. But he was a seaman second class; there would be no wings. For several years Harold worked his way up in the enlisted ranks, qualifying as an aircraft radioman and knocking around in both big oceans from Pearl Harbor to Guantanamo. He also began what became a lifelong habit: buying dictionaries and memorizing the meanings of new words. That way, a guy with a grade-school education could talk with anyone about anything.[162]

Sometime in the summer of 1940, Harold was in a serious plane crash. He spent six weeks in the Norfolk Naval Hospital, and when he was released, he met a woman. Her name was Elsie. Like Harold, she was the child of immigrants—her mother had come to America from Syria. But that was about all they had in common. Elsie was emotional; Harold was logical. She stood barely five feet; he was more than a foot taller. Still, something clicked, and they were married that same year.

Soon after, Harold's four-year hitch in the navy was up for renewal. He took a chance and refused to reenlist unless he was guaranteed pilot training. His timing was excellent. By the spring of 1941 war looked more and more likely, and the need for fliers was growing. The requirement that pilots be officers and have some college was being waived. So in April Harold left for Pensacola; in October he got his wings.[163] While training he learned that he had congenitally low blood pressure, which meant he blacked out easily under the g-forces generated in fighter planes. So he was assigned to the "boats," the patrol planes, and sent to San Diego in November.

Within weeks he found himself aboard the aircraft carrier *Enterprise*, due home at Pearl Harbor on December 7, 1941, after delivering fighter planes to marines on Wake Island.[164] But heavy weather caused Admiral Bill Halsey to reduce speed, delaying the *Enterprise*'s arrival by a day.[165] Harold had missed his date with destiny, but he didn't have to wait long to fight the Japanese. By April he was stationed in Perth, western Australia, flying patrols in PBYs. He stayed there more than a year, during which his first son was born. A San Diego newspaper photo from the time shows Elsie wearing a heart-shaped locket and Harold's navy wings pinned to her dress. In her lap is a little boy. The caption reads,

> Harold Stang Jr., nicknamed "Boogie," will at last meet his dad, Harold Stang Sr. This picture will introduce the 10-month-old lad to his father. Stang, chief aviation pilot in the Navy, has been overseas since March 1942. "Boogie" greeted the world in August.[166]

The headline said, "This young man's father is in far-off Australia." But by the time the picture was printed Harold was on his way to his next assignment, taking aboriginal spotters and scouts in and out of Japanese-held territory on the north coast of New Guinea. Even flying only at night, the planes regularly ran a gauntlet of enemy gunners. Harold patched the bullet holes with duct tape and kept going. This went on until the area got too hot and his squadron was finally ordered home. In November 1943, twenty months after he shipped out, Harold met Boogie in person.[167]

June Dohner's father owned the drugstore on the corner of the courthouse square in Kokomo, Indiana. In the fall of 1942, she was twenty-one and beautiful, taking time off after three years at Stevens College in Missouri.[168] Big news in town was the pilot training base the navy had just opened nearby. The station was so new that the runway wasn't even finished; the first class of twenty cadets took off and landed on grass. They called it the "U.S.S. Cornfield."[169]

June's mother and her mother's best friend, whose son June was dating, decided to open up a canteen for the navy boys. They found second-floor space in a building on Main Street, hauled up a jukebox, bought some Cokes, baked some cookies, and opened the doors. The night it opened, June was there to help. One of the first fliers through the door was a lanky guy with a big grin. He walked straight over to June and said, "Hello. Thanks for waiting for me." She laughed. He introduced himself: "First name Bill, last name Benn. Not first name Ben." She laughed again. He said he liked the music on the jukebox and asked her to dance. He was a very good dancer. They talked. He was a city boy, had probably been to sophisticated clubs and dated sophisticated girls. But he was gracious and gentle. He had a serious side. And he was kind—she could tell that too.

Neither June nor Bill ever went back to the canteen. He began visiting her at home whenever he could scrounge a ride into town. They chatted with her parents, who then retired to a sitting room upstairs. Bill and June stretched out in front of the fireplace and filled in the blanks in their backgrounds. Winter was coming on, and Bill often talked about his high school summer on the shore, how he'd loved the ocean and the beach and would like to show it to her someday.

One night in front of the fireplace, he turned to her and said, "I really do love you." He was the first to talk about marriage, and by Christmas he had bought a wedding ring. Soon after, he left for Pensacola to finish his training.[170] Bill got his wings in May 1943 and married June the same month, at the Main Street Christian Church in Kokomo.[171]

His father didn't come; he didn't approve of his son marrying a non-Catholic. But Nellie made the trip. She and June hit it off immediately. After the ceremony, Bill, June, and Nellie boarded a train back to Minneapolis to introduce her to the rest of the family. Between Kokomo and Chicago, June dozed while Bill and his mother chatted. Once she woke without opening her eyes and heard Bill say, "Nellie, she's everything I ever wanted." She let the train rock her back to sleep.

They stayed overnight at a hotel in Chicago. When they arrived, Bill and June went to their room, and his mother went to hers. Five minutes later, the phone rang. It was Nellie, wanting to know whether they'd like to go to dinner. Bill said he'd call back. June hugged him and said, "Don't look at the bed!" She laughed and told him his mother had had a long day. She was in a strange city in a room by herself. They would take Nellie to dinner, and they would have their own time later. So they did, and they did.

Their first home together was in Hollywood Beach, Florida, a resort north of Miami that had been turned into a "navy town" for the duration. A gunnery school came first, followed by the U.S. Naval Air Navigation School housed in the plush Hollywood Beach Hotel. Bill and June lived a block away in a second-story apartment, right on the beach.[172] When Bill went off to "work" during the day, June volunteered as a lookout and plane spotter. Early in the war, dozens of freighters had been torpedoed offshore by German U-boats, and a coast watch had been kept ever since. June sat in a cupola on the roof of the hotel, staring into field glasses for hours. She never saw anything except seagulls and navy trainers, but it helped pass the time.[173] Sometimes Bill would be on flights overnight or for several days. Navy regulations didn't allow him to tell her where he was going, but he got around the rules by sending her funny telegrams:

SHOO SHOO, BABY, FROM THE CANADIAN CLUB.
I'LL BE THERE SOON.

Most nights they ate alone in their apartment listening to records, often dancing after dessert in the darkening living room. Other evenings they spent with friends. The navy social scene in Hollywood was warm and relaxed, not like at some bigger bases. They were all young, and they all wanted to make the most of their time together. There were parties, usually pretty tame. There were days off; Bill loved being back on the beach, and June took to it even better than he'd hoped. A photo shows them sprawled on the sand, Bill wearing his aviator sunglasses, June in her two-piece suit, squinting into the sunlight. They were a handsome, happy couple. They made quick and close friendships. It was like one long honeymoon.

New Year's Eve 1943 they bought whistles, made newspaper hats, and invited some friends over. There were drinks and hors d'oeuvres. Sometime after midnight only Bill and June and the couple from downstairs remained. Bill got a mischievous look and suggested they go skinny dipping. Oh no, they couldn't do that. Bill laughed. It was the middle of the night, he said. They'd wrap themselves in towels, drop them by the water, and be up to their necks in ocean before anyone saw them. That sounded logical somehow. They sprinted across the sand and dove into the water. They were laughing and splashing when one of the girls said, "What about the guards?" The coast guard patrolled the beach on horseback throughout the night to prevent infiltration from the sea. Like June in her cupola, they never saw any Nazis. But they were out there nonetheless, and now they would surely see the two couples and order them out of the water. The four looked both ways down the beach and dashed back to the apartment. Inside, Bill said he was sure if the guards knew what they were doing, they would understand. After all, it was New Year's. He went to find them. Ten minutes later, he returned and said they'd gotten the all clear. Well, it was a special occasion. So back across the beach and into the waves one more time. The stars were still out when they ran home, holding hands.

That spring Bill was ordered to report to VPB-117. San Diego was a bigger town, Camp Kearny a bigger base. The beach was bigger too. It went on for miles, lazy Pacific rollers washing ashore with the morning fog. And the social scene was different. Couples weren't all the same age; rank was more apparent and important. But Bill and June didn't pay much attention. Just blocks from the famous Del Coronado Hotel with its red roofs, they rented the maid's quarters in the home of a retired admiral. They had their own entrance and could come and go as they pleased.

The work was more serious. Bill didn't tell June he was training for combat. He said he was involved with a special project in the squadron, one that made use of his engineering skills. It might take him overseas, but he would probably be back in a few months.[174] He first flew with

Harold Stang on June 1. By July, they were a team and had their own crew. Harold was solid, serious. Bill kept everyone at ease. His receding hairline earned him a nickname, "The Brow," and he laughed along with the rest. When Bill was at the base, June again volunteered, working in a converted A&P grocery store riveting instruments into control panels for B-24s. They made new friends and became regulars on nights when a favorite piano player was working at the Coronado. The days rolled in and receded like the waves. Whatever time they had, it would have to be enough.

Word came that the squadron would ship out in August. The night before, Bill and June dressed in their best. They had dinner and then visited their friend at the Coronado. He played their favorite song, "I'll Be Seeing You."

Back home, Bill laid out his khakis for the morning. When he got into bed, June quietly asked whether he wanted to make love. He didn't think so; he was too sad.[175] The next day at dusk June went to the end of the runway at Camp Kearny. Bill's plane rolled into place for takeoff. Harold ran up the engines; Bill leaned out the window and waved. Desert dust blew. First the roar and then the plane itself faded into the evening sky. They were over the ocean in minutes.[176]

June stayed in San Diego for a few days and then left to live with her parents while Bill was away. The train trip to Kokomo took two days, and she spent the whole time in a dressing area off the women's washroom; there were no other seats to be had.[177] In Hawaii, Harold and Bill continued to complement each other in the cockpit. Harold was old-school. He could read waves so well he knew how far they were from land without looking at a map.[178] Bill handled all the "slide rule stuff." It was a good combination. The navy told families that any Christmas packages for men overseas had to be mailed by September 15. So June filled three shoe boxes with tokens and trinkets—writing paper, pencils, socks, a miniature Christmas tree. And she made plans to visit Bill's family.

Harold and Bill flew their first combat patrol from Tinian on October 4. They had six more missions that month, ten in November. Most were fairly routine. They bombed and strafed a Japanese freighter. They shot at a plane they listed as "probable," meaning they hadn't seen the plane crash, though it likely had.[179] On the long flights the roar of the engines prevented much conversation, so they developed private jokes and gestures. Bill carried a picture of June in his pocket; she was reclining on a couch, wearing a robe. Whenever it looked like trouble might be coming, he would pull out the picture and wave it at Harold, as if to say, "Don't forget, we want to go home."[180]

On December 1, they transferred to Tacloban, and almost immediately the war hit closer to home. Their first patrol in the Philippines took them over Bataan and Corregidor, where Bill's family friend Lawrence Meade had died in what became known as the Death March. Bill wrote his mother,

> Tell Rena that I flew over where Lawrence died and saw all that country. I really had a lump in my throat. I felt I was making history all over again and I'm proud of it. You tell Rena we are paying the dirty Japs back tenfold.

The bitterness didn't sound like Bill to her, but the rest of the letter felt more familiar:

> I hope you and June are having a nice visit. Write and tell me all about her. Just think, I'm way out here and still just a few days from home. I don't really feel like I'm far from home.[181]

All this time Bill was writing June too—recalling times they'd made love, talking about starting a family, about his friendship with Harold, telling her he'd received one of her Christmas packages.[182] On December 18 he and Harold flew through a typhoon that battered Bill Halsey's fleet, sinking three destroyers and killing almost eight hundred men.[183] On Christmas Day they headed north-northwest, toward the China coast. On the way, they broke through the overcast and found themselves right over Manila Bay. In the harbor were hundreds of Japanese ships, marshaled to oppose the coming American invasion of Luzon. The Liberator was quickly flanked by eight enemy fighters, four on each side. Maybe they were training, maybe they had no ammunition, but for whatever reason, the fighters stayed just out of gun range. Waist gunners in the crew actually motioned them to come closer, but no shots were fired. They flew on, landing at Tacloban thirteen hours after takeoff.[184]

The intensity of the patrols was draining. On December 30, Bill wrote Nellie again:

> Don't send me any more packages because I'll probably be home before they arrive. We are flying a great deal. It's quite tiring and rather a strain so I sleep nearly all the time I'm not flying. Glad you and June had a nice visit. I knew you would love her once you got to know her. She is a dear sweet girl. The longer I know her the more I love her. I'm glad she has gotten herself some clothes. I really enjoy dressing her up. Well, love to all and write often.
>
> Billy Boy

The next morning, New Year's Eve, they took off again for the China coast. They were attacked by a Zero and took advantage of some cloud cover, but it was an otherwise uneventful flight until monsoon rain draped the field as they approached Tacloban in the dark.[185] Ralph Sanders, the air bomber and the youngest member of the crew, was standing on the bomb bay catwalk, leaning forward and watching the pilots. Rain had overwhelmed the windshield wipers. It was pitch-black except for searing streaks of lightning. The tower said conditions were zero-zero. Dangerously low on gas, they came in anyway. Ralph watched the altimeter on the instrument panel unwind, like a clock running backward, and heard the engines roar as the plane pitched upward again. Harold and Bill couldn't see anything. They tried again with the same result and then circled in the storm for twenty more minutes, waiting for a break. The squall squatted over the runway, the fuel situation went past critical, and they had to make another pass. Visibility was still nil; they lowered and locked the landing gear, lining up where the strip should be. Two hundred yards from the runway, all four engines quit. They'd been in the air for more than fourteen hours; they needed only twenty seconds more.

Ralph Sanders thought they'd landed and hit the ground too hard. But the plane didn't bounce, and then everything went black. He came to in a tangle of metal, took a breath, and got a mouthful of ocean. Slowly he realized the wheels had hit water, not land, and the plane had flipped on its back. He felt water rising toward him. Then he realized his leg was trapped. He tried to yank it free but couldn't. The water came up to his chest, to his chin. Finally, he could breathe only through his nose. But the plane stopped sinking. The auxiliary rubber fuel tanks in the bomb bay, drained hours earlier, had enough air in them to keep the plane half afloat, at least for a while. Maybe they shifted something in the wreckage as well, because his leg began to work loose. Ralph swam free of the fuselage just as a landing craft from the base roared up and lowered its ramp right on his head.

Most of the crew had been aft and were thrown clear. Amazingly, they had mainly minor injuries—cuts and bruises, a badly broken leg. Those in the bow were not as lucky. Ralph Sanders spent nine months in the hospital and had to have skin grafts to repair his leg.[186] Navigator John Studebaker went through the cockpit window headfirst. He had a broken arm, broken collarbone, and badly cut leg.[187] Harold Stang had fared worse. When they found him in the water, his left arm seemed barely attached to his torso. He had lost a lot of blood. They took him straight to the surgeon, who looked him over and said, "I'm going to have to take your arm." Lying on the table, Harold reached up with his still-good right hand, grabbed the doctor by the collar, and pulled his face close. "If you do that," he said, "tomorrow morning I'll go out to the garbage and find it. Then I'll bring it back here and shove it up your ass." When Harold woke the next day, his arm was still attached.[188]

The only one who didn't clear the crash was Bill Benn. He spent the night in thirty feet of water, upside down, still strapped into his seat. At dawn an officer rowed out with a navy diver, who brought Bill in. The doctor said he'd died instantly of a fractured skull.[189] When word spread through the squadron, some didn't believe it. By now they knew how random and ridiculous things could get, but this was Bill. He was special, he was smart, he was charmed. Nobody told Harold Stang at first, and when they did, he was inconsolable. The navy put him on a hospital ship and sent him home to Elsie. When he arrived, doctors told her never to ask about the accident.[190]

In Kokomo, June's parents were hosting a small New Year's Eve party. She stayed for a while but excused herself early and went to her room. Earlier in the day she had written Bill, reminding him about last New Year's Eve on the beach and promising, "We'll celebrate when you come home."

Two weeks later, her father answered the phone one evening and spoke softly for maybe a minute. He came back to the living room and sat next to June. He told her the call had been from one of Bill's relatives. "He had terrible news, June. Bill died in a plane crash on December 31."

When the words exploded in her ears, it seemed the concussion would be enough to knock the earth off its axis. June and her mother sat up until dawn in two chairs, facing each other in front of the fireplace, crying. In the days that followed, disbelief turned to anger. How could God do that? Bill had so much to offer. As the first in Kokomo to lose a husband in the war, June immediately became "the widow." She hated the attention, the sincere but useless attempts to console.[191] Better somehow were the earnest, awkward notes from navy friends:

Wherever Bill went he made friends with his cheery smile and good word. His memory will continue to do so, I'm sure. I only wish I could help in some way.[192]

June, no one can ever take away the memories of your happy days in Hollywood. You and Bill were always having so much fun together that it was a pleasure to be in your company. Not trying to be a Pollyanna but those times are something that many married couples never experience—the complete happiness and joy of living that you found there.[193]

There was a memorial service in the church where they had married. A red carpet was laid over the snowy steps. The American Legion put a picture of Bill on a table. The minister spoke. Someone sang. A bugler played "Taps." Only when an officer gave her the folded flag did June cry.

Some time later, the navy mailed back the two Christmas packages Bill never received. They were waterlogged, smashed. With them came his billfold. Inside was a note from her.[194]

An Open Book

Harold Boss's life was an open book, tapped out in a tent on a borrowed typewriter. Autobiography helped plug the holes in idle hours, especially now that he wasn't flying. Yet his memoir was more than a way to kill time or avoid awkward encounters. It had drama. It had humor. It had plenty of romance.

But let's begin at the beginning: May 1942, in Buffalo, New York.

> I wandered into the main post office with nothing else on my mind other than to buy an air mail stamp. While standing in line, I came face to face with Uncle Sam saying, "The Navy needs you," followed by the Navy's top-ranking flier smiling from his fighter plane adorned with Jap flags. "You, too, can fly with the United States Navy."[195]

When he saw that poster, Harold was twenty-two years old. He had a good job building airplane engines in a former Chevy factory, and he had a good time in the evenings as a blue-collar man about town. He also still lived with his mother. She had divorced his father years earlier, and Harold now shared a home with her, her second husband, a grown stepsister, and a nine-year-old stepbrother. It was a full house, and maybe that was on Harold's mind as he climbed the five flights of stairs to the recruiting office on the top floor.

An old Chief Petty Officer nailed me as his own and the siege was on. We discussed my trade and I meekly asked if it would be possible to sign on as an Aviation Machinist Mate Third Class, in view of my experience along those lines. "Son, take it from me, earn yourself a commission in naval aviation."

I saw the way out and used it. "Sorry, I haven't the required college education, and besides I'd rather be a Machinist's Mate," I responded. Then he said, "In view of the urgent need for aviators, the college education requirements have been lifted and I'm sure you have a high school diploma." That did it.

An officer and a gentleman. And a pilot! Girls loved fliers, and Harold loved girls of all kinds. Girls liked him too—blonde hair, bright blue eyes, a ready wit. But his best girl was his mother. He was, said a family friend, "the great love of her life." So when he got home and broke the news, she immediately cried and kept crying.[196] The only consolation was that his first post was literally right down the road—Civilian Pilot Training at the Buffalo airport. It didn't go that well. On his final check flight, he committed the cardinal sin of landing his Piper Cub downwind, rolling more than a mile before he could bring it to a stop: "The sight is still the talk of the hangar pilots around the Buffalo airport. But somehow I managed to pass the requirements, both of flying and ground school."[197]

Next he left for real, for preflight training in Chapel Hill, North Carolina. The emphasis there was on learning to do things the navy way and on physical conditioning:

> The only thing I had done in an athletic way since high school was to build up my right arm bicep lifting foaming glasses of beer off the bar. I carried 186 pounds of malt muscle on my 5'9" frame, thereby achieving the look of a duck waddling down the way. This, of course, had to go.
>
> Boxing left the greatest impression. The weight limits in this so-called body building sport stopped at 175 pounds for heavyweights. All those unfortunate enough to fall over that mark were designated "unlimited." I was unlimited, and expendable. My first

bout was a classic long to be remembered by our coach. My opponent turned out to be an ex-Marine just returned from the forward areas for flight training. He towered at a height somewhere less than 11 feet and his arms dangled about eight feet long.

The bell rang, the Marine threw his right, and—lights out for me, although it was only 10 o'clock on a bright winter morning. This routine was repeated with disgusting regularity for a period of days and in between said murder, my Marine friend, with a benevolent arm around me, would say, "It hurts me more to do it than it does you."

Harold was finally saved by a case of the measles and a nurse. She was a WAVE officer, and her name was Jerry. Having no desire to go back to boxing, Harold played the invalid, and Jerry played along.

"Jerry, (I called her Jerry when alone as we were buddy buddies by this time) it's a shame we can't get together when I'm finally evacuated from here as I sure would enjoy dating you." I, of course, knew this was impossible as a naval officer associates only with other officers—or so it is said in the book. Jerry smiled, thought my little speech over and gave out these golden words of knowledge: "In the Navy it's not what you are supposed to do, but what you can get away with."

This advice still guides me in dubious moments. "But where could we possibly go that we wouldn't be seen? The town is so small you could hold your breath and walk around it leisurely." For her sake I knew that this thing would have to be handled with discretion. Jerry again coped with the situation by producing a cute apartment belonging to a friend of hers, and so started a series of Saturdays that helped make me think there was more to war than blood, sweat and tears.[198]

After thirteen weeks, Harold had lost twenty-eight pounds and shipped off to E-base in Glenview, Illinois, outside Chicago. More ground school and more time in the air. The flying was more demanding than before, including aerobatics, and again it didn't go that well. But again, the girls made up for it. Overnight liberty was granted every other week.

For some unexplainable reasons Chicago liked us, and for very substantial reasons we liked Chicago. The people—especially the young, good-looking and otherwise attractive girls—took us to their hearts. Some, in fact, took us to other places, including their apartments. My gang haunted the Celtic Room of the Hotel Sherman, meeting some of Chicago's most attractive women, who drank up our beer.

We pooled our money and one or two predetermined cadets would engage a room or, if possible, a suite of rooms to do, as one might say, our big-time operating. To find anywhere from 10 to 20 cadets and dates having a party in one room was nothing out of the ordinary. And 0400 was no different than 2000.

Problem was, a lot of check flights with instructors took place on Sunday afternoons, following Saturday nights. One bad flight meant a "down check," and two meant you washed out and were shipped to nearby Great Lakes Naval Training Station to become an ordinary seaman.

I found myself in this perilous predicament twice, mostly because of the Hotel Sherman, but was successful in obtaining extra time by the Board. The Board consisted of three to six instructors who decided if the cadet in question rated additional time in which to get squared away. This time granted, the real sweat job was to convince two check pilots you had gotten the word, and then on to the next stage. It all turned out for the best as my luck and talking ability held out.

And so it went. Harold zigzagged across the country, every stop marked by the names of bases, places—and women. Intermediate flight training in Corpus Christi found him struggling with instrument flying, both in the air and on the ground in the Link trainer. His Link instructor was a WAVE named Kay, and naturally she took pity on him.

On dates, instead of making violent love under a beautiful Texas moon, Kay would think up horrible radio problems she forced me to solve. It was the oddest love affair ever, as when, in an affectionate mood, instead of the age-old kiss, Kay would give out with a pretty A-. or N-. and received in answer a simulated fading or building radio beam. The Navy sure changed my ideas about a lot of things, but that kiss substitution was the tops.

At times the Link was more trouble than actual airplanes, but Harold eventually qualified in the flying boats. The last hurdle to earning his wings was Morse code. He swore off the social life; no dates, not even any movies, while he went to extra study sessions in the evenings. But still he couldn't get past eight words a minute, and it took twelve to graduate. After six weeks he broke his ban on women and attended a dance hosted by a sorority at a local college. There he met Jo ("She had a most beautiful body and long black hair that flowed freely over her shoulders"), who ditched her date to go home with Harold ("I floated back to the base at 0600 on clouds") and made it clear she wanted to see him again ("When a girl of Jo's desirability made a statement like that, who was I to not obey?"). Once again inspired by a woman ("Jo supplied the motive that two hours a day and no movies failed to instill in me"), he passed at last ("through the grace of a radioman's failing eyesight").

Did anyone ever admonish Harold, tell him that women are not playing cards to be shuffled before he deals the next hand, that something he missed in the classroom or in the air might one day be crucial to him or his crew? Some of his instructors or fellow cadets may have tried. Later, some in the squadron did too. But he had an easy smile, he made more fun of himself than anyone else, and he wanted you to have a good time too. So he squeaked by. On December 18, 1943—nineteen months after he signed up—he accepted his commission and wings as Naval Aviator C-12597. "Did I say accepted them?" he later wrote. "I almost knocked the admiral off his sea legs getting that piece of paper out of his hands." Jokes aside, it was probably his proudest moment. In their commissioning pictures, most young aviators struck a serious pose, trying to look menacing and world-weary at the same time. Ensign Harold Boss beamed. He cocked his hat, smiled until his cheeks creased, and wore his new status like a crisply tailored uniform.

After Corpus Christi came a short stint at the Banana River Naval Air Station in Florida ("We had a few girls at the River and did our best to entertain them"), followed by orders to report to Hutchinson, Kansas, for training as a copilot in a PB4Y-1. Harold had never seen a Liberator in person before, and his first visit to the cockpit was discouraging:

> The entire width of the plane was just covered with instruments. Later on, I snuck out to a plane and sat there for an hour counting all the gizmos a pilot had to push up, push down, flip up, flip down, turn on, turn off, twist on, twist off, switch on, switch off, in addition to all the instruments. I threw in the towel at one hundred sixty.

This plane was different and more daunting than anything he'd flown before. Also different—and maybe more daunting too—was a woman he met in the nearest town, forty miles from base.

> Edith lived in Wichita, and Kansas seemed the place a fellow should go to find his mate. I not only liked Edith and she me, but I also fell in love with her whole family, three sisters and all. They took me in as one of the gang, and so filled an empty space my wanderings in the Navy caused to exist—the affection and enjoyment of being in a family group.

Maybe Harold had had enough fun by now. Maybe he was just homesick. While in Hutchinson, he received orders to report to his new squadron in California, so maybe edging closer to actual combat made him more serious about his work and his life. It's not clear exactly how far his relationship with Edith had progressed.

> Her Dad looked to me for moral support as here was one man fighting a losing battle with five women. "Be sure to come back soon, as I take a lot of guff from these females." With this kind

of backing and diplomatically staying on the right side of the women who did the cooking, I settled down to a contented life. I enjoyed my work. Edith and her family were dear to me. This continued for six weeks and the basic mysteries of a PB4Y cleared up and the time came to resume the odyssey. After five good-byes to Edith and family, I finally left for San Diego.[199]

Harold's crew had been put together on paper back at Hutchinson, but the men had never worked together until they gathered at Camp Kearny in June 1944. The plane commander was Lieutenant Bob Garlick—tall, handsome, quiet, a lawyer from California in his late twenties. The other officer, Ensign Bob Massey, had left college to join the navy. Unlike Harold, Massey hadn't become a pilot on a whim. He fell in love with flying as an eight-year-old when a family friend took him up for the first time. He sold newspapers to pay for lessons and got his license on his sixteenth birthday, the earliest age allowed. On dates in college he would tell his wife-to-be, Reggie, "You can have a hamburger or you can have a soda, but I can't buy both because I have to spend that extra dime on gas for the plane." Massey believed in mastering anything he did and later set up a safety school for the navy.[200] He was, in short, almost the exact opposite of Harold Boss. Practicing navigation one night at Kearny, he and Harold shot the stars and plotted their positions. Massey's calculations put them about a half mile from where they were standing; Harold had them somewhere near Detroit.[201]

The rest of the crew came from across the country. One was a kid radioman from Missouri named Bill Swink, who had failed an Army Air Force physical for being too thin but later learned that the navy had no problem with skinny fliers. On long, uneventful missions, Bill was fond of using his parachute as a bed and happily sleeping the hours away undisturbed. As a result, the crew gave him the nickname "Rip Van Swinkle," and it stuck.

If Harold was missing Edith back in Wichita during this last period of training, he nevertheless sought solace with another WAVE ("a female fellow-in-arms who restored my faith that a uniform did not basically change a woman"). After ten weeks in San Diego and six more of shakedown in Hawaii, he left for Tinian and combat. Bob Garlick had developed a reputation as a pilot who could get a lot from a gallon of aviation fuel, so his crew was sometimes assigned the slightly longer sectors. On one mission, flying *Dirty Gertie*, they found themselves off course and low on fuel. Harold wrote about it later:

> The boys were ordered to throw everything possible over the side. Strip Gert, make her light and save that precious gas. First, the bomb bay tanks, now sucked dry, went out the bomb bay doors. The oxygen system was ripped out. Ammunition and guns, flak suits, tool kits, camera, even all the top deck turret that could be broken off followed over the side. Every piece of Gert's gear not essential to flying went. Still, all hands feared we would never make it. And when the dim lights of the camp broke through in the distance, they looked bigger, brighter, and better than Times Square on New Year's Eve. The coral runway would not have felt better if it was made of diamonds.

He didn't mention that he'd been pestering his pilot to let him navigate on a mission. Bob Garlick had given in, and Harold had taken them hundreds of miles off course before the error was discovered. The flight lasted more than fifteen hours, and they had so little gas left that two of the four engines quit before the plane even taxied off the runway. After that, Bob Massey always did the navigating.[202]

Later, on Leyte, things got even more hectic. Aircraft action reports show that on December 9 they shot down a single-engine Japanese seaplane. The wings came off when it hit the water, and they saw the pilot slumped in his cockpit as they strafed the sinking wreckage.[203] On another flight they were escorted by five Japanese fighters who stayed just out of gun range until they broke off and headed home. On New Year's Eve, coming back from the China coast, they came across a Tabby, a Japanese transport plane. The Tabby's starboard engine was smoking, and the cockpit was burning brightly when it went in. A lone survivor hung onto the tail as they turned for Tacloban.[204]

Nearing the base at twilight, the tower told them enemy planes had gotten into the landing pattern. One was behind them, and gunners on the ground would try to shoot it down. Holding course, they watched while red antiaircraft tracers arced up and just over the cockpit. They were flying through the Fourth of July. It was mesmerizing. It was terrifying. Harold Boss began to cry.[205]

Crying wasn't that uncommon. It was a natural reaction to stress and fear, and it had been a long month for everyone in the squadron. But almost inevitably, incredibly, most crewmen would be there three mornings later, standing next to the nose wheel in the predawn darkness. They came back, they climbed in, they buckled up.

Harold Boss never did. He could have just quit. Others in the squadron had turned in their wings, and there was no caustic rebuke from the commander, no "damn you" dialogue with their peers. Nobody called you a coward (certainly not to your face). The truth was, almost everyone understood. Some guys could drink more; some could lift more weight. When it came to fear, some seemed truly waterproof. It rolled right off them. For most, it was more like the weather; dread came and went. But when it settled in and stayed, the panic just pounded you. It was like living under a waterfall, and you sank or you swam. Those who survived hardly blamed those who went under. Besides, admitting that you couldn't go on took its own kind of courage. You weren't going to be transferred out, which meant you still had to live with your friends and with yourself. Gordon Forbes, a navy pilot who flew similar missions and wrote a novel about it after the war, put the problem succinctly: you could quit, but you couldn't hide. That's probably why more didn't do it.

But Harold tried to have it both ways, to save face and save himself at the same time. The next day he began complaining of headaches, sinus problems. The pressure changes on the flights would make it worse, he said.[206] Again, this was hardly unheard of. In Forbes's novel, a nervous Lieutenant Junior Grade Tim Brady fights a running rearguard action, coming up with assorted ailments to confound the squadron's flight surgeon.[207] In Harold's case, no medical records survived. It's likely the squadron doctor prescribed the usual treatment: ground him for now, schedule another exam, wait and see what happens. But as January stretched into

February the squadron made its own diagnosis: Harold had "the willies," and the headaches were just an excuse.

He wasn't an outcast, but he wasn't part of the regular rhythm in the squadron anymore either. His friends flew and fought. He kept more to himself and worked on a memoir, titled *The Blue Monsters*. He wrote about pilots:

> Lt. (j.g.) Jan Carter is a huge man towering head and shoulders over the rest of the boys at six-foot-four and weighing two hundred forty pounds. As is typical of most large men, his heart is as big as he is tall.

He wrote about Commander Harold McDonald, the squadron CO:

> The Captain ran a taut but happy ship. He would often join us at the O Club, being sociable with all including the lowly Ensigns.

He wrote about funny incidents during training or in the islands. He wrote dramatic accounts of squadron planes ditching or being shot down. He wrote from memory about a typical patrol with his crew. The passage ends with Harold daydreaming as the plane nears base:

> "What the hell are you doing out here in the Philippines?" my other self asked me. It seemed funny, and the events of the three years that had passed since I left my home in Buffalo flashed through my mind.[208]

It was the last chapter.

Left untended, a life story decomposes like an animal that dies alone on the prairie. The rest of Harold's tale is like that. Time has left us only bare bones and questions. We know that around the third week of March, two things happened: He was promoted from ensign to lieutenant junior grade. And he was ordered to report to Manus, a busy rear base and staging area in the Admiralty Islands north of New Guinea.

While there, Harold borrowed a plane from the local navy base, flew it into the side of a ship in the harbor, and was killed.

The story the squadron heard was that Harold had been showing off for a nurse he had met. That wasn't mentioned in the official accident report filed two days after the crash, which his friends never saw. But when I tracked it down, preserved on grainy microfilm, the report answered some questions and raised others.[209]

The accident happened just before 5 p.m., and there was no doubt about the cause:

> Pilot was observed to be "flat hatting" and giving stunting exhibition over harbor at altitudes between 10 feet and 3,000 feet. Had just zoomed ship and pulled up in a wingover and was making another pass at ship and failed to pull up and hit ship.

In a wingover, the pilot puts the plane in a climbing turn until it almost stalls and then lets the plane fall through the rest of the turn until he pulls out headed in the opposite direction. In the section of the report labeled "Analysis," the investigator found

> that this airplane was observed by witnesses aboard the vessel in question and aboard another vessel in the vicinity to make several fast diving approaches into close proximity to the USS Admiral E.W. Eberle at altitudes approximating or below the level of the bridge (about 60 feet), zooming sharply over or banking away from the ship on each occasion. That one of the above mentioned approaches was made by the airplane in question entering from a very low altitude a maneuver resembling either a half-roll with a diving pull-out or a steeply banked diving turn during recovery from which the airplane flew toward the ship in question at an extremely low altitude and at high speed and eventually struck the ship's hull about 12 feet above the water line, completely piercing the hull and forming an approximately round hole about five or six feet in diameter, then dropping back to the water and sinking within 10 or 15 seconds.

The *Eberle* was a troop ship, more than six hundred feet long. Later it would set a transpacific speed record carrying more than forty-six hundred soldiers—also a record—home from Japan. But that day it had just dropped anchor on its first mission since being commissioned two months earlier.[210]

The plane was an SBD Dauntless, a dive bomber that had gained fame in the Battle of Midway but had recently been retired from the fleet. Pilots had nicknamed it "Slow But Deadly" and "The Barge." Harold had never flown one and hadn't flown anything in almost three months. So how did he get into the cockpit?

> That Boss did not receive an SBD "cockpit check-out" by a quali-fied Naval Aviator prior to his first flight in SBD No. 06912 on the afternoon of March 25, 1945. That Boss verbally falsified his previous flight experience when requesting permission by phone of the CNAB Operations Officer, a non-aviator, to fly the SBD airplane in question.

In short, he talked his way in.

But what was Harold doing down at Manus in the first place? The report answers that question too:

> That a flight physical examination directed by the Commander Aircraft Seventh Fleet (Logistics Section) Personnel Officer and commenced at the Acorn 24 Dispensary on the morning of 25 March had not been technically completed in the case of Boss, who had been instructed by the examining flight surgeon to return next day for completion of the examination.

Did the navy want to settle once and for all whether Harold was fit to fly? What did the doctor tell him? Did it look like he was going to pass the physical? Why did he have to come back the next day? The accident report concludes with some cryptic speculation:

That, however, two factors should be considered as possibly contributing to a temporary condition of irresponsibility on the part of Boss which led him to obtain the airplane in question under false pretenses and thereafter to violate established flight regulations and prudential rules of safe flight: (1) An emotional disturbance connected with his alleged recent engagement and forthcoming marriage. (2) An undue eagerness to fly after a period of about 2.5 months in non-flight status.

What recent engagement? Was it to Edith from Wichita? Or someone he'd met since? How did the investigator know about it? And was Harold really "unduly eager" to fly or just the opposite? He had to know that buzzing the *Eberle* like that, no matter the outcome of his physical, would likely get him grounded again. Was that what he wanted?

In some ways, that explanation makes the most sense. Like problems with his ears, grounding would have kept him out of combat, at least for a while longer. And he certainly would not have expected to die on a "joyride." If we were writing the story, not Harold—and if it were a novel, not a memoir—we might choose that as the surprise ending, drenched in irony.

But there's one last possibility, raised by the reference in the report to an "emotional disturbance." Distraught over serious complications in his love life or fearful that a flight surgeon might order him back into a bomber—or both—did Harold Boss take his own life?

I don't think so, because of something I found elsewhere in the report. In a section titled "Injuries to Pilot," the investigator typed "fatal." Next, under the heading "Name & Rank of Other Personnel," he typed "Carlson, E.P., S1c USNR. Dead. Collision with ship."

A sailor on the *Eberle* was also killed and five of his shipmates injured. They never knew what hit them.[211] But what was twenty-year-old Seaman First Class Evert Parker Carlson of Plainfield, New Jersey, doing in the back seat of that SBD? Was he stationed at the airfield when Harold showed up? Was he ordered to go along by Harold or an officer at the base? Did he want to get some hours toward flight pay, on what was supposed to be just a local familiarization flight? When they started stunting, did he whoop it up on the intercom? Or was Carlson screaming in anger and terror, pounding on the canopy, trying to get Harold to stop? Whatever his reaction, nothing we know suggests that Harold would have involved someone else in his own suicide. He was neither an accomplished airman nor a serious student of flying, but he always believed he could pull it out in the end. So far, he always had.

Evert Carlson's obituary—just 109 words, published 46 days after his death—said he was "killed in an airplane crash while flying over the Admiralty Islands."[212] The navy didn't tell Harold's mother much more; they said he had been getting in some flight hours when he hit a ship. They also told her that his body had never been recovered, and she grabbed that single thread like a lifeline. For years after the war, she wrote and visited members of Harold's crew across the country.[213] Couldn't he have gotten that canopy open as the plane sank and swum to the surface in the confusion? Couldn't a head injury have caused amnesia and left him, nameless, to start a new life somewhere else? The men were polite and sympathetic. They didn't know all the details, they said. But most of what they did know they kept to themselves.[214]

Even decades later they didn't reveal everything. Especially at first, my questions about Harold met with averted eyes or the sliver of a smile. They put the same face on his memoir. Sometime after he died the squadron added an appendix to *The Blue Monsters*, titled "In Tribute to Lt. (j.g.) Harold J. Boss, USNR." It included excerpts "from letters by his buddies":

> I was very happy to have the honor of being a friend of Harold. He was one of the best-liked men in the squadron, or that I have ever met.

> A fine lad that was admired, liked and sought after by his fellow officers. Wherever Boss went there was song and laughter.

There was no mention at all of the accident. The appendix concluded,

> And so this book closes as of March 25, 1945 when Lt. Boss fulfilled his final and fateful mission on earth.

Had Harold been able to write the ending himself, he probably wouldn't have chosen one that veered so swiftly from comedy to tragedy. It wasn't his style. So instead, we leave the last word to the last person who saw him alive. After the war a priest came to see Harold's mother. He said he'd been standing on the deck of the *Eberle* that day. He didn't tell her he'd watched with growing concern as the plane swooped like a swallow in the late-afternoon light. He didn't tell her that some on board swore and shook their fists at the pilot, while others egged him on. So we'll never know exactly what that scene was like.

But the priest did tell Harold's mother that when the Dauntless failed to pull up from its last dive and headed straight for the *Eberle*, he walked to the rail and looked down a second before the hit. What he saw, he said, he would never forget—beneath the canopy, as though looking through clear ice, Harold's frozen face and his bright blue eyes, wide open.[215]

Dear Barbara

Poverty is raw, pitiless. And war mangles—it doesn't care whom. Only surviving redeems either. Surviving and surpassing. Finding a way and a place to live the life you imagined.

Joe Papp did.

His earliest memory was of his mother's casket being lowered into her grave. She and his father, both Hungarian immigrants, had met and married in South Bend, Indiana, and she died giving birth to their seventh child. Joe was not yet three years old.[216]

He was sent to live with his mother's sister and her husband, but two years later his father remarried and brought Joe back home. By then a brother and sister had been "adopted" by relatives in New Jersey; they were in their teens before they learned that their "parents" were really their uncle and aunt and they had siblings they had never known about. Joe's stepmother began weeding out the rest. She beat his oldest sister so often that she went to live with another family for whom she'd been a nanny. The stepmother shaved another sister's head and sent her to a convent. The only good thing was that the stepmother sometimes packed a bag and left for weeks or months at a time.

His father, though, was even worse—an abusive drunk who never held a regular job. So from the time he could remember, Joe had to help out. He weeded onions ten hours a day for ten cents an hour. At the end of his first six-day week, his pay packet held $5.50, instead of the $6 he was owed. He told his boss about it. The boss said, "You want a job, don't you?" When he brought the money home, his father took all the rest (except a nickel) to buy whiskey.[217]

There was never enough of anything, especially food. Joe often carried "lard sandwiches" to school for lunch. When they were especially hungry, he and his older brother George would sneak under the fence of a nearby junkyard, steal a piece of brass, and sell it back to the owner for a few cents. The next day they'd steal something else and sell it back again. The owner, saying, "This looks awfully familiar," hired them to do odd jobs, which helped a little.

As the Depression deepened, George took off on his own, riding the rails. Nine years old, Joe was left to fend for himself and his younger sister. He made the meals, kept the house, and bought what food he could. His father had a lathe in the basement, which he sometimes used to do small jobs for people. The house had no electricity, so Joe learned to "pull the belt"—to haul a leather strap, hand over hand, to power the shaft that turned the lathe. He would do it until he felt his arms would fall off. If he tired, or if he brought his father the wrong wrench from his toolbox, or sometimes for no reason at all, Joe would get punched out. There were drunken rages, fights with the neighbors. Late in life, asked what he missed, Joe said without a trace of self-pity, "I miss my mother, because I never knew her. And I miss my childhood, because I never had one."[218]

Then, when he was fourteen, deliverance—Joe's father died. It must have felt like someone had taken a crowbar and uncrated him, prying him loose from life in the shadows. Joe moved in with an older sister and her husband. He could now keep some of the money he earned, so he saved $25 and bought a beat-up Model T Ford convertible. He took the engine apart to fix it; then he took it apart again just for fun. He repainted the car bright yellow with red trim and lettered snappy sayings on the sides: "We stop for redheads and back up for blondes." With no car radio, he installed an ancient windup Victrola in the rumble seat so he could have music on rides to the lake. He bought gas a gallon at a time, at fourteen cents a pop.

But he was restless, eager for something new. Halfway through high school, Joe left to join the Civilian Conservation Corps (CCC). It was a year of living military style in a barracks with two hundred other boys, and he loved it. He earned $1 a day working as a surveyor, building raccoon pens, and helping create a twenty-seven-acre lake that is still there, near Fort Wayne. On one of his visits home, he met Martha Newland, who lived next door to his sister. Soon he was regularly hopping the fence to visit the girl everyone called Markey. When his hitch with the CCC ended, he found a job in a factory, working a lathe.

Besides Markey, he also he fell in love with flying. The one extravagance he remembered from his childhood came when he was four years old and his father paid $5, an enormous sum, to let Joe fly with a barnstormer in a blue Waco biplane. He'd wanted to go back up ever since. Now that he was earning steady money at the factory, he could afford flying lessons in a thirty-seven-horsepower Piper Cub. He was twenty years old, and halfway to his license, when he and Markey married. Their wedding picture shows Joe looking serious in his only suit and Markey, almost as tall, with a corsage pinned to her dress and smiling eyes beneath her curls.

Ten weeks later came Pearl Harbor.

Joe volunteered and chose the navy because he hoped they would let him fly. He saw the war not in terms of danger, or even adventure, but as an opportunity. In the service, you couldn't tell who'd come from the slums; everyone wore the same uniform, ate the same food, and followed the same rules. And everyone had the same chance to prove himself. Joe intended to make the most of it. After boot camp he graduated in the top 10 percent of his class as an aviation mechanic and was the only one picked to become an engine overhaul specialist. That took him to the West Coast and eventually to Commander E. O. Rigsbee's flag unit, where he was head mechanic on the admiral's plane. It was a cushy job, but when Rigsbee formed VPB-117, Joe begged to go to war. Most guys he knew never traveled more than fifty miles from where they were born, he told Markey. This was a chance to go halfway around the world.[219]

His plane commander was Nick Carter, big and boisterous, from Arkansas. Joe was plane captain, head enlisted man, and chief mechanic. Carter trusted him completely, even let him log some time at the controls when he or the copilot wanted a break. They got their first taste of combat in Tinian, including an encounter with some Zeros near Iwo Jima. But the real baptism came when they moved to Leyte. In two months based at Tacloban, they shot down four planes and sank five ships.

The squadron's move to Mindoro in February was supposed to make things easier, but on one of their first flights to Indochina, they spotted a three-ship convoy of Japanese freighters near the coast, covered by a single-engine Jake seaplane. The Jake broke off and headed for land; Carter chased. Fifty feet above the jungle, the bomber's shadow skittered over the treetops. They closed the range and showered the seaplane with tracers. It cartwheeled into the canopy, crashed, and burned.

Carter turned back toward the freighters, still off the coast and now without air cover. The largest was more than 150 feet long. A big, but not easy, target. They would have to start their run miles away, and when ships saw a bomber low on the water, they immediately turned broadside to it, minimizing the time the plane would spend over their decks and maximizing the number of guns they could train on it. Over the intercom, Carter asked the crew whether they wanted to take a shot. All said yes.

He put the plane into a five-degree dive to gain speed and to give the top turret a better firing angle. Going three hundred miles per hour, seventy-five feet off the water, they dropped two five-hundred-pound bombs. According to the later action report,

> The first bomb struck 40 to 50 feet short and apparently exploded beneath the vessel and the second struck it in the side. The vessel appeared to be lifted and hurled over. A large column of smoke was observed.

They had hit the target. But the target had also hit them:

> Antiaircraft hits were received in the fuselage and five of the PB4Y-1s personnel were wounded.[220]

Standing between Carter and his copilot, Joe had a front-row seat. He could see the faces of the gunners on the ship and their shells sparking off the plane's aluminum skin. At first, the danger didn't register; he thought, "I'll never forget this. It looks just like a movie."

Then a round came through the bow turret, missing the gunner's ear by two inches, and slammed into the flight deck. Joe had his hand on the copilot's back and felt the shrapnel hit him. Two crewmen took the copilot aft to look at his wounds. Joe sat in the empty seat for a few minutes; then he noticed that blood was pooling inside his flight suit. Soon one of his feet started swelling and he was getting short of breath. So they carried Joe back as well, laying him down between the waist guns where he stayed until the swelling and the bleeding slowed. Then he went forward again to see whether he could help.

Things weren't looking good. Besides Joe and the copilot, two other crewmen had minor shrapnel wounds, and an Army Air Force weather observer, along for the ride, had wounds in his legs, face, and arms, as well as a shattered kneecap. It looked like all might survive the long trip back home. But they weren't as sure about the plane itself.

Because they had chased the Jake over the jungle, they didn't have enough gas to reach their regular base, so controllers told them to head for a recently captured Japanese fighter field on northern Mindoro. Joe adjusted the fuel-air mixture in the engines to conserve gas; then he started to think about what would happen if they made it back to Mindoro.

The field they were heading to had a dirt runway, much shorter than usual for a B-24. And there was another problem. During the attack on the ship, shrapnel had shredded hydraulic lines throughout the plane. Joe told Carter that on landing the flaps wouldn't work, and the brakes would fail the first time he touched the pedal. Joe thought of something that might help slow the plane on landing. He gave the waist gunners his own parachute and one other and told them to unpack the chutes, tie the cords around the gun mounts next to the waist hatches, and throw them out the hatches as soon as the plane touched down.

When they finally reached the field, Carter brought the plane in as slowly as he could, almost stalling. The wheels touched, the chutes went out the window, their lines broke, the brakes failed, and the plane kept rolling. Now they were just along for the ride, and it seemed to last for minutes. Near the end of the runway the landing gear collapsed; the plane kept plowing forward on its belly, nosed into a drainage ditch, and split in half, tail in the air. Amazingly, no one was hurt in the crash. But those with wounds were quickly taken to a nearby field hospital.

Doctors pulled shrapnel from Joe's arms and chest, decided to leave the rest until later, and told him to stay for a few days. His bed was in a ward where most of the men were very badly hurt, some in full-body casts. Anytime a transport plane was due to leave the field, the worst cases would be wheeled out in the hope that there would be space to take them back to a rear area for better care. Most times, the planes left without them. After a day or two of watching this routine, Joe wanted no part of the hospital. One morning he got dressed, simply walked away, and hitchhiked back to the squadron's base.

When he got there, he found two things on his bunk: his torn parachute, folded neatly, and a letter from Markey, telling him he had a brand-new daughter. Joe sat and thought about the last two days: the shells exploding all around him, his wounds and the flight home, the crash landing, the boys in the hospital. He was very lucky, he knew. And now this! He decided he would use some of the silk from the parachute to have a dress made for his baby girl.

He asked in town about a seamstress and was directed to a bamboo house on stilts. Climbing up, he introduced himself to a Filipino woman sitting at a foot-powered Singer sewing machine, made in Joe's hometown of South Bend. He tried to explain what he wanted, and she eventually understood. What kind of dress would he like? Joe didn't know. The woman reached under her bed and pulled out a five-year-old Sears catalog. Together they looked at pictures of baby clothes, until Joe pointed to one. The woman said she could make it. The only problem was that she had no buttons; Joe gave her the ones from his uniform. Come back in two days, she told him.

When he did, he thought the dress was perfect, right down to the ruffles. Joe gave the woman $10 and told her to keep the rest of the silk. He mailed the dress home to South Bend, along with a pair of pajamas made for Markey.[221] Then Joe went back to work, flying twenty-six more combat missions, sixty-one in all. He even volunteered for several missions after the rest of his crew went home, including three flights with my dad. Joe had made chief petty officer, and he wanted the extra flight pay—he had a daughter to take care of now.

When Joe was finally relieved, it took him more than a month to get to South Bend, where Markey and baby Barbara were waiting on the train platform. Back home, the men who'd held the veterans' jobs while they were overseas weren't about to give them up. Joe found work first as a machinist and then at the local Studebaker plant. A year later, when Studebaker cut back hours, Joe went looking again. At a company that said it wasn't hiring, he filled out an application anyway and was on his way out the door when a supervisor called him back. "It says here you were a chief petty officer, so you must have something on the ball. Come back Monday morning."

He stayed thirty-one years. The company was among the first to make what has become the most overlooked of American inventions: the automatic door at the supermarket, the mall, the airport. Especially early on, there were problems with design and reliability. With his tenth-grade education, Joe was hired as an assistant to the graduate engineers on staff, and when he made a suggestion to one of them about how to solve a particular problem, the engineer sarcastically said, "If you think you can do better, go ahead." So Joe did. He ended up with six patents in his name,[222] like number 4046167:

A mechanical accumulator for holding and supplying a volume of hydraulic fluid under pressure comprising a variable volume fluid pressure chamber including a piston and a cylinder member, a plurality of coil springs acting on one of said members for biasing the same toward the other of said members to minimize the volume of said chamber and pressurize the fluid therein, etc.[223]

It sounded simpler when Joe explained it, and it worked perfectly. He remained a self-taught mechanical genius, a tinkerer in the great American tradition. And he took the same hands-on approach to everything. When it came time to own their first house, he and Markey bought an acre outside town. Joe designed and built the place by himself, after work and on weekends. He started by digging out the basement with a shovel. They moved in around the time their son, George, was born in 1952.

During those years his family and friends rarely asked about his war experiences, so Joe never brought them up. But there were occasional reminders. For years after he first came back, he would eat only with the utensils from his navy mess kit; he never explained why. His daughter Barbara remembered as a little girl briefly hearing a story about the dress he'd had made for her in the Philippines, but the dress itself had long since been tucked away in the attic. Now and then a piece of shrapnel in Joe's side or back would rise to the surface, and Markey would pluck it out, like removing a splinter. But the rest of that time in his life stayed mostly out of sight.

The days and the decades rolled by. Joe was a good father, sometimes stern and always eager for his children to succeed. While digging the basement of their first house, he brought a blackboard into the pit and drilled little Barbara on her arithmetic as he shoveled dirt into a wheelbarrow. He believed in family, in work, and in paying his own way. He owned three homes during his life and never made a mortgage payment. He was sixty-nine years old before he had a credit card.

After the kids were on their own, Markey took him to Las Vegas a few times, often paying for the trip with her blackjack winnings. They were married fifty-two years before she died in 1993. Watching as her casket was lowered into the ground, like his mother's so many years before, was the hardest thing he ever did.[224]

Eventually, Joe decided to move from the home he and Markey had shared into a smaller place. That's where I first visited him. He showed me his photos and his logbook. He told me how, in packing up a lifetime of memories from the old house, he came across baby Barbara's dress of parachute silk. And he said he'd had an idea.

Joe's time came a few years later. Congestive heart failure slowly sucked the life from him. The only relief came from breathing bottled oxygen. Worst was when the doctor told him he couldn't drive anymore because he might pass out or pass away behind the wheel and hurt someone.

His brain and the rest of his body were fine, but he knew the score. Still, he didn't want to go to an extended-care facility. So they put big oxygen tanks in his house and attached long tubes to the masks he could wear while moving around. I pictured him alone in his kitchen or in his favorite chair, tethered to the tanks, shuffling to open the door for neighbors who brought him groceries or the hospice worker who checked on him daily, unmasking himself to answer the phone or have a bite of dinner.

And he settled in to wait. Joe wrote some letters, watched a little television. He didn't complain; he said he wasn't afraid. I called him from time to time, and often the talk turned back to his days in the squadron. One day he told me a story he'd never shared with anyone.

It had happened before they'd even shipped overseas, while training at Camp Kearny. He'd agreed to help a friend tune his Model A Ford, so right after muster one foggy morning, they were about to cross the parade ground when they heard the roar of a B-24. From the straining sound of the engines, Joe immediately knew the plane was in trouble. It came out of the low clouds, hit the ground, and headed straight at them. Instinctively, Joe jumped back. His friend, five feet away, didn't; the bomber's wingtip cut him open.

Two seconds later, the plane hit a nearby building and exploded in flames. One crewman, on fire himself, burst through the bomber's molten aluminum skin and rolled to the ground. He and two others survived. In shock, Joe watched the plane burn with eight men still inside. There were more muffled explosions, and he noticed something lying next to his feet. It took a second before he realized he was looking at a human heart. It took another second before he kicked it back into the fire, so no one else would have to see it.[225]

In those months I sent him some books as well, because Joe loved to read—about flying, about physics, about famous Americans. That's where he died, in his reading chair, on January 9, 2010. He took a nap and didn't wake up.

Barbara, who had just spent a week visiting at Christmas, drove overnight from her home in Maryland. She and her brother buried Joe next to Markey, five pieces of shrapnel still in his back. The next morning she went back to sort through his things at the house. His bedroom came first.

She opened the top drawer of his dresser, and there, right where she couldn't miss it, was her baby dress from the Philippines. She knew immediately what it was. Then, on his writing desk, she saw a yellow pad with her name on top. Several pages written in his own hand. The tears came before she finished the first paragraph:[226]

Dear Barbara:

In the process of sorting through the things I would keep and the things I didn't need to take to the new house, I came across your little silk dress I had made for you sixty years ago. You don't remember it because you were one year old when you wore it, then it was put away, out of sight and out of mind.

Upon seeing it again, it brought back memories to me of an eventful day: February 11, 1945. Since this mission had so much to do to provide the material for the dress, I thought you might like to share the whole day with me.

We lifted from the runway just as the sun was beginning to rise . . .

Snapshots

Why do the dead look so wise?

Beyond the edges of the cracked and faded photos, they seem to stare at something forever lost to us. We want to see what they see. We want to populate the pictures with stories. But these are not paintings, fictions. These are real men. They lived within a frame of facts, most of which are lost now too. So we search their faces for clues. We end up staring back at them. And we cannot turn away.

Here's Bill Loesel, for instance, four years old. He's standing in front of his family's house, a violin tucked under his chin, bow in the ready position, almost as tall as he is. His grandfather had been a master violin maker in Germany; his father is principal violinist and concertmaster for the Pittsburgh Symphony Orchestra. His mother is a pianist with the orchestra; that's how they met. Little more than a decade later, both would lose their jobs when a new conductor revamped the orchestra. Bill, at the time, was in high school, a bright student and good musician, looking forward to college. But now there would be no money. After graduation he got a job and took classes on the side. Then came the war.[227]

So the next picture we have is likely his formal portrait as an aviation cadet. It's a head-and-shoulders shot of a handsome young man in his dark uniform, close-cropped hair beneath his hat, wide-set eyes focused just past the camera to his right. He is barely in his twenties, and we know more about what's coming than he does at this moment. Yet he seems serene, as if he's already seen it all and then some. Or maybe he's just trying to look confident and grown up, so his mother won't worry when she passes the picture on the mantel.

Next is Bill's official commissioning photo, showing him seated from the waist up. He's wearing dress whites, shoulder epaulets with the single ensign's stripe, and, above his left breast pocket, the Wings of Gold. His hands look relaxed, and this time he holds his hat pressed between his right arm and his side, military style. It's only months since the previous picture, but he's already perfected the sincere, yet ironic, smile.

The first snapshots from his time in the squadron were taken in Hawaii, on the way out. They've flown from Oahu to Hilo, on the big island, and they're probably on liberty because they seem to be in some kind of park. Five pilots lean against a railing in khakis and ties, one or two wearing aviator sunglasses. The sky behind them is blank, which means the sun is high. The ones without glasses, including Bill, are squinting, and it makes their smiles seem forced. No one in the picture has yet flown a single combat mission.

The next time we see him, he's on Tinian. Almost all the photos they sent home from the front were posed—no candid portraits, no action scenes. Nothing that would worry anyone. Like the censors and the war correspondents, the men managed the news. So in this shot, Bill and two buddies are standing in front of a tent. He wears shorts, no shirt, athletic socks, and sandals. The others are dressed similarly, and all three are wearing elaborate bandages—on their legs, on their arms, on their hands and torsos. It is the first month of combat, and the picture seems a deliberate joke intended to reassure the folks back home (and maybe themselves). In the shot the three are literally laughing at danger. In two months' time, the fellow on the far right would be navigator on a flight that crashed in the water, seconds short of the runway, in the middle of a monsoon rain. He would be hurled through the windshield, suffer multiple serious injuries, and live.

Jump ahead to January 1945, on Leyte. Another smiling group shot, the men this time standing in front of a swamp. They never know quite what to do with their hands: crossed in front, held behind the back, one or both resting on a hip. It is impossible to read their futures in their faces. The navigator two to Bill's right had already been shot down with the rest of his crew by a Japanese Zero, survived ditching in the ocean, been rescued with six others by Philippine guerillas, hidden on a nearby island, and sailed a native outrigger through the night to get back to the American lines. Four decades later, he would retire as vice president of a pharmaceutical company. Next to him stands a blonde kid who would become a famous test pilot for Boeing, flying everything the company built for the next fifty years. The buddy on Bill's left would be a successful sales rep in Ohio.

By now Bill himself had flown more than two dozen missions with his plane commander, Harold McGaughey. Much older, in his late thirties, Mac had been something of a legend from his first day in the squadron. Around Camp Kearny they said he'd been a professional barnstormer and racing pilot. Amelia Earhart had asked him to navigate on her around-the-world flight. He'd worked with Jimmy Doolittle, who later led the daring bomb raid on Tokyo six months after Pearl Harbor.[228]

Mac had joined the navy early in the war but because of his age hadn't been given a combat assignment. So he badgered the Bureau of Aeronautics until he finally got his ticket with VPB-117. Besides being a plane commander, he became engineering officer and devised a bypass that made the squadron's engines more powerful when flying fully loaded at low altitudes, which was almost all the time. Balding, with heavy eyebrows and a broad nose, he also served as father confessor and Dutch uncle to many young ensigns and lieutenants.

And once they reached the combat zone, his legend only grew. Mac quickly became the most aggressive pilot in the squadron. And he always finished what he started. Their first week in Leyte, he spotted a camouflaged cargo ship and made a low-level run while the plane's gunners and the ship's antiaircraft crews both blasted away. At the critical moment the bombs failed to release. So they retired to a distance until the bomb release was fixed and then attacked again. When they came in close, someone noticed smoke coming from amidships. A second later the ship exploded beneath them, rocking the plane like a giant uppercut. The official action report described what happened next:

> Its camouflage of trees and branches were hurled up in the path
> of the aircraft as were parts of the ship and bodies of personnel

aboard the ship. The aircraft flew through the debris. The number four engine was lost due to the fuel line being severed. The number one prop was damaged by flying metal. Wings were perforated by flying metal. The open bomb bay was blown full of leaves, sticks, dirt and debris. The terrific explosion of the ship lifted the aircraft from 200 to 700 feet altitude.[229]

The shrapnel, some of it human, pocked the plane on all sides. Men instinctively patted themselves, feeling for blood. There was none. The report didn't mention that the wing was also nearly blown off, bent at the root. Somehow they limped home.

Two days later, on the third anniversary of Pearl Harbor, they shot down a Japanese floatplane; then they found four ships anchored in a harbor. The first bomb run sank one. On the second run, the bombs again failed to release. Most pilots would have stopped there. A second or third run on a defended ship was risky; you had lost the advantage of surprise and had to fly low into the teeth of antiaircraft fire. Plus, in this case, you were being fired on by not one but three ships. They fixed the release mechanism, and Mac made a third run. His last two bombs sank a second ship. Then he dropped down to fifty feet off the water and started strafing the remaining ships. They made fifteen runs and fired four thousand rounds of ammunition. The nose gunner had to stop shooting because his turret filled with empty shell casings. It was the OK Corral in the air, and Mac was Wyatt Earp. The last two ships went down burning just as the Liberator ran out of bullets.[230]

During those first days in the Philippines, Mac and crew also shot down two Japanese planes. As with the ships, he was direct and calm in the middle of a melee. Only once, a few weeks later, did they see him rattled. Skimming low near the Indochina coast, they spotted a Nell, a twin-engine Japanese bomber, flying above and ahead of them in the same direction. Unseen, like a sniper, they closed from below and behind to within fifty yards. The first bursts, maybe ten rounds, incinerated the Nell's engines, which sprayed oil all over the Liberator's windshield. The Nell lost power and fluttered directly in front of them. Mac pulled back on the yoke and the throttles; the engines made a sickly, gagging sound.

Somehow they avoided a collision, but now they were headed straight up, in danger of stalling themselves. The airframe shivered; they hit right rudder and brought the plane around in time to see the Nell diving straight toward the water. The crew watched as its port wing came off, it went into a violent spin, and seconds later it exploded into debris—"like confetti," one remembered.[231] There were none of the usual whoops, no celebration of the kill. Several admitted later that they had said a silent prayer for the men in the Nell on its way down. Visibly shaken, Mac told his copilot to take them home.[232]

His reputation made Mac a magnet for people who wanted to hitch a ride into battle. One was a navy radar expert, Nelson McCaa, who knew he could count on Mac to get him close to enemy targets so he could learn more about Japanese countermeasures. Another was Henry McLemore, a syndicated columnist for the Hearst newspapers. McLemore's columns were colorful and popular, and he'd learned that a flight with Mac had a good chance of producing a good story.

But what riveted readers back home didn't always sit well with everyone in the squadron itself. Some considered Mac a hero; others thought him reckless (or worse). Mac didn't talk much about it himself, so it was hard to know why he took such chances. He wasn't a braggart; he didn't have a personal hatred of the Japanese. Maybe he wanted the medals. Or, in the end, it might just have been that a cockpit was the one place in the world where Mac felt most comfortable. Imagining being shot down was like imagining being murdered in your living room. It didn't seem likely.

After a while, though, some in his crew weren't so sure. At least one, maybe more, asked to leave. Mac didn't begrudge or belittle them. He didn't try to talk them out of it either.

What about Bill Loesel? He was hard to read. Quiet, studious, an ace in the classroom back at Pensacola. Not much seemed to upset him. He had a wry sense of humor—"the chuckler," one friend called him.[233] Whatever he was thinking, in the air or back at base, he didn't share much. Like Mac. So Bill and the rest of the crew flew on.

On January 29, 1945, Mac took them two hundred miles south of Okinawa to what the Japanese considered "home islands." Their first target was Tarama Jima, and they attacked low and fast. Four ships at anchor were literally sitting ducks, sunk in a row on one run, while the machine guns set several more afire. Mac pulled up into the clouds, reloaded the .50-calibers, and headed for Miyako Jima nearby. More than one hundred small ships were in the harbor. They came in even lower, twenty-five feet off the water, the props kicking up spray. Bombs destroyed two ships, and the gunners set at least ten more on fire while also strafing soldiers, trucks, buildings, and anything else on the beach. The official report of the mission listed six large and ten to twenty smaller ships sunk, along with "1 horse (estimated one-half ton) drawing cart, dead."[234] Mac won the Navy Cross that day, the citation praising "his exemplary leadership, his cool courage, and his superb airmanship."[235]

A week later, the squadron moved from Leyte west to Mindoro. On their first mission from the new base, Mac's crew came across a convoy of tankers protected by a single Japanese floatplane, called a Paul. Mac played a cat-and-mouse game, feigning attacks on the ships to draw the Paul beyond the range of the convoy's antiaircraft guns. Eventually the Japanese plane broke off and headed for the coast. Mac followed, but he had to skirt the convoy to avoid antiaircraft fire. That gave the floatplane a twelve-mile head start. Most pilots would have let it go, but Mac chased the Paul for an hour until they finally got within one hundred feet and shredded it with one burst.

> The aircraft pitched forward in a vertical dive and the pilot was catapulted completely clear over the nose. He wore a chute but it did not open before his body hit the water. The Paul, streaming flames, crashed into the sea in a vertical dive.[236]

Three days later, near Cam Rahn Bay, they ran into another convoy, this time guarded by a destroyer, destroyer escorts, and another floatplane, a Jake. That was a lot of firepower for one Liberator to tackle, but Mac went in after the Jake, which ran for the protection of the destroyer. They flew into what even Mac described as "intense AA fire of all caliber, completely bracketing both the Jake and the PB4Y-1. The PB4Y-1 continued chase within one-half mile of the destroyer and then broke off, taking violent evasive action."[237] The words don't begin to capture the chaos and the stress—not just on the men but on the plane itself. At any moment, everything could have come apart. But as they pulled up and away, the Jake tumbled into the water and burned. It was Mac's fifth confirmed kill, officially making him an "ace."

The only photo of Bill Loesel on Mindoro shows him, thinner now, walking down a path through a bamboo thicket. If we had been there, we'd have heard the tall stalks rubbing against each other like the legs of a giant cricket. In the picture the light is from behind, almost spectral. Bill's hair glows, but his face is in deep shadow. And it is, for once, a candid shot; someone walking ahead must have turned around and snapped it. A note on the back says, "Jungle on Mindoro, February 16, 1945."

At 4 a.m. the next morning they took off again, heading south, this time toward Borneo. At 9:45 Mac's radioman sent a message to base:

First report. Destroyed troop barge loaded with troops. Many dead. Many survivors. Continuing patrol.

Fifteen minutes later, another transmission:

Bombed and sank one patrol vessel. Continuing on mission assigned.

Later they radioed an estimated time of arrival back on Mindoro. Then, silence.[238] All next day the squadron searched but turned up nothing. Less than two weeks later, Americans invaded Palawan, a Japanese-held island in the Sulu Sea between Borneo and Mindoro. The first wave focused on the main city, Puerto Princesa, and the Japanese airfield nearby. They met no opposition; defenders had retreated into the hills. After the area was secured, an American survey team found the charred skeleton of a PB4Y-1 on the beach near the airfield at Puerto Princesa. It was *Pop's Cannonball*, Rigsbee's old plane, which Mac had been flying. A matter-of-fact report was filed:[239]

Wreckage of plane was found and examined by party from Fighter Command 13, AirSea rescue, and the following information was furnished by them:

No. of plane: PB4Y-1, 38735

Natives say plane crashed 17 February 1945 about 1200 hours on beach five miles north of strips on east coast of Palawan, P.I.

According to natives, all persons aboard, 13(?) in all, were killed.

Plane was burning before it crashed and exploded, scattering parts of bodies over widespread area.

Names found on parts of clothing and cushions were "Commander Rigsbee," "Harold McGaughey," and portion of another "A.G. Corp" with at least two or three letters of name missing.

What happened? Palawan is almost three hundred miles long and only thirty miles wide. The flight plan for that sector usually sent the returning plane up the western coast. But for some reason, that day Mac crossed over to the eastern side, where the airfield was.[240]

There was a report of a three-word radio message: "We are hit!"[241] The island had been bypassed; the Japanese garrison could defend itself, but it couldn't attack anyone. Still, there was the airfield, a target of opportunity. Compared with what Mac and the crew had already been through, it must have looked easy. But as when the ship blew up beneath them, the violence punched back, trying to knock them out of the sky. And this time they couldn't slip through its fingers.

Men from Graves Registration went to the wreck site:

Personnel of 601 Q.M. Co. (GR) searched the area and gathered together all the parts of skeletons they could find, consisting of three skulls and miscellaneous bones. Individual bodies could not be segregated as the bones were not together but scattered over widespread area.

Like confetti. On March 12, the remains were buried together, along with a copy of the report, in a single grave on Palawan.[242] Now Mac and the men had been bypassed too. The war went on and was won. A few months after that, Henry McLemore wrote his final column about Mac, called "A Fine Pilot and Fine Man":

This story is for Mrs. Ray McGaughey of Macomb, Ill., and is in answer to her letter asking about her son, Lt. Cmdr. Harold McGaughey, who was killed in action over Palawan Island, the Philippines, last February.

I missed being with McGaughey on what proved to be his last flight by just fifteen minutes. The truck, which was bringing me to Manila from the hills where the Forty-Third Division was fighting, broke down and the PT boat on which I was to travel to the air base left without me.

The next day, McGaughey's Liberator was shot down. I don't know the details, but he must have been jumped by half the Jap air force. Otherwise they never would have gotten him, because he could handle the big Lib as if it were a Mustang or a Corsair or a P-38.

McGaughey was no pink-cheeked kid. He was in his late thirties, and with years of commercial airline flying behind him. It was only by pestering Washington Navy brass half to death that he finally got assigned to combat duty. He served under Admiral Wagner's command, and his squadron had one of the toughest—and least publicized—jobs in the Pacific theater.

His job was to search and destroy. Working alone, these Navy Libs would take off before dawn and return after dark, searching the seas for enemy ships, and coming in for mast-high bombing when they found them. These Libs seldom flew higher than 200 feet. No one wore a parachute. And they took on everything—single handed.

I took a ride with McGaughey a couple of months before his death. It was just about a year ago, at Leyte, when Mac horsed the Lib into the air from the Leyte strip and started on the search leg that carried us far out into the South China Sea.

About 2 in the afternoon Mac, speaking over the inter-com, asked the crew to be extra alert. "That pip you see on the radar," he said, "is Luzon. I am going in to have a look at Manila and the suburbs."

He lowered the Lib until it was not more than 25 feet off the water. "They'll have trouble picking us up," he said.

The crew and the extra passenger were nervous—mighty nervous. But not Mac. To look at him, he might just as well have been flying between Dallas and Chicago.

At fifty feet we swept over Corregidor. The United States markings on our wings must have looked as big as moons to the startled Japs as we barreled over Manila. We took a tree-top look at Bataan, and then headed for home.

But we hadn't sunk a ship or knocked down a Jap plane. This bothered Mac. "You see," he said, "if we get something, the crew will get a nip of brandy when we get home. The surgeon'll let us have it for medicinal purposes."

We were about half an hour from home and the light was getting dim over the Visayan Sea, when Mac spotted a low-flying dot miles ahead of us. He turned on the coal and started after it. He came up behind it, and there were the big "meat balls" of Japan on the wings. It was a Topsy, trying to sneak back to a Jap island base.

He kept closing on the Topsy. At no more than a hundred yards he told the nose gunner to open up, and the nose gunner, whose brother had been killed only a few weeks before, unbuttoned the transport job with his fire. The first burst of the "Fifty" streaked just over the nose of the Jap ship. The second burst cut it in two, just as if a giant hand had pulled a zipper the length of it. It burst into flame and dove into the sea.

Mrs. McGaughey, there was no finer pilot and no finer man in the Pacific theater than your son. The men who served under him loved him, and the Japs who had to fight him must have hated him. He did his share—and more.[243]

The column appeared shortly before the crew's remains were moved from Palawan to an air force cemetery on Leyte. Three more years passed before they finally came home, to Fort Scott National Cemetery in Kansas.[244] On April 29, 1949, the remains were interred in what the local newspaper called "the largest group burial in the history of the cemetery." A minister and a priest presided. The Veterans of Foreign Wars provided pallbearers and an honor guard. Flags were folded and given to families. Mac's mother and father were there, along with his widow, Kathryn. Her last name was Tucker now. In all, more than fifty mourners came from a dozen states. They had suffered and sorrowed without ever knowing each other. And now that the hurt had hardened, like a broken bone that leaves you with a limp, there seemed little to say. They likely shared stories and small talk and finally, in silence, a grief as pure and prolonged as the last note of "Taps." Bill Loesel was one of only two crew members for whom no one came.[245]

More than a year later, Mac's mother came back to see her son and couldn't find him. She went home and wrote the quartermaster general:

Dear Sir:

Having made a trip October 1 to Fort Scott, Kansas, National Cemetery, where our son, Lt. Commander Harold Meade McGaughey and his eleven plane crew are resting (we hope), we felt pretty bad finding no stone up, since they were brought there April 20, 1949. As soon as this stone is up, which we hope very soon, as we will be going back soon, will you kindly send us a picture of it. Thank you.

Mr. and Mrs. Ray McGaughey
Macomb, Illinois

The army wrote back and said the delay had been caused by "a study which was made of the proposed design for such stones." The study had now been completed, and work would begin soon. Then, when the tablet arrived, someone noticed that the name of one crewman had been misspelled. The final, corrected, stone was laid in 1952.[246]

So the last photo we have of Bill Loesel is the only one in color. It shows a gently sloping hillside with grass as green and kempt as any golf course. Fort Scott is one of the oldest national cemeteries; the graves here go back to the Civil War. It's also one of the smallest, only twenty acres. Unlike Arlington, where the headstones march to the horizon and beyond understanding, it is an intimate place. Halfway up one row, just beyond the shade of a black locust tree, it's easy to see a break in the ranks of the upright markers. In the space lies a tablet, flush with the ground. Death is democratic; the twelve names are listed alphabetically, rather than by rank. Bill and Mac are near the middle. Between them—as he often was, sitting on the flight deck, chatting away another long mission—is radar expert Nelson McCaa. In front of and behind them, on the plaque as in the plane, are the rest of the crew. A headstone one grave over bears a single name, U.S. Army sergeant Richard P. Rudd. He is the brother of Robert J. Rudd, Mac's radioman, who sent the final message. Their parents asked that they be buried together.[247]

The prairie light lingers. We stare at the stone as we stared at the snapshots, but the marble gives up nothing but names. So we chisel two last facts into memory.

The family story said Bill Loesel left behind a fiancée, Patty Renner. Her name had changed, but I found her. We would talk on the phone many times, and I would learn how she later married a man who became an alcoholic. They divorced, but she was very close to her three children. She would tell me how she and Bill had met in high school, how he had "made me feel safe and content and happy," how they had decided to wait until he returned from his tour before getting married, how she had kept his letters and medals for many years after.

But that first day, after I introduced myself and explained why I was calling, we talked for only a moment before there was a silence. Then sobs, muffled at first. From experience, I'd learned not to interrupt. More than sixty years passed in sixty seconds, followed by six words: "Yes, I loved him very much."[248]

The family story also said Bill left behind a footlocker with all his navy mementoes perfectly preserved—dress whites, neatly strapped in; a shoe-shine brush; instruction manuals, maps, and papers; notes from his classes at Pensacola; dog tags. When the squadron shipped it home, his mother and father opened it only once. They stared without speaking, hardly touching what was inside. Then they closed it like a casket and buried it in the attic.[249]

The Flying Cowboy

The word "courage" comes from the French *coeur* and, before that, the Latin *cor*, meaning "heart." For a long time it referred to any strong emotion. Gradually it came to describe a specific strength: valuing something or someone more than your fear, or even yourself.

In war, of course, courage is celebrated, even consecrated. We visit the monuments and read the accounts. Distilled and dulled to language you can put on a plaque, the military citations tell us what heroes did, but they don't tell us why. Probably because it's hard to know, even for the heroes themselves.

But when does courage cross the line?

Your answer might depend on where you were born, how you were raised, or what you hoped for the future. Tom Mulvihill and George Parker had fought literally side by side, many times. But they saw themselves and their jobs very differently. The resulting controversy splintered the squadron, lasted longer than the war itself, and reverberated to the highest reaches of the high command.

Thomas Patrick Mulvihill Jr. inherited his toughness from a father who had set out for wide-open Montana from Pennsylvania, alone, at age fourteen. He worked as a jockey and, after he grew too big, got a job on the railroad. Tom Sr. married, saved his money, and bought land, one piece after another, around Columbus on the Yellowstone River in the southern part of the state. Almost as soon as Tom Jr. could walk, he worked—his daughter sent me a picture of him on horseback at age four, helping herd cattle. But the boy never really took to ranching; he always seemed to be looking for something else over the next rise.

He found it in Missoula, while he was away at college. In the classroom, he was a very good student—a math whiz, a speed reader. But when a barnstorming pilot came to town and Tom went for a ride, everything else took a back seat. During the Depression he worked for the Work Projects Administration to pay for lessons and his license. He also took up with a girl from Columbus he'd known since grade school, whose father had been president of the local bank before it folded during the Depression. They married and moved to Miles City, where Tom did anything to stay in the air. He flew charters. He made maps. He ran his own flight school, training pilots who would later fly with both the navy and the army.[250]

Five months before Pearl Harbor, Mulvihill joined the navy. He was later assigned to an air delivery unit at the naval air station on Terminal Island, near Los Angeles. The job was to test and deliver new planes, built in the nearby factories, to navy bases across the country. While there, he met a young lieutenant from Arizona named Dan Moore and another experienced pilot about his age, Harold "Mac" McGaughey. The three flew just about everything the navy owned, from fighters to bombers to flying boats, racking up hundreds of hours. They also took advanced instrument training, flying for months with commercial airlines. Tom and Mac especially became fast friends. Because of their age, they were not likely candidates for combat, but they kept making their case to any brass who would listen.[251] Finally, in early 1944, they got their chance when they and Dan Moore were assigned to VPB-117.

Mac became engineering officer, and Mulvihill was named flight officer in charge of training crews. Tall and thin, with a sharp tongue, he reserved much of his ire for the younger copilots and navigators, most of whom had no combat experience and were fresh from training. One was Isaac George Parker, from Seattle, whose father owned half of what was then the largest civil engineering firm west of the Mississippi. The military was in his blood. He was a direct descendant of Captain John Parker, who had commanded the Minutemen at the Battle of Lexington. He had gone to a military boarding school. At the University of Washington, he signed up for the Reserve Officer Training Corps and took Civilian Pilot Training; then he left to join the navy in 1943 and was assigned to the squadron a year later.[252]

The first time Parker flew with him, Mulvihill yelled repeatedly. But Parker was eventually named to his crew, and once in the war zone, it was clear the older man intended to make his mark.[253] A reporter from the *New York Times* visiting Tinian wrote a long article about the squadron:

> Men like Lieut. Comdr. Tom Mulvihill, the flying cowboy from Columbus, Mont., can't be kept out of a fight. They gave him a four-motored plane and told him to do routine searches, so he tears into every lighter, more maneuverable Japanese plane he sees, making his PB4Y do tricks that most fliers considered impossible with heavy bombers.[254]

The article described an early patrol on which they came across a two-hundred-foot cargo ship. The Liberator's guns cut sailors down on deck and knocked others into the water. Then bombs wracked the hull and blew debris higher than the plane. Turning for home, north of Iwo Jima, they spotted a Japanese bomber known as a Kate closing on them from below. Mulvihill turned toward the Kate, passed it, and did a wingover, putting the bomber above and behind the Kate. Flying so fast that Mulvihill had to pull back the throttles to keep from overrunning it, and diving so steep that the top turret was able to fire straight down, gunners set the Kate on fire and it exploded, so close that the Liberator flew through the smoke.[255] As the *Times* reporter noted,

> It is not the victory over the Kate that is the point of this story—it is the wingover, and the fact that Mulvihill made a four-motored Liberator turn inside of a fast light bomber. Everybody in the air force knows that such a thing cannot be done—everybody except Mulvihill, who did it.[256]

Mulvihill got the Distinguished Flying Cross (DFC) for that day's work. He and Mac made a $100 bet as to who would sink more ships during their tour, and they liked to schedule special joint missions. In October, two Liberators from another squadron had been jumped by eight Zeros near Iwo Jima, shooting down six of the fighters. A week later, Mulvihill and Mac flew the same sector together, cruising off the coast of Iwo Jima, daring the Zeros to come out and fight. None did, so they settled for sinking a cargo ship and some barges.[257]

In December, the squadron moved to Leyte in the Philippines. On one mission during the first week, Mulvihill found three Japanese cargo ships holed up in an island harbor surrounded by high, wooded hills. To attack them he had to dive almost straight down and pull up abruptly, but he never hesitated and set all three afire. On the way home, he found three more hiding near another island, this time in the shadow of vertical rock cliffs one thousand feet high. He first tried bombing them from above the cliffs; when that didn't work, he dove straight at them, again pulling out just in time. He made eight such strafing runs while his tail gunner, Farney Edwards, deliberately ricocheted rounds off the cliff and into the ships, all of which burned and sank.[258] It was a little like trying to juggle knives while swinging from a trapeze (and working without a net), but it earned Mulvihill his second DFC, which cited "his exercise of extreme courage and resourcefulness in flying into secluded enemy harbors, and skillful maneuvering of his plane in attack that resulted in the destruction of the enemy ships encountered."

Mulvihill was winning citations, but the squadron's number one responsibility was reconnaissance. Attacking targets of opportunity, especially on an outbound leg, meant that the full search sector might not get covered. The problem became serious enough that Admiral Frank Wagner, head of the Fleet Air Wing, ordered crews not to carry bombs.[259] There were also complaints from Mulvihill's own crew. Some of the men said he went after targets immediately, on instinct, rather than sizing up the dangers first. During runs on Japanese ships, he twice told his air bomber that if he didn't hit the target, he'd crash-dive the plane into it.[260] Coming back to base after one flight, he was told to circle in a given area and then ordered to leave because an enemy plane had been spotted nearby and night fighters were on their way to attack. He told the tower,

"If they can get me, let them have me." He refused to move and was mistakenly fired on by friendly antiaircraft batteries.[261]

Mulvihill also frequently flew planes other pilots had rejected for mechanical problems because, he said, with his experience he could "get by with them."[262] Before one flight, his copilot and chief mechanic had refused a plane because engine performance during warm-ups was well below accepted limits. When Mulvihill found out, he said they would fly the plane anyway.[263] Another time, despite the possibility of seeing Japanese planes within minutes of takeoff, he didn't wait for malfunctioning bow and tail turret guns to be repaired.[264]

It wasn't any one incident but rather the accumulating weight of worry that eventually led to stress fractures within the crew. Sometime in early November, copilot John Sullivan left to replace a copilot in another crew who had quit flying. He didn't come back, and his spot wasn't filled; George Parker became both copilot and navigator. That same week Mulvihill's radioman asked to quit because he was becoming too nervous.[265] He later flew many missions with another crew and had no problems.[266] Meanwhile, his replacement was gone from Mulvihill's crew in less than a month.[267]

All the while, the missions kept coming. To the China coast, to Formosa, to Okinawa. The last week of January, commanding officer Harold McDonald was promoted to Fleet Air Wing; Mulvihill, the executive officer and next in line, became VPB-117's CO. Ten days later, the squadron moved west to Mindoro, and on his first mission from the new base, Mulvihill came upon a Japanese airfield in Borneo with several parked planes. He dove in, destroyed three fighters, received two holes in his own wings from antiaircraft positions, and won his third DFC.[268]

Then, on February 17, his best friend, Mac McGaughey, didn't return from patrol. The next day Mulvihill went searching for him. He didn't find anything but decided to attack Japanese antiaircraft positions protecting a town on an island near Borneo. His bombs missed, but the Japanese scored several hits on the plane. One hot shell fragment landed on Parker's chest. Another round sailed over the radio operator's head just as he bent to pick something up.[269]

Back at base, Mulvihill wrote Mac's wife, telling her, "We all bargain for death out here, it could well be my turn next." He showed the letter to Parker and asked what he thought of it. Parker said he didn't like the idea of Mulvihill thinking he would be killed while Parker was sitting next to him.[270]

It seemed to the crew that Mac's death had somehow raised the stakes for Mulvihill; after that the flights became even more hectic.[271] The last week of February they brought along a navy liaison officer whose specialty was coordinating airplane searches with attacks from nearby submarines. They found a convoy of three Japanese tankers, protected by four destroyer escorts and six Jake floatplanes—a formidable force. Mulvihill chased one of the Jakes through heavy antiaircraft fire and shot it down. They later radioed the convoy's position, and an American sub attacked and sank several of the ships.[272] That earned Mulvihill his fourth DFC. The fifth came less than two weeks later, when he made two runs on a large Japanese cargo ship and sank it off the coast of Indochina.[273]

Early in a flight on March 11, his plane developed a fuel leak, and the crew could smell fumes throughout the plane. On the homeward leg over Borneo, they came upon a Japanese oil refinery. Mulvihill lined up at tree-top level to attack large oil storage tanks. As they approached, Parker told the bow gunner not to strafe on the way in so that they wouldn't trigger an explosion directly in front of the plane. Mulvihill said, "The hell with that; go ahead and hit them on the way in." Just as he spoke, the waist gunner reported that he had fired into a tank alongside, which had exploded and nearly blown off the back half of the plane. Mulvihill changed his orders.[274]

Most in the crew were now having trouble sleeping. Many were losing weight. Parker was among those just hoping to somehow make it through. He wrote home on March 14,

> For some reason the time has passed quite quickly since the last time I wrote a letter. One reason may be that there is so much "scuttlebutt" (rumors) going around. The very latest is that we will leave about a week or better after Dad's birthday (early April) for that long journey back home. Don't count on this as there are a good many reasons why this will not go through.[275]

They left the next morning on a mission to the coast of Indochina, where they spotted a small cargo vessel in a harbor. Mulvihill immediately threw the plane into a steep dive to gain speed for an attack. But he was going too fast to pull up at the normal level, and he passed over the ship no more than thirty feet above the water. The crew felt a shudder, as if the plane had been hit by antiaircraft fire.[276] When they returned to base they saw that the top of the ship's mast had torn away the radome, which hung just below the belly of the Liberator.[277] Mulvihill said he thought the wind had blown it off, and anyway they could have survived hitting the mast of a ship that size. The crew disagreed; they felt that if they'd been a few feet lower, the mast might have torn open the plane's underside and tossed it into the water.

The next morning Mulvihill called Parker to his tent and told him that he'd ordered another crew to fly a dusk strike on a convoy holed up at Cap St. Jacques on the coast south of Saigon. Mulvihill said he would follow up with an attack of his own at dawn the following day. Parker pointed out that if a squadron plane had already attacked once, they had lost the element of surprise, adding, "We probably won't get away with it." Mulvihill said, "Well, we will try." By the time Parker got back to his tent, scuttlebutt about the mission had reached the enlisted crewmen. At least four went to see Parker and told him they wanted to be transferred from Mulvihill's plane. Parker said he would go talk with him.

When he again found Mulvihill in his tent, at first Parker didn't tell him about the crew. Instead, he said that he, Parker, would like to be transferred. Mulvihill asked why. Parker said he felt they were getting into too many unjustified attacks, but he would fly with any other pilot in the squadron. Mulvihill refused, saying Parker had done too good a job "to throw it away this way." He pointed out that the crew had only seven or eight patrols left to fly and told him to think it over. Parker said he wasn't going to change his mind and that the rest of the crew felt the same way. Mulvihill said to bring all of them to his tent after noon chow.

When the crew arrived, Mulvihill was sitting on his bed, Parker in a chair. The men stood or sat on the floor. Mulvihill told them they were going to talk, man to man, as if they were civilians. Then he said, "I hear some of you don't want to fly with me anymore." Several said that was true. Mulvihill turned to Parker and said, "Mr. Parker, you have made up your mind. You are through flying, and I will take your wings." Parker said nothing. Then Mulvihill spoke to the crew, asking each, "Do you not want to fly anymore?" All said they would be happy to fly with any other pilot in the squadron. To each, Mulvihill said, "You will fly with me or you will fly with no one." He was slapping a notebook against his leg; everyone in the hot tent was sweating.

The men started to explain. Several said McGaughey's crew had all been killed, and they were afraid they were next. They talked about the near misses, the aggressiveness of the patrols. They said every time they were scheduled for a mission, other crews joked they'd be flying search patrols looking for their wreckage. Mulvihill said that being in a crew with such a reputation was something to be proud of, not ashamed of. The men said they were proud, they believed they'd done their share, but they felt their luck was running out. During the discussion some in the crew suggested that they could simply avoid what one called the "suicidal" attacks: cover the sector, attack enemy planes as long as they were not protected by shore batteries or warships, attack enemy shipping when it seemed to make sense. Mulvihill cut them off: "Do you mean you want me to fly negative patrols?" No, they said, just not to tempt fate so much. Mulvihill said he wouldn't make such promises; he didn't want to "fill [his] mind with percentages" like that. He told them to think it over and let him know the next day. They did, and none had changed their minds.[278]

The question for Mulvihill then became what to do about it. Another crew in the squadron had lost its pilot, who had been sent back stateside, and they were waiting for his replacement. Mulvihill ordered this second crew to fly missions with him. They also refused. Meanwhile, Parker's request for transfer to another crew had been sent to a board of investigation, which heard the story and sent him back to the squadron to fly with a different pilot. But someone higher up must have overruled the board, because before he could fly again, Parker was ordered to face a general court-martial. Ensigns James Gray and Hugo Prell, the officers in the second crew that had refused Mulvihill, were put up for court-martial soon after.[279]

As far as anyone knew, nothing like this had ever happened before. Parker, meanwhile, referred to the incident only obliquely in a March 23 letter home:

> Here is word of your wandering boy. . . . Some of my experiences the past week will help me a lot in the future. None have involved flying. Have been working with a very competent lawyer to enable me to write up a statement I may be called to submit. You will no doubt be very curious as to the type of statement I am writing. Would like very much to tell you but it may spoil my chances. Will tell you all about it as soon as I can.[280]

A few days later, Mulvihill put a statement into the official files of each crewman:

> The designation of combat aircrewman is hereby revoked and the right to wear the aircrewman's insignia is denied. This man, due to his refusal to fly as an aircrewman with his regularly assigned patrol plane commander, citing the patrol plane commander's increased aggressive contact with the enemy as reckless and dangerous to his well-being, it is recommended by this command that this man never be allowed to act as or be designated as an aircrewman again.

Also in their files were recommendations for commendations, including several pending air medals. On Admiral Wagner's orders, Mulvihill removed all the recommendations from the files.[281]

Then a sudden twist: On April 8, Mulvihill was relieved as squadron commanding officer. Now he was in limbo; he couldn't fly without a crew, and he couldn't order anyone to fly with him because he wasn't in command. Still, he kept trying. He went to Leyte, recruited a complete crew from the pool there, but couldn't get the men assigned to him. He made himself available to the squadron as a standby pilot but was never called. Parker was also at loose ends. In a letter to his family, he said his big excitement came two nights a week, when they served ice cream with evening chow. He also tried to explain briefly why he had so much free time:

> My not flying is only temporary as far as I can tell now. To make my story short: I refused to fly with one man and because he was the C.O. he tried to do a lot of things which are very unreasonable. . . . As yet we still have no idea as to the outcome. There are three of us officers and eighteen enlisted men who didn't want to fly with him.[282]

The trial began May 17, 1945, at Clark Field, on Luzon. The judges were ten naval officers. The lawyers were officers too. Counsel for the prosecution was Charles Kickham from Boston. He had two years at Harvard Law before joining the navy in 1942.[283] The defense attorney, Jake Dickinson, was a little older. He had graduated from law school and gone into practice in his hometown of Topeka, Kansas. His brother had been the only war correspondent in the landing barge with Douglas MacArthur when he splashed ashore for his "I have returned" photo op. Dickinson himself would later be admitted to practice before the U.S. Supreme Court.[284]

But I never would have known what happened at George Parker's trial except for two women, a lifetime later. After following some leads, I finally found his widow. George had died years before, but she had kept a carbon copy of the trial transcript—hundreds of sheets of onionskin paper—on a back shelf in the closet.

Then one day I was looking through some VPB-117 action reports when I noticed a familiar name: Jake Dickinson. So he was not just a defense lawyer assigned by the navy. He was familiar with Parker's story from firsthand experience. He had joined VPB-117 in January as an aircraft intelligence officer, briefing pilots before their missions and writing up action reports when they returned. In fact, he had written reports on eight of Mulvihill's flights, including the last one.

Most pilots liked and trusted Dickinson and knew he was a lawyer, which is why Parker and the other pilots asked that he represent them. Dickinson knew he would have to cross-examine Mulvihill on the stand, no holds barred, even though six weeks earlier he had been taking orders from the same man. But he never hesitated and threw himself into Parker's defense.

I found Jake Dickinson's daughter, who filled me in on her father's story and sent copies of his letters home. In one of them he told his wife about the upcoming trials, wording the letter carefully so it would get past the censors:

> To the best of my knowledge the cases are without precedent in several respects and consequently are going to be very difficult and tiring to try. . . . I am going to be quite distressed if I lose since the pilots in question are personal friends of mine and I am thoroughly in sympathy with them in the situation which led up to the filing of the charges.[285]

Parker's trial was first, and as it opened Mulvihill was the prosecution's star witness—confident under Kickham's questioning. He said he didn't think the Japanese were "hot enough" to shoot him down, and he had "a certain feeling of luck." He admitted he had ridden his crew hard, especially during training, and agreed that he often sought out the most difficult assignments:

> As flight officer, and executive officer and finally captain, I felt it was my place to lead out flights often, and to take any patrols and attacks that were possibly a little harder to accomplish. I went on the premise that no pilot could ever say that I have done something you have not. They never claimed that.

And he spoke candidly when questioned about his risk/reward calculations, especially in the last months of his tour:

> Q: Was the aggressive character of your flights of a combat nature increasing in aggressiveness as your tour of duty came to a conclusion?
> A: I came out to do as much as I could in the time I had to do it, and there was one other pilot in this occasion that I felt has exceeded

me, Lieutenant Elder. I had in mind a number of attacks I had intended to make at that time. The intended targets in French Indo-China had been thrown open, we were permitted to bomb bridges, railroads, and there were fat targets over there. They were not particularly dangerous targets, but the crew brought up the question in the meeting, "do you think it's worth risking our lives and the aircraft on those inland targets?" I told them that was not their problem. That it was within the bounds of reason, that anything we destroyed would hinder the enemy's prosecution of the war, and that when we took our oath of office, and their oath, that in fact we had promised the United States government to die if necessary, that they didn't throw open those targets if they didn't want us to attack them.

Q: What was the attitude as to the safety of yourself and your crew during these missions?

A: Well, I did the best I could, I felt that the crew, that includes myself, was, as I said before, as good if not the best trained and operating crew; that was their, and my, only insurance. There is no attack, no combat flight, that is conducive to a long life. You don't have to get shot down, anything can happen. It is the only feeling I have, that our training would bring us home.

Q: Did you ever, in your combat experience, run up against the problem of deciding whether a specific target and its ultimate destruction was worth your plane and its entire crew?

A: I never made that decision. I attacked anything I thought I could get away with, even though it meant the destruction of all hands.[286]

Jake Dickinson's cross-examination was lengthy and pointed. An exchange about the attack on the oil tanks in Borneo was typical:

Q: As a matter of fact, an armor-piercing incendiary is designed especially to set afire and blow up oil tankers and oil tanks, is it not?

A: It is certainly designed to set a fire. I don't think there is an explosive charge in the incendiary.

Q: Oil and oil vapors are known to be explosive as a matter of common knowledge, are they not Mr. Mulvihill?

A: I've always labored under that impression.

Q: You then knew that you were ordering your bow gunner to fire incendiary bullets into an explosive target directly ahead of a plane which you were flying at tree top level, did you not?

A: That's right.

Q: Is that one of the instances which made you distrust Mr. Parker's judgment when he ordered the bow gunner to withhold fire?

A: I had seen an ammunition ship blow up under another airplane and it had survived the explosion. I felt that I could fly through any explosion or that I would fly by any explosion which might have occurred as the result of our strafing. However, I purposely countermanded my orders to strafe on the way in, told the bow gunner not to strafe those tanks that came up over the bow or directly in front of us.

Q: But that, Mr. Mulvihill, was only after a tank had exploded alongside and almost blown your plane up, is that correct?

A: You said almost blew the plane up. The parts of that airplane, the tail section, had recently been salvaged for further use. They certainly didn't suffer much damage. Yes.

Q: So on that occasion, his judgment turned out to be good, did it not?

A: That was a good decision.

Q: And your judgment endangered your entire plane and crew, did it not?

A: I expect that's correct. Certainly it is dangerous just to start with.

Q: You were adding to the danger of the attack by shooting armor-piercing incendiaries into an explosive target ahead of you, were you not?

A: Yes, that's the reason we got as many as we did.

Q: Do you feel, Mr. Mulvihill, that that was a prudent attack?

A: They tell me that oil keeps the fleet at sea, and, in my opinion, destroying oil came under the classification of knocking out those targets which I felt I could get away with.

Q: You mention that you could fly past an exploding tank. Do you mean to tell the court that, flying at tree top level, you could have maneuvered a PB4Y1 around an oil tank exploding in front of you?

A: I wouldn't be afraid, and I think it could be successfully done. To fly over an exploding oil tank, it has been done successfully.

Q: And you were willing to do it on that day with your plane and your crew, is that correct?

A: I went in there to get all the tanks that I could get, any way I could get them.

Q: Without regard to consequences, is that correct?

A: I felt that I'd get away with it.

Q: Do you feel, Mr. Mulvihill, that the members of your crew had legitimate reason to be slightly nervous about that attack?

A: I would hardly say, slightly.

Q: And with good reason?

A: Definitely, that is definitely playing for keeps.

Q: And you were knowingly subjecting your plane and your crew to a very great risk, were you not?

A: Yes.

Q: You did that intentionally?

A: Every attack I have ever made, I did that intentionally.

Q: You intended to keep on doing the exact thing in the future?

A: When the intended targets in French Indo-China were thrown open, I had a number of similar projects in mind.[287]

It was getting to be pretty good theater, and more spectators, especially pilots, were showing up to watch. Dickinson and Mulvihill sparred back and forth. On flying with bad equipment:

Q: Mr. Mulvihill, it was also after Lieutenant Brooks was shot down that you made your crew take off without their guns working, was it not, as you testified previously in this case?

A: It was after Lieutenant Brooks was shot down.

Q: Did you feel you might have been subjecting your plane and your crew to an unreasonable and an unnecessary risk by making them take off with inoperative guns?

A: That was relative to the importance of the patrol. At that time good search patrols were imperative. I knew that the guns were not in such condition that they could not be fixed.

Q: How did you know that?

A: I asked the ordnance man. They had been fixed before we reached the Verde Straits.

Q: But, Lieutenant Brooks had been shot down between Leyte and the Verde Straits, wasn't he?

A: Yes.

Q: And if you had been shot down or had been attacked by Jap fighters at the same place Lieutenant Brooks was, you wouldn't have had your guns working, isn't that correct?

A: Some of it. I think it was one bow gun that wasn't working.

Q: How about the tail guns?

A: I don't remember.

Q: As a matter of fact, they weren't working, either?

A: I don't know. I do not remember. It may be true that they were not working, it could have been true. I do know that we had some ordnance trouble that morning. All I heard of the trouble was what it took to fix. I went out on my patrol.[288]

On winning medals and competing with other pilots, especially Art Elder:

Q: On his next to last patrol he [Elder] came home with one man dead and five wounded, did he not?

A: That sounds familiar to me, although I'd been detached. While I followed his career, more or less, I'm not sure of that point.

Q: As a matter of fact, you followed his career with a great interest because you wanted to outdo him, didn't you?

A: I certainly would have liked to outdo him. I wager that Lieutenant Elder is the best combat pilot that I have ever met.

Q: And you were willing to have yourself, your crew and your plane destroyed in an effort to outdo Lieutenant Elder, were you not?

A: I never made any attack in which I planned on being destroyed.

Q: The question is not what you planned, but what you were willing to have occur.

A: I was willing to put myself in a position where it might occur.

Q: And, of course, your crew and your plane along with you?

A: Definitely, they were in the same aircraft.

Q: You were aware that Mr. Elder might be recommended for a Navy Cross for either or both of two missions which he flew, were you not?

A: I made the order initiating that recommendation.

Q: You yourself were determined also to get a Navy Cross before the end of your tour of duty, were you not?

A: I'd certainly be proud to earn one.

Q: And you were going to try to earn one, weren't you?

A: I was trying to earn one, yes, and for that matter I was trying to earn the Congressional Medal of Honor.[289]

On fatalism and risk:

Q: You have also said that you don't care if you come back from this war, hadn't you?

A: No, I never said I didn't care.

Q: How did you state it?

A: I made this statement, that when I came out here, I came on the basis that I wasn't coming back.

Q: Didn't you tell your crew on one occasion at Tinian, that you had lived a full life, seen all you wanted to see, and that you didn't care if you came back?

A: I do care.

Q: What did you tell the crew?

A: I don't believe I told them that.

Q: Did you say something to that effect?

A: I told you what I said to that effect. I felt that is the way, that by figuring I wasn't coming back, I would not have my mind all cluttered up. I felt then, and I feel now, that under certain circumstances I was expendable.[290]

All this was interesting, Dickinson felt, especially for pilots in the room and throughout the navy. It might well set a precedent about what rights crews had when flying with pilots they deemed unsafe. But it was peripheral to what he considered the indisputable core of his case: that Parker could not be charged with disobeying an order, since no official order had been given. He zeroed in on the issue during cross-examination, talking about the meeting between Mulvihill and his crew.

Q: When did you make up your mind that someone had disobeyed some orders you gave?

A: When they said they would refuse to fly with me.

Q: You have just testified that at that time, you didn't think there had been a refusal, is that correct?

A: That is correct. I now want to change that. It was at the end of the conversation—then.

Q: You say in your statement, that you did not understand that an order had been disobeyed at the time of that conversation—that you gave a false answer there.

A: The start of the conversation I had no feeling that the order, or any order that I would give, would not be obeyed. At the end of the conversation, when they refused to fly with me, I felt that my orders would be disobeyed.

Q: You felt that they would be disobeyed if they were given?

A: I knew they would be disobeyed.

Q: And that is the reason you gave no orders, is that right?

A: That is correct.

At that moment Dickinson felt the trial was over. Mulvihill himself said no order had been given.

Of course, Dickinson went on anyway. As defense witnesses, he called eight pilots from VPB-117 and four more from another squadron.

All said basically the same things. That they didn't think chasing a Jake across a convoy of warships or attacking oil tanks head-on made sense, and they would not have done so themselves. That they would not have flown planes with the engine or gun troubles that Mulvihill described in his testimony.

And, to a man, they said requests not to fly with a particular pilot were frequent, beginning in training and right through their combat experience. Some had done so themselves. In every case they knew about personally or had heard of, the request had been granted. Some cited Bus Miller, commanding officer of VP-109, who won a Navy Cross, Silver Star, and six DFCs but had two complete crews ask to be transferred along the way.[291] A few told personal stories of having requested not to fly with a pilot, only to have that pilot and his crew later killed due to overaggressiveness or pilot error. As one put it, "Asking a man to fly with someone he considers unsafe is like asking him to commit suicide."[292]

Two others testified that, in talking with Mulvihill about taking chances as plane commanders, they had said they would do what was asked of them but not unnecessarily endanger their planes or their crews. In both cases, Mulvihill had asked, "Didn't you expect to come out here and be killed?" Both pilots had believed he was serious. Both had said no. Mulvihill had acted "very surprised."

Dickinson also called two members of Mulvihill's crew. Among other things, they recalled specific times when Mulvihill told them he did "not expect to come back from this tour alive" and asked them "what we had to live for." They said they were certain he meant it.[293]

Closing arguments took three hours. Prosecutor Charles Kickham described military graveyards he saw on Los Negros and Pelileu as he traveled to the combat zone and compared the refusal of Mulvihill's crew with "our young men on Iwo Jima" who were being ordered into "the face of imminent death." He agreed that Mulvihill "treated his crew like a race horse" and "lashed them to the hilt." But, he said, the conversation in the tent between Mulvihill and the men amounted to an order, "even though not stated in so many words," and they had no choice but to obey.

He also touched on the challenge, and the importance, of the trial:

It could be said, and I speak only for myself, that I have enjoyed, as a lawyer, working on this case. It is a key case in Naval law. I have enjoyed this case, and my previous association with it has been far more pleasant than you may ever suspect.[294]

When it was his turn, Jake Dickinson disagreed with almost everything Kickham had said, including whether he had enjoyed the proceedings: "Certain facts in this case have been brought out that are, personally, extremely distasteful to me. I don't like this case. I don't like any part of it, and I state to this court frankly, that I wish I had never heard of it." Nevertheless, he drove home his arguments one more time. He said that, based on things Mulvihill had done and said—and didn't dispute—the crew was more than justified in not wanting to fly with him. Citing the testimony of a dozen pilots, he said that asking to fly with a different pilot was a "generally understood" privilege and that Mulvihill was "the one man in the history of Naval aviation" who refused to grant it. But these were side issues, Dickinson said. The prosecution's job was to prove Parker had disobeyed a direct order, and Mulvihill himself had said on the stand that he never gave an order. He asked the court to give Parker a "full and honorable" acquittal, which in naval procedure was used when "the court wishes to place the highest stamp of approval upon the actions of the accused."[295]

As final arguments ended, Dickinson felt he had "never so thoroughly won a case" in his life. Kickham later said he figured the odds of conviction at only about three in ten.[296] But after deliberating for a full day, the jury brought back a verdict of guilty.

Dickinson wrote his wife,

I do not believe that the case will ever stand up on appeal—or rather, review—and I wasn't particularly surprised at the verdict, but nevertheless it was a bit of a shock to me. I still have the other two cases to worry about. Naturally the outlook in them is not too favorable at the moment, but the fight is far from over.[297]

There were rumors. Admiral Wagner had a long history in naval aviation. In 1926, he led the first exercise that proved the effectiveness of dive-bombing tactics. He'd been in charge of the air wing that had to retreat to Australia when the Japanese invaded the Philippines in the wake of Pearl Harbor. He believed in the navy and in the chain of command. Some claimed to have seen a letter from Wagner to members of the court, saying he would be "pleased with a conviction" in Parker's case. Not long after the trial finished, the senior member of the court, Commander Frank P. Brown, was having drinks at an O Club with some fellow officers. In an affidavit signed and filed two months later, the officers said,

> Commander Brown did not mention the sentence or the details of the case, but from his statements it was obvious the sentence was severe. He said that he felt pressure was on this case from the entire Naval Air Corps and that Parker had to be convicted regardless of circumstances, for the future welfare of the Naval Air Corps.[298]

Parker was sentenced to be separated from the navy and to serve five years in prison at hard labor. He wrote home and explained in detail, for the first time, about the case and the trial. Dickinson went to work on an appeal and told Parker that if his father had any friends in Washington, DC, it would be good to contact them. He also began preparing for the trials of the two pilots from the second crew who also had refused to fly with Mulvihill.

By now the whole situation was a cause célèbre throughout the navy. Dickinson tried to explain to his wife:

> The charge in the cases is disobedience of orders by refusing to fly with the ex-skipper of the squadron, and my clients are three co-pilot ensigns. Among the defenses is the claim that he was an unsafe pilot and that it is the privilege of a naval aviator to decline to fly with one whom he believes to be unsafe. You can imagine the various types of dynamite involved since such a case has never been heard of—that is, resulting in a court martial— although pilots have often refused to fly with other pilots before. Add the part that Naval aviation is a voluntary service plus a large

handful of interesting facts, stir well, and you have an amazing concoction.[299]

The second trial opened in July, and Dickinson's first move was to ask that three members of the court at Parker's trial be disqualified from the second case. He claimed they were prejudiced and won the argument. All three (including Commander Brown, the presiding officer) were removed. The prosecution called many of the same witnesses, including Mulvihill, and made many of the same arguments. This time, though, Dickinson also challenged the court to weigh evidence and administer justice without regard to rank. He wrote to his wife,

> It is interesting to watch reaction when I inquire whether a judge will give equal weight to the testimony of a seaman and a commander; and whether they believe the defendant to be innocent although the admiral has filed the charges; and whether they believe that a commanding officer should be upheld as against the contention of his subordinate. One just isn't expected to ask such questions but I am asking them and they suddenly find themselves in the position of having to answer under oath, even though they outrank me and would rather not.

The trial lasted twenty-seven days and, toward the end, was being argued seven days a week, well into the evenings. As Dickinson was preparing his closing argument, he got a cable saying that his mother had died. He couldn't leave.[300] On August 1, 1945, Ensign James Gray was found innocent and given the "most full and honorable acquittal" that Dickinson had requested for Parker. The case against the second defendant, Ensign Hugo Prell, was dismissed before it ever began. Admiral Wagner later tried, unsuccessfully, to get both of them "disenrolled"— that is, thrown out of the navy.

Dickinson was elated:

> It is a wonderful feeling to be able to help people out sometimes when they are in desperate need, but always being in the center

of a maelstrom gets awfully wearing at times. . . . My grateful client has bestowed on me a bottle of Black Label which I think I will bring home and maybe put under glass as a memento. I don't think I will be able to drink it.[301]

He also felt the later verdicts would be a big help in support of George Parker's appeal.

Parker himself, meanwhile, remained at the squadron's base on Mindoro. Taking Dickinson's advice, his father's lawyer wrote the family's congressman and senator, each of whom served on his respective house's Naval Affairs Committee, asking them to look into the case. For his part, Parker tried to make the best of an awkward situation in camp. He wasn't in jail, but he wasn't allowed to fly either. He wrote home that his duties involved "sleeping, eating, going to shows, eating and sleeping." He had long talks with the squadron chaplain. He and members of the two crews that refused Mulvihill formed a softball team in the base league; they called themselves "The Outcasts."[302] But he said the majority of fliers openly supported him: "I can look anyone around here in the face. People around here know what the story is and they are for me. Anyone I ask a favor of does anything they can do to help me."

Like Parker, Mulvihill was not flying. When they bumped into each other in camp or at the O Club, nothing was said. Mulvihill tried to get Parker put under guard and confined to his tent, but he was overruled. After that, Mulvihill stopped going to the O Club altogether.[303]

In July, Parker learned that his sentence had been reduced from five years to one. But the summer dragged on, and so did the appeal. Then:

Guess some good news comes in stretches. The announcement of the end of the war came during intermission of the stage show "Oklahoma" last night. About two hours later I was told I was going back to the States. I am to report to San Francisco and will very likely be restricted all the time I am there.[304]

The Japanese had surrendered, but George Parker's personal war went on.

Smiling Dan

Some actions, some events, cleave a life in two. A single decision—good or bad or both—and the arc of someone's story becomes forever divided into the before and the after.

For Dan Moore, that moment came April 6, 1945, somewhere over the South China Sea. It didn't involve contact with the enemy. He'd seen plenty of that already, and he and his crew had acquitted themselves well. Instead, that day he was involved in a conflict of conscience—one that left him seriously wounded and shadowed him for much of his long life.

He was born at the height of the "war to end all wars." June 1917 saw German airplanes bomb London for the first time,[305] and the earliest American troops arrived in France.[306] But in southern Arizona that summer, Folsom Moore and his wife, Ola, were welcoming a baby boy. A newspaperman and member of the International Workers of the World, Folsom had been sent a few years earlier to cover the border war between America and Mexico. He stayed and settled in a place called Bisbee, more than five thousand feet up in the Mule Mountains and only eight miles from the Mexican border.

The town sat alongside, and on top of, one of the continent's great deposits of copper ore. At the turn of the twentieth century, it was booming—the biggest city between Saint Louis and San Francisco.[307] And when the Moores arrived, it was still going strong. The largest mine, the Copper Queen, was owned by the Phelps Dodge Corporation, along with the *Bisbee Daily Review*, where Folsom became business manager and then publisher in 1922. As a boy Dan hiked the "high lonesome" trail into the stronghold of the great Apache chief Cochise. He did well at Bisbee High, Class of 1934, delivering a speech titled "A Student's Impression of the New Deal" at graduation. From there it was on to the University of Arizona, and after that, its law school. He was into his second year there when America's first-ever peacetime draft caught up with him.[308]

The Selective Service Act of 1940 assigned a random number to each potential draftee in towns across the country. The lower the number, the sooner you would be called.[309] Dan was number seven in Bisbee; his best friend was number one. When they heard the news, they went out and got drunk. But then came the obvious morning-after question: What next? Another of his friends had a pilot's license, but Dan didn't know anything about airplanes—he thought they would fly faster if they didn't have wings. Still, the idea appealed to him, and he decided he'd rather volunteer than be drafted. He was allowed to finish the school year, and the navy officer who signed him up encouraged Dan to recruit some friends. So in June 1941, he and thirty or so others left for Long Beach, California.

The syllabus for potential pilots was simple: you had ten training flights, after which you either soloed successfully or washed out. Dan wasn't getting the hang of it. His instructor, who had flown for the navy and was also a lawyer, told him he was thinking too much. He should just relax and do what he was told. So Dan did and soon found himself on the Golden State Limited headed across the country to Jacksonville, Florida, for flight training. He did very well with the classroom work and spent most of his air time in PBY flying boats. Weeks and then months went by. On December 7, after watching Gary Cooper in *Sergeant York* at the movie theater, he and a buddy came outside to learn that America was once again at war.

Then things began to happen quickly. Dan was asked whether he wanted to fly PBYs or fighters. He chose fighters and was sent to the Miami Naval Air Station at Opa-Locka. Training on Stearman biplanes, learning more and more about what an airplane could do, he became comfortable and confident in the cockpit. In March 1942, he earned his Wings of Gold.

Next stop was Floyd Bennett Field in Brooklyn, near a Grumman Aircraft plant on Long Island that was churning out hundreds of navy fighters a month. Badly needed on the West Coast for the Pacific Fleet, many were shipped by rail. But the demand was so great that the navy also began using pilots to ferry planes cross-country, and Dan was assigned to the unit. Most often, he flew the Grumman F4F Wildcat—twelve hundred horsepower and a top speed of more than 320 miles per hour.[310] A big step up from the Stearman.

The trip usually took three days, the first from New York to Atlanta. Day two was the longest, Atlanta to somewhere in Texas, as far west as he could get. The last leg brought him to California. I picture him beneath the clear canopy—watching for weather, checking the gauges, the vibration and noise becoming almost background music as the continent scrolls by beneath. Young and strong, smart and serious, almost a lawyer and already a pilot. His world ahead as wide as the sky.

Then Dan was picked to learn how to fly multiengine planes, mostly DC-3s, that ferried navy brass and VIPs from one base to another. It was a crash course—just one month. After that, he was scheduled for ninety days of extra training on actual airline flights, based out of a naval air station near New York City.[311]

There he ran into a college classmate, and while they were out on the town, she introduced him to a friend. Hilda Jane Young had been born and raised in Canton, Ohio. Her mother died when she was four, and her father remarried. She was a cheerleader in high school, a champion amateur golfer, beautiful by all accounts. A woman who knew her own mind and how to take care of herself. When a high school boy one seat behind pinched her on the butt, she turned around and knocked him cold with one punch. And when the principal tried to admonish her, she pointed out that she didn't start it.

She had trained to be a nurse and worked in a hospital for several years. Then she decided she wanted to see the world. In those days an airline stewardess had to be a registered nurse, and good looks were considered part of the package. Hilda had no trouble getting hired by American Airlines. Based in Chicago, she made frequent flights to New York. Her picture also appeared in ads for the airline.

After his friend introduced them, Dan took Hilda to the dance floor, where he was immediately, and irrevocably, smitten. Before that first night was over, he blurted out that one day he would marry her. Hilda looked at him and said, "Oh, save your corn for someone else."[312]

But they continued to see each other whenever both were in town, which was often enough. He remained ardent. She was still skeptical, if no longer dismissive. At one point, maybe in part to test her own feelings, she asked for a transfer to the West Coast. As Dan's luck would have it, not much later he was sent to California as well. And the rest, as they say, is family history. Dan and Hilda were married on April 24, 1943, followed by a reception at his parents' home in Bisbee. She wore a tailored suit and a wide smile. He was in his dress blues, on his sleeve the one and a half stripes of a lieutenant junior grade.

Based now at Terminal Island near Los Angeles, Dan ferried PV-1 Ventura bombers from California to Seattle and to the East Coast until December 1943. That's when E. O. Rigsbee was assigned to lead a new squadron, VPB-117. One of his first acts was to ask an Annapolis classmate at Terminal Island to recommend his best three pilots who had experience flying multiengine planes. He tapped Harold McGaughey, Tom Mulvihill, and Dan. Mac and Mulvihill had more years of experience. But by then, Dan himself had twenty-three hundred hours in the air; was licensed to fly anything the navy owned, from fighters to bombers to seaplanes; and was certified to fly on instruments in any weather.[313]

Trouble was, all that training and experience wasn't much use to him when he first came to the squadron, because Rigsbee assigned him a new role: procurement officer. The list of what VPB-117 needed was long, and battling the bureaucracy was more than a full-time job. Dan made requests. He sent memos. He asked for favors. And he got back mostly lip service. In the end, Commander Rigsbee intervened, and just in the nick of time. The supply ship for the squadron—five miles out to sea, headed for Hawaii—had to turn around and take on extra equipment for VPB-117.[314]

The ongoing struggle with the bureaucracy had left Dan little time to train with his own crew. Copilot Marvin Barefoot had grown up on a farm in Oklahoma with one brother, four sisters, and his favorite horse, Buck. He served in the National Guard and then joined the navy, first as a sailor before earning his wings.[315] Navigator Swede Johnson was from North Dakota. Most of the rest of the crew—including an eighteen-year-old ordnance man and waist gunner from Arkansas named Gene Kern—were young and eager, if untested. But once they left the mainland, their time at Kaneohe gave them a chance to catch up on some of the practice they'd missed in San Diego. Six weeks later, they arrived in the war zone on Tinian.

At first, the biggest threat they faced didn't come from the Japanese. Another crew had been assigned to search southwest over open ocean, looking for Japanese picket boats—small ships that act as sentinels to warn the fleet of enemy activity. But the original crew had to return to base with engine trouble. So Dan and his men took over the search, and they ran into rough weather almost immediately.

They never saw any ships, but by the time they reached the end of the sector and turned for home, the sun was setting in the west and the weather was rapidly getting worse. They flew into the storm at five thousand feet, and immediately Dan and Barefoot had to literally wrestle with the controls to keep the plane level. Rain poured into the fuselage from every direction; ammunition boxes broke loose. They kept going lower and lower, hoping to find a better altitude. Finally they were flying one hundred to two hundred feet above sea level.

Then, suddenly, they broke into clear skies over calm seas. Dan remembered a book by Joseph Conrad he had read as a boy, *Typhoon*. It told about a ship caught in the eye of a hurricane—and how the captain realized that he had to reverse his course in order to reach his destination. So Dan told Swede Johnson to do just that when they reentered the storm.

They flew on through the darkness for hours more, past the point where they thought Tinian should be. It was after 3 a.m. when Swede reported seeing a light and radar picked up a signal from Saipan, the island nearest to home base. Dan radioed that they were almost out of fuel and asked them to clear the field on Tinian. They landed at 4 a.m., with barely enough gas to taxi off the runway. Commander Rigsbee was waiting for them as they left the plane.[316]

The rest of their time on Tinian was relatively uneventful. They flew cover for a damaged American submarine, found a ditched navy flying boat, helped search for Glen Box and Bill Pedretti's crew, and attacked some Japanese cargo ships on a mission with Rigsbee. They also flew some long, boring negative patrols on which they saw almost nothing but ocean, horizon to horizon.[317]

Then the squadron was ordered west, to Leyte. And it was immediately apparent that they would be much busier and more at risk.

Their first flight in the Philippines, December 2, took them north and west from Tacloban. They found three Japanese destroyers and got a few flak holes in their bomb bay as a result. But shortly after, they had a chance to turn the tables when they ran across a Japanese Zero near Lubang Island. The fighter attacked first, from above and behind, but Dan reversed course sharply and came at the Zero head-on, bow guns blazing. The fighter banked to the bomber's left, and Dan kept turning too, with the top turret and waist gunner Gene Kern firing. They sparred and parried for another minute or so before Dan was able to get behind the Zero at one thousand feet.

The Japanese pilot tried to break off by heading for the water and weaving. Diving after him, Dan closed the gap, and his gunners sent a final burst from above. The Zero crashed and burned on the island.[318]

So this, at last, was the real thing—air-to-air combat like in the newsreels, tracers and flames and shards of aluminum skin peeling away. Everything heightened, every instinct in play. But it was only the first act.

Two days later, they bombed but couldn't sink a couple of Japanese cargo ships. On December 6, flying at one thousand feet, Gene Kern spotted something below. It was a Japanese Jake, fifteen miles away and only fifty feet off the water. A long-range, single-engine seaplane, it could carry bombs and a crew of two or three, including a rear-facing machine gunner. The Liberator began to stalk from behind until within a mile of the Jake; then Dan pushed the yoke forward and went into a dive. The bow gunner's name was Richard Henry (R. H.) Thomas, and the crew called him "Right Hand" because he was a straight shooter. He opened up when they got within fifteen hundred feet, and the Jake's starboard wing caught fire. As they passed over, the tail turret got in a last burst as the

Jake crashed into the water and burned.[319] One of its pontoons broke off, and a surviving crew member clung to it. Dan circled back, and gunners strafed the wreckage. The pontoon sank, but the crewman survived.[320]

Meanwhile, at her parents' home in Ohio, Hilda was getting ready for Christmas and sending loving letters to Dan. He wrote her too, but not as often, maybe in part because letters from the front were subject to serious restrictions. You couldn't say where you were based, what your work was like, or almost anything about what you had seen or done.

None of Dan's letters to Hilda survived. But hers to him were more frequent, and some from December 1944 and January 1945 were saved. Reading them now, handwritten on crinkly thin air mail paper, yellowed with age and bearing six-cent stamps on the envelope, we know much more than she did then about what was happening with him—and how different their days were, half a world apart.

She began all the letters, in order, with Roman numerals. So the one from December 17, 1944, was "Letter XXXI":

> One week from tonight is Xmas Eve and my darling, I shall be thinking of you and missing you so much. But I shall also dream about next Xmas and how we will be able to look back on this one and thank the heavens that we have each other.

She says she's mailed him a cigarette lighter, a book, and some magazines. She thanks him for money orders he sent, describes the blizzard they're having in Ohio ("it's beautiful but so very, very cold"), and tells him to make sure he's eating well and getting his rest.

> And don't forget for one second that I'm thinking of you and that my heart is with you.

A dozen time zones away, back in the Philippines, December 17 began early for Dan and his crew. At a 3 a.m. briefing they were told that intelligence reports believed Japan's last two big battleship-carriers, the *Hyuga* and the *Ise*, might be holed up in Cam Ranh Bay in what is now

Vietnam. Dan was to fly in and see. Theirs would be the first navy aircraft to penetrate the harbor, and they would have no wingman, no fighter escort, no bombs.

The seriousness of the single-plane mission became clear when the crew members were issued survival kits that included instructions for finding friendly forces if they were shot down; Free China flags to show they were allies; French Indochina paper money; orders to give only name, rank, and serial number if captured; and two sets of dog tags—one to wear around the neck and the other on the wrist, in case the wearer's head was blown off.[321]

They took off from Tacloban at 4 a.m. in a driving rain that continued through the islands and into the open ocean—keeping them close to the water until they were within five miles of Cam Ranh Bay, when it eased up. So into the bay they went. But there were no big ships; they would later learn that around the time they left Tacloban, an American submarine spotted the *Hyuga* and the *Ise* leaving the bay, heading south toward Singapore.[322]

That didn't mean they were out of the woods, though. The Japanese also had an airfield in Cam Ranh Bay, and when Dan's crew looked down, they saw more than twenty Zeros lined up, some already beginning to take off. But the rain clouds that had caused such problems earlier now became a life saver. The Liberator simply disappeared into them, and the fighters couldn't find it.

They flew on for some time, out of range of the Zeros, before breaking out into blue skies and bright sunshine. Later—after fourteen hours in the air and nearing home in evening twilight—Gene Kern looked out his port waist hatch and saw two Japanese troop transport planes called Tesses. They were low to the water, maybe a mile ahead. Dan and Barefoot checked to see whether they were covered by fighters, and when they saw none, they dove toward the transports.

The bow gunner opened up on the trailing Tess, and its port engine caught fire; waist gunner Joe Mullen and tail gunner Frank Wharton followed up, and the plane crashed into the water. Then bow gunner R. H. Thomas started firing on the lead plane, which had gone low to the water and begun weaving back and forth. One of its engines soon began to burn, and the Tess lost control and crashed into the ocean. There were no survivors in the first plane. Five passengers from the second Tess were seen swimming in the wreckage—some on the port wing, others holding onto a floating tire. The Liberator went back and strafed them, but the crew couldn't tell whether anyone had been hit. Decades later, Dan Moore told me he regretted that decision for years.[323]

Three days after, on December 20, Hilda wrote letter XXXII:

Just a note to tell you I love you, my darling.

Back in the States, she and Dan had become good friends with Harold Riede, an aircraft intelligence officer, and his wife Evelyn—who may have let something slip about the squadron's location:

Ev said in her last letter that you and Harold are somewhere on Leyte. You are in the midst of everything and very busy. I only hope you take care of yourself and get as much rest as you can.

She tells him it's still cold and snowy in Ohio and closes by saying,

I love you and I miss you so very much. You are in my thoughts constantly, sweetheart. All my love, Hilda.

On the same day in Leyte, Dan and the crew went out again, this time north to the island of Luzon. Two days earlier, a typhoon off the coast had capsized and sunk three destroyers in Admiral Bill Halsey's fleet. And the storm was still raging. On their outbound leg, water poured through seams in the fuselage, followed by an electrical fire that filled the plane with smoke. They opened the bomb bay doors and even the cockpit windows to draw out the smoke. But they couldn't find where the fire had come from.

As they reached the north coast of Luzon, they spotted four flights of Japanese Zeros headed in the other direction. Dan and Barefoot discussed giving chase but decided to stick to their mission. So they turned south, breaking out into afternoon sunshine and catching a one-hundred-mile-per-hour tailwind. Near the port of San Fernando, they found a group of Japanese ships packed together in the harbor, offloading ammunition—a target both dangerous and inviting. Successfully bombing one or two ammunition ships could easily cause a chain reaction, destroying them all. They decided to try.

But they assumed they had already been spotted, so rather than coming in low and slow, thereby giving the Japanese guns a better shot, they climbed to five thousand feet and became a four-engine dive bomber. With the typhoon tailwind at their back, heading down and gaining speed, antiaircraft fire passed just below the plane. "It looked like we were walking on fire," Dan remembered. Bomb bay doors opened—but the bombs didn't drop. They would later learn that the earlier smoke in the plane had come from an electrical fire in the bomb-release mechanism. The crew tried everything; one even kicked at the bombs to knock them loose, nearly falling from the plane himself. So they pulled up, hoping to fix the problem and make another run.[324]

And then—at the open hatch near the rear of the plane, on the side away from the Japanese guns, Gene Kern had the bulky K-20 camera in hand to record the results of the attack when he noticed a sweetish smell. He looked toward the tail turret and saw that one of the doors had been blown off. Then he saw that tail gunner Frank Wharton had been hit, and his blood had spray-painted the inside of the fuselage.

Gene got on the intercom and called the cockpit, saying he thought Wharton was dead. Swede Johnson was sent back to help, but there was nothing to be done. With waist gunner Joe Mullen they spread out a parachute, pulled Wharton from the turret, and laid him down. The top of his skull had been sheared off, brain matter exposed. He surely never knew what hit him.

But now the Liberator was still in the middle of a melee. Even though they'd broken off the attack, they were vulnerable, especially if a Japanese plane saw the damage and attacked from behind. In fact, they had spotted an enemy floatplane fighter on the beach during their dive. Through the intercom, Dan told Gene to go to the turret and see what, if anything, was still working.

All the plexiglass windows had been blown away, and it was hard to keep from being sucked out of the turret. Gene couldn't pull back the handle on the right-hand gun, which meant Wharton had been shooting when he was hit. But Gene was able to fire the left-hand gun. And the turret could be turned with a hand crank.

So he sat in Wharton's seat, put on the headphones, and told Dan the situation. The wind whipped through the turret, and they were still more than three hours from Tacloban, at least half of that time over Japanese territory. Dan told Gene to stay in the turret and watch for trouble; then he asked whether he was all right. Shaken, Gene said, "I'm cold." There was a pause before Dan answered softly, "I know."

If a buddy dies on a battlefield, you have to keep moving, leave him behind. But if he dies in a plane and it's still flying, you carry him home. It gives you a long time to think about what happened and why luck left you untouched. For the next hour, Dan called Gene on the intercom every five minutes or so to see how he was doing. Once they were in American airspace, Gene climbed out of the turret. They landed at Tacloban at about 6 p.m., and men from Graves Registration were waiting, ready to remove the body.[325]

Wharton was from Texas, short and wiry, quick with a quip, a good friend. Nineteen years old.[326] Sometime that same night Dan, Barefoot, and Johnson, along with some of the crew, went to see about him. When they arrived, they found Wharton's body already wrapped for burial. In the hot, wet climate, the dead were interred as soon as possible. But his personal effects had not been removed. So Dan cut open the shroud, likely seeing the damage to the corpse for the first time. Then he took Wharton's dog tags and a ring from his hand, went back to his tent, and put them in an envelope along with a letter he wrote that night to Wharton's mother, Cora, in Houston. Dan told her that Frank had been struck by a shell but left out the worst details.[327]

Still the letters, and the missions, kept coming.

On Christmas day, Hilda wrote how pleased she was to get a letter from him the day before. Dan must have referred obliquely to some combat encounters, likely with the Zero and the Jake. And maybe he had talked about the issue of taking a life in war, because she told him he had weighed the incidents and "come forth with the right answer."

Then she moved to a happier topic, describing her Christmas presents, including an electric iron from his parents. She asked whether he would have any presents to open and get "something decent to eat." She told him to get his rest and closed by saying, "Good night sweetheart, and know I love you as much as any person can love another—and that's real much."

On flights that same week, Dan and the crew spotted several Japanese destroyers and came under fire for their trouble. They also pursued, but couldn't catch, two enemy planes. Then the new year began with two negative patrols, no enemy contact.[328] But the first week of 1945 ended with a bang.

Their search sector on January 7 took them to the island of Taiwan and the China coast. Fifteen miles offshore, three hundred feet above the water, and a little after noon, they spotted a Japanese floatplane called a Pete passing more than one thousand feet above. Pulling back on the yoke and pushing forward on the throttles, Dan climbed and turned to chase. In less than two minutes they'd gotten within gun range. The top and nose turrets opened up and kept firing as they got within three hundred feet.

The Pete's wing flamed up but then immediately went out. The pilot did a wingover and dove for the water, heading in the opposite direction. Dan turned after him, his gunners firing as they closed the distance again. This time the Pete's other wing began to flame. The fire continued, and the floatplane's port side pontoon and other debris flew off. The Pete first turned right, then left, and then pulled up into a stall at about five hundred feet. As it began to fall, Dan's crew saw something but couldn't tell whether it was the pilot jumping out or just a puff of smoke. A few seconds later, fully aflame and out of control, the plane crashed into the water.

It was the fifth Japanese plane he and his crew had destroyed. Dan Moore was officially an ace.[329]

Meanwhile, back home Hilda wrote about how her letters "always sound like some sixteen-year-old gal, but I love you anyhow, and that's the text" of everything she writes.[330] A week later, she was delighted the day she got four letters from him—"it's the nearest thing to actually talking to you; I've read them and re-read them." But soon after, another blow. They had both expected a leave for Dan sometime early in the new year. But now it had been canceled. It might be six months more before Dan could come home.[331]

By then Hilda had returned to Bisbee, staying with his parents. And Dan was struggling with something besides lost leave and the daily drama of life in a war zone. In the book for the squadron's first reunion, there is a picture of him standing in front of his tent on Leyte. It's captioned "Smiling Dan Moore of Bisbee, Arizona."[332] But beneath the surface, there was a different story. Inklings show up in a letter he wrote to his father around mid-January. Dan said that he was "getting along OK, though quite fatigued from time to time" and that his experiences were teaching him a great deal:

> I think I have obtained a fairly thorough knowledge of how to lead men; what their fundamental needs are; what truly great and admirable abilities they, at the very least, potentially possess; that the price of leading is first to serve—a price that is seldom fully discharged; and the most bitter lesson of all—that there are times when negation is the best course . . . don't help or promote disaster, but it is best not to try and prevent it. This was the hardest lesson to learn, and one of the best.

He said he believed he had always done the best he could, and "in my failures I have been able to prove that the responsibility lay elsewhere. This latter fact has earned me no phony friends and has greatly discomfited some people."

He talked about seeing his crew "put through more grueling tests than any other—one man violently killed before their eyes—and yet they follow and will even try to do so when sick, this while other crews fall apart when men exercise their prerogative of refusal. My faith in them has been returned a thousandfold."

He wrote that "the enemy has suffered materially from my hands in both apparent and not so apparent ways, [and] from the fact that this is least important to me you can glean some idea of the nature of the battles I have fought and am still fighting. I have thought of late that the seeds of opportunity always exist in the foulest soil. In part this may be true. I have tried to grasp these opportunities, and feel that I have to some extent succeeded."

Then, a little incongruously, "And it has all been fun."

His family might have been a little worried, or at least surprised, by some of what he wrote. It didn't sound like Dan. But then he closed the letter with a request to his father that seemed more familiar:

> I shall make you a committee of one to give big hugs and kisses to all for me. And give my sweetheart some special. I have delegated everyone to do so, but it will be more in character coming from you as a man.
>
> Don't worry about me. I am getting along OK and feeling fine. My health has never been better. The chow is lousy and I'm not especially comfortable. But there's no easy way to fight a war.
>
> Love from your son,
>
> Dan[333]

Two weeks after Dan wrote that letter, Harold McDonald was relieved as commanding officer and sent to the Fleet Air Wing. So the next in line, Tom Mulvihill, became VPB-117's CO. And a week or so later, the squadron moved to McGuire Field on Mindoro.

North and west of Leyte, the new base put squadron crews within range of the China coast, the Tonkin Gulf, Indochina, the Mekong Delta and Saigon, the coast of Thailand, and Borneo. And Mulvihill intended to make the most of the opportunities.

VPB-117 (and, for a few weeks, three planes from VPB-111) was the only navy outfit at the field. The rest were all army bombing and fighter squadrons, as many as ten at any one time.[334]

Mulvihill erected an eight-foot-tall sign at the base. In bold letters it proclaimed,

VPB-117
The Best Damn Search and Low Altitude
Bombing Squadron in the World
Air Force
Pacific Fleet
"The Blue Raiders"
Lt. Cmdr. T. P. Mulvihill, USNR
Commanding
15 Planes and 15 Crews Flying
Lone Patrols Day and Nite
October 1944 to ___

The billboard included spaces that recorded the number of planes VPB-117 had shot down, as well as probables and planes destroyed on the ground, ships sunk, and ships damaged.[335]

But by then there were also serious problems within the squadron. We wouldn't know as much about the rest of the story if it were not for another VPB-117 pilot, a good friend of Dan's. He was, by the time I found him, very old and very ill. I spoke with his daughter, told her what I was doing, and asked whether her father might help fill in some blanks. She shared my request, and he refused—said it was a long time ago, and it shouldn't be "rehashed." He died less than six months later. But a lifetime before, when he was relieved and returned from the war zone himself, he had sought out Dan's parents in Bisbee and spent two days explaining what had happened. Dan's father then wrote to Hilda and Dan's sister, Maggie Lu, relaying what he heard.

Those letters survived. At the time, and for decades after, Dan himself couldn't or wouldn't recall much of the story—in part, maybe, because he'd blocked it out himself. And out of respect for Dan's friend, I've not used his name in the excerpt that follows. But there is little doubt that his, and Folsom Moore's, account is the best we have of what happened.

Probably the clearest explanation of events came in a letter Dan's father sent to Maggie Lu on July 15, 1945:

As we knew, he wrote, there was much dissension in that squadron. _____ says that Dan spent a lot of his time trying to quiet the dissension and that he was able to do so until the end. But when he could go no further he made two moves which were in violation of regulations, and had to suffer the consequences. . . .

Mulvihill had trouble with his crew, and they refused to fly with him again. This included the ensign who was his co-pilot. Mulvihill could do nothing to the crew, but he put the ensign on notice and sent him before a general court martial. He ordered two other ensigns to go up as his co-pilot; both refused and he has them up for court martial. Dan worked very hard on this, endeavoring to straighten it out.

The Admiral sent a committee of three squadron commanders to check the status, but they backed Mulvihill against the rest of the squadron. Then the Admiral sent his personnel man over, and he reported to the Admiral the exact status. Then Dan made his mistake. He radioed the Admiral on a combat frequency, emphasizing the urgency of listening to Lt. Dean's recommendations.

When his radio reached the Admiral's Chief of Staff he was in the air, on his way to another squadron, but his destination was changed and he was on the ground at the headquarters of VPB-117 within 30 minutes after Dan sent the radio—and an hour later Mulvihill was relieved of command.

When Dan landed, he was immediately grounded and confined to quarters for ten days. That was the punishment for violation of regulations regarding use of the combat frequency for messages not pertaining to combat. After his ten days he was called in to Manila with Mulvihill and a day or two later was called back alone. When he returned he had evidently been severely reprimanded and the following day became delirious. A couple of days later he was again delirious and was sent to Guam. After that, the squadron heard nothing of him.

One of the mistakes Dan made, his father wrote, was going directly to the admiral rather than through channels. But in fact, Dan never spoke personally to Admiral Frank D. Wagner, Commander Aircraft, Seventh Fleet. His two face-to-face meetings were with Captain C. B. "Doc" Jones, commanding officer of Fleet Air Wing 17—who, Dan recalled, "reamed me out real proper."[336] And the "personnel man" who contradicted the findings of the three squadron commanders was Lieutenant John Marvin Dean Jr., also from the Fleet Air Wing. I hired two different military researchers specifically to search for the reports from the other squadron commanders and from Lieutenant Dean. Neither could find either.

After the reports of Captain Jones's and Lieutenant Dean's investigations had been made and read, the air wing sent Harold McDonald back to VPB-117 with a short and simple message. He told the squadron they had to "straighten out this mess" and gave them twenty-four hours to come up with a plan.[337] On his flight the next day, Dan made his ten-word radio broadcast: "Squadron morale at critical low. Request immediate investigation. Continuing patrol."[338]

So why, I asked him once, did he take on the role of peacemaker and go-between in the first place—especially since just a few months earlier he'd written that it was "best not to try and prevent disaster"? Dan said he'd changed his mind because he and Mulvihill were now the last of the five original fliers first assigned to VPB-117 back at Camp Kearny. Rigsbee had been relieved, McDonald had been kicked upstairs, and McGaughey had been killed. He felt an obligation to hold things together, or at least to try. Besides, he thought his law school training would help him explain the situation and defend himself better than the other pilots.

I also asked, if he had known ahead of time how it would turn out, would he have done the same thing anyway? Dan said yes.[339]

After his second episode of delirium on Mindoro, he was flown to Guam by a squadron pilot. And at some point, Dan was transferred to Aiea Naval Hospital on Oahu, opened in 1942 to treat casualties from the Pacific theater.[340] It was built to handle a little over sixteen hundred beds. But these were the months following the battle of Iwo Jima, and more than fifty-six hundred patients were being cared for.[341]

When Dan arrived, they took his flight log. They took a photo of Hilda in a small silver frame that he kept in his pocket. He was disoriented. Somewhere along the line, he had gotten the idea that what he'd done with his broadcast would somehow help Japan win the war.[342] He believed he had disgraced his family. He tried to break out of the hospital—climbed out a window and hurt his head before he was caught.[343]

He stayed in Hawaii for several weeks. But at some point—maybe because Aiea was overcrowded, maybe because the doctors felt Dan needed better psychiatric care—they decided to send him back to the States. So they put him in a straightjacket and locked him in a cell in the hold of a ship. Two others were in cells nearby, and they tapped out messages to each other in Morse code as they sailed to California.

The ship arrived in Oakland on June 17. When Dan walked down the gangway and saw Hilda standing on the dock, he cried.[344] The next day she was allowed to see him for twenty minutes in the naval hospital at Imola.[345] A few days after that, Dan wrote his parents, trying to explain:

> Things are coming along rather roughly and the future is obscure. . . . The past few months have been like a nightmare to me. Things should improve—they must. . . . Don't worry about me. I am somewhat foggy and do extremely foolish things sometimes, but basically my mind can function as well as any person's.[346]

Next they put him on a train for a four-day cross-country trip he hardly remembered. When he got to the East Coast, he was first sent to Bethesda Naval Hospital in Maryland. As publisher of one of Arizona's most influential newspapers and a Democrat, Folsom Moore knew U.S. Senator Carl Hayden well. So the day after Dan arrived, on June 27, Hayden wired his father back home:

HE WAS ADMITTED TO THIS HOSPITAL YESTERDAY AND IS UNDER OBSERVATION AND TREATMENT FOR A RATHER SERIOUS MENTAL ILLNESS. INITIAL OBSERVATION WOULD INDICATE THE TREATMENT WILL NECESSITATE A RATHER PROLONGED PERIOD OF HOSPITALIZATION AND INSTITUTIONAL CARE. . . . I AM ADVISED BY HIS

PHYSICIAN THAT THE CHANCES FOR ULTIMATE RECOVERY IN THIS CASE ARE PROBABLY GOOD.

The next day, the head of neuropsychiatry at Bethesda wrote to Hilda, explaining that they had "expedited" Dan's transfer to St. Elizabeth Hospital in Washington, DC.[347] Built before the Civil War, it was the government's largest hospital "devoted entirely to the care of nervous and mental disorders." And Dan was only one of many such cases. More than one million American servicemen suffered some sort of psychological injury during the war. In 1943, the army was discharging ten thousand soldiers a month for psychiatric reasons. In just over three months during the Battle of Okinawa, twenty thousand marines became psychiatric casualties.[348]

Dan's parents and Hilda arrived, and seeing them buoyed his spirits. In the weeks since leaving the squadron, he'd convinced himself that, because of what he'd done, no one would have anything to do with him.[349] Now he knew that wasn't true. But Hayden had been right to warn that the process would take time.

St. Elizabeth's was in a beautiful setting, high on a hill overlooking the confluence of the Anacostia and Potomac Rivers. Inside the walls, though, the picture wasn't so pretty. The war had increased the number of patients being treated, and two navy men had died violently the month before Dan arrived.[350] Walter Freeman, former director of St. Elizabeth's Blackburn Laboratory, had been a pioneer in the use of lobotomies to cure depression and other psychological disorders after leaving the hospital. And he later performed the procedure on an estimated forty-five to fifty patients at St. Elizabeth's in 1945.[351]

The staff also used electroshock and other therapies. Like a lot of patients, Dan didn't much like the hospital food. But early on, he noticed that those who didn't eat often showed up the next day looking very subdued. "Like zombies," he said. So he made sure he cleaned his plate.

When he was allowed to go outside, Dan and Hilda had a favorite bench above the rivers—a peaceful place where they could talk, hold hands. Just be alone, together. Sitting there she told him, over and over, that he was not crazy. That this too would pass. And slowly, he began to believe.[352]

There were even some lighter moments. One day an orderly interrupted their reverie to tell them they were wanted back inside. Arizona's other senator, Ernest McFarland, had come to visit Dan and gotten lost in the hallways. When someone asked who he was, he explained. But they assumed he was a delusional patient instead, and it had taken a while to straighten things out.[353]

Mostly, though, it was a time of work and worry. Dan working with doctors and Hilda and on his own, trying to understand what had happened to him. And worrying that he might never again be the person he'd been just a year before. At first, things seemed to be going well. After staying a week or so, Dan's parents felt comfortable enough to head back home. And Hilda settled in Washington to help in any way she could.

From the beginning, the doctors said they expected Dan's recovery to take several months. And, as with her letters to Dan in the Philippines, the ones Hilda sent his parents from Washington are the best record we have of what was happening at the time. Progress was fitful. One step forward, then a setback, followed by an encouraging rebound. In the last week of July, Hilda wrote Dan's parents and said he was homesick for Arizona—all he wanted to do was "go to the Grand Canyon and sit until he feels like doing anything active again." She added that two things "very apparent in Dan" were a lack of self-confidence and periods of depression, although she felt there had been improvement in both areas. And he had gained back some weight. As for herself, on days when she wasn't allowed to see him, she visited "the different buildings of interest" in Washington, read books, and washed and ironed clothes.[354]

Early in August, Marvin Barefoot, finally relieved from the squadron and back in the States, came to Washington and had a "wonderful visit" with Dan. But Hilda worried that the doctors were "firmly convinced that Dan has a mental disease, even though they are not able to diagnose it definitely." As a result, she was down in the dumps herself. And any time Dan seemed at all depressed, his grounds privileges were denied, which only made matters worse.[355]

A few days later, Hilda wrote again, explaining why she had sounded so despondent in her last letter:

Lt. Black, a patient in Dan's ward, hung himself and Dan stumbled upon the body when it was found—accidentally, by a group of patients, Dan being one of them. This had a severe reaction on Dan and I was greatly worried about it. The patient had had his parole privileges and was coming along fine but evidently became desperate and acted upon impulse, with the subsequent result.

But she also recounted a hopeful conversation with Dr. Weil, the "Navy doctor in charge at St. Elizabeth's." He told her that if Dan continued to make progress, he would recommend his release in about seven weeks, or roughly the middle of September.

Between now and then, he said, Dan would need to understand that, back on Mindoro, his actions hadn't been due to bad food or poor living conditions or overwork. He simply had reached his breaking point. As soon as Dan understood and admitted that, he would be on the road to recovery. And Dr. Weil told Hilda that she, not the doctors, would be the best person to explain this to him. Hilda said, "I came away from the interview happier than I've been in a long time."[356]

So the next day she spent hours talking it over with Dan. And she wrote his parents, explaining the conversations. Dan's father wrote back, agreeing with her and the doctors and suggesting that Dan send letters more frequently as a way of reconnecting with his life and his interests outside his navy experience.[357] Four days later—on August 14, 1945—Dan wrote his parents, telling them Hilda "sends her love and communicated to me her desire and yours that I write."

He said he was doing well, asked his father to send some cigars if possible, and urged them to keep writing him too. "P.S.," he said. "Don't worry about me."

And then, hastily scrawled at the bottom of the page, "Jap surrender just flashed! Hurrah!"

At last, the long war was well and truly over. But Dan Moore's private battle would continue.

Young "Rip" Swink
COURTESY OF EMMY SWINK

Gene Kern with wings
COURTESY OF ROSIE KERN

Galen Bull, pilot
COURTESY OF ERIC BULL

E. O. Rigsbee at Annapolis, 1930
COURTESY OF RIGSBEE FAMILY

Lieutenant Commander Rigsbee, 1943
COURTESY OF RIGSBEE FAMILY

Rigsbee on USS *Currituck*
COURTESY OF RIGSBEE FAMILY

E. O. Rigsbee, farewell speech COURTESY OF *THE BLUE RAIDERS*, NAVY DEPARTMENT
LIBRARY

Bill and Marilyn Pedretti
COURTESY OF PEDRETTI FAMILY

Emily about to crash, October 31, 1944 COURTESY OF BOX FAMILY

Bill and June Benn,
wedding
COURTESY OF PAT BENN

Bill and June Benn, on beach COURTESY OF PAT BENN

Harold Stang, young pilot
COURTESY OF HAROLD STANG JR.

Elsie and "Boogie" Stang
COURTESY OF HAROLD STANG JR.

Joe Papp, Navy
COURTESY OF BARBARA MANSFIELD

Joe Papp, plane captain
COURTESY OF BARBARA MANSFIELD

"Mac" McGaughey on Leyte
COURTESY OF *THE BLUE RAIDERS*, NAVY
DEPARTMENT LIBRARY

Bill Loesel with violin
COURTESY OF LISA SUTTON

Bill Loesel with his wings
COURTESY OF LISA SUTTON

Bill Loesel and buddies on Hilo, late
summer 1944 COURTESY OF LISA SUTTON

Bill Loesel and buddies on Tinian, October 1944 COURTESY OF LISA SUTTON

Bill Loesel and buddies on Leyte, 1945 COURTESY OF LISA SUTTON

Bill Loesel on Mindoro, February 16, 1945
COURTESY OF LISA SUTTON

Tom Mulvihill and his plane
COURTESY OF LAVELLE SAIER

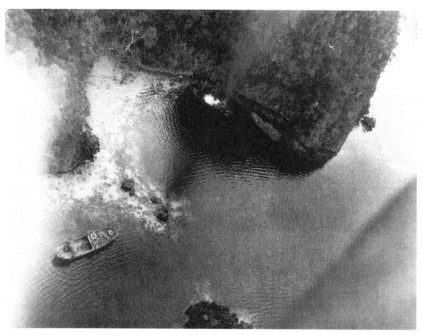

Attack on enemy shipping on Busuwanga Island, Palawan, Crew 3,
December 7, 1944 OFFICIAL NAVY PHOTO

Dan Moore on Mindoro
COURTESY OF MOORE FAMILY

Lieutenant Junior Grade Daniel E. Moore, wedding COURTESY OF MOORE FAMILY

Lieutenant Junior Grade and Mrs. Daniel E. Moore, USNR, April 24, 1943
COURTESY OF MOORE FAMILY

Smiling Dan Moore
COURTESY OF *THE BLUE RAIDERS*, NAVY
DEPARTMENT LIBRARY

VPB-117 billboard on Mindoro
COURTESY OF MOORE FAMILY

Marvin Barefoot and "Swede" Johnson COURTESY OF GENE KERN

Lieutenant Junior Grade Jake Dickinson, George Parker's defense attorney
COURTESY OF LINDA SPALDING

Art Elder, Guadalcanal, 1943, plane commander, VPB-117, 1944–1945
COURTESY OF AIR GROUP ONE

Tom Hyland in Philippines, pilot, VPB-117
COURTESY OF ELLIOT SCHREIDER

Bill and Mary Quinn,
the early years
COURTESY OF QUINN FAMILY

Above: Stan and Mary Sayre,
wedding COURTESY OF MARY
SAYRE (DAWSON)

Left: "Sally" and "Dort"
Brownlee, wedding
COURTESY OF JIM BROWNLEE

Joe Lowder
(center standing) and
Pete Hourcade (below)
COURTESY OF LOWDER FAMILY

Pete Hourcade
COURTESY OF ALICE DURSANG

"The four buffoons" at Lake Arrowhead, California COURTESY OF KITTRELL FAMILY

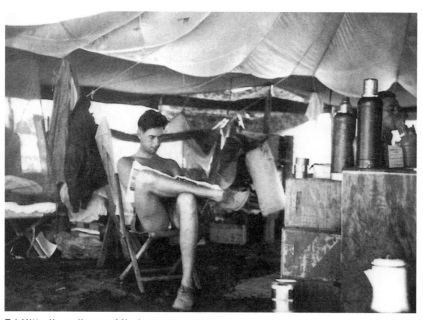

Ed Kittrell reading on Mindoro COURTESY OF KITTRELL FAMILY

Left: "Those wonderful Carters three"
COURTESY OF KITTRELL FAMILY

Below: Dad and I on his wedding day
to Lorraine COURTESY OF KITTRELL FAMILY

Bob Faxon with puppy on Mindoro
COURTESY OF REBECCA KNOWLES

John Bourchier
COURTESY OF BARB CANNY

Bob Faxon on Mindoro COURTESY OF REBECCA KNOWLES

Presentation of Legion of Merit
to Captain Rigsbee from
Admiral Sprague, 1946
COURTESY OF RIGSBEE FAMILY

Presentation of Presidential Unit Citation to VPB-117, 1947
COURTESY OF RIGSBEE FAMILY

Manila American Cemetery COURTESY OF ANA MARIA KEATING

Bill and June Benn, the day before Bill shipped out COURTESY OF PAT BENN

Bill and June Benn, the night before Bill shipped out COURTESY OF PAT BENN

Bill on bike—Pat Benn's favorite picture
COURTESY OF PAT BENN

Bill Benn's marker, Manila American Cemetery COURTESY OF ANA MARIA KEATING

Headstones blurring into silence, Manila American Cemetery
COURTESY OF ANA MARIA KEATING

The original eighteen VPB–117 and ground crew photos. These pictures were taken in 1944 at Camp Kearny, California, sometime between February 1, 1944, when the squadron was commissioned, and August 1944, when they left for the front. ALL THE FOLLOWING CREW PHOTOS COURTESY OF SUSAN BANTON.

Back Row: Taliafero, Voelzke, Cox
Middle Row: Jamieson, Ensign Allsopp, Skipper and Squadron Commander E. O. Rigsbee Jr., Lieutenant Osborn, Chief Lassey
Front Row: Brewer, Riggs, Manners, Stockton, Maughn

Crew 2

Back Row: Jones, Holzrichter, Yates, Ishie, Shacklett
Middle Row: Grant, Lybarger, Shelton, Bolton, Rodden, Blood
Front Row: Ensign Allen, Lieutenant Golden, Commander E. McDonald

Crew 3

Back Row: Meany, Bandas, Cox, Wallace, Edwards, Heikkinen
Middle Row: Hess, Glunt, Hornick, Pfister
Front Row: Lieutenant Commander Mulvihill, Ensign Sullivan, Ensign Parker

Crew 4

Back Row: Haralson, Eldridge, Rudd, Beveridge, Otto
Middle Row: Martin, Miller, Freethy, Womack, Brown
Front Row: Ensign Bullock, Lieutenant Commander McGaughey, Ensign Loesel

Crew 5

Back Row: Martin, Presley, Lamar, Kellogg, Sommers
Middle Row: Collins, Craig, Pierson, Bagwell, Carlin
Front Row: Ensign Pedretti, Lieutenant Box, Ensign Henry

Back Row: Trotter, Chatman, Nelson, Tedrowe, Allen
Middle Row: Sullivan, Hooper, Taylor, Thompson, Long
Front Row: Lieutenant Brooks, Ensign Roberson, Ensign Sager

Back Row: Doane, Goodman, Wydeen, Lane, Ragland
Middle Row: Price, Deeter, Crawford, Brown, Kelly
Front Row: Lieutenant Castleton, Ensign Williams, Ensign Currin

Back Row: Cotcher, Keith, Grace, McCarthy, Peruso, Fliezar
Middle Row: Wade, Siders, Anderson, Alianell
Front Row: Ensign Slye, Lieutenant Conners, Ensign Bull

Back Row: Tonsick, Davis, Thompson, Bellafiore, Blanchard
Middle Row: Diller, Baker, Smaluk, Thomas, Dobbins
Front Row: Lieutenant Squires, Ensign Wise, Ensign Endahl

Crew 10

Back Row: Ticen, Zander, Davis, Wilson, Ennis
Middle Row: Wharton, Coleman, Mullen, Thomas, Kern, Williams
Front Row: Ensign Johnson, Ensign Barefoot, Lieutenant Moore

Crew 11

Back Row: O'Shaughnessy, Turnbaugh, O'Brien, McCrillis, Hall
Middle Row: Epler, Swink, Talbott, Peterson
Front Row: Ensign Massey, Lieutenant Garlick, Ensign Boss

Back Row (Not in Order): Wilson, Grimes, Rinaldi, Grunow, Hosticka, Turley, Beals, Wagner, Allred (missing the name of one of the original Crew 12 members)
Front Row: Lieutenant Walker, Ensign Kilgore, Ensign Nagel

Back Row: Palmer, Mallett, Stephenson, Donnelly, Evanovich
Middle Row: Chesson, Gleason, Zaluga, Kelly
Front Row: Ensign Fishman, Lieutenant (jg) Quinn, Ensign Beaudoin

Back Row: Tomaselli, Mehron, Martinez, Conrow, Sanders
Middle Row: Woods, Brown, Bottjer, Evancik
Front Row: Lieutenant Stang, Ensign Benn, Ensign Studebaker

Back Row: Bates, Holt, Mical, Stallings
Middle Row: Ferrell, Turner, Carter, Schaut, Smith
Front Row: Lieutenant (jg) Rhodes, Lieutenant (jg) Canny, Ensign Long

Crew 16

Back Row: Wardlaw, Lawrence, Magoon, Burgan, Plunkett
Middle Row: Shaulis, Eichenberg, Papp, Cormier
Front Row: Ensign Crawford, Lieutenant (jg) Carter, Ensign Pistotnik
Not shown: Crew member Blakely

Back Rows (Not in Order): Strickland, Latham, Anderson, Larsen, Engh, Handsfield, Self, Fondren, Forkner
Front Row: Lieutenant (jg) Kittrell, Ensign Bloomquist, Ensign Simonich

Back Row: Judson, Cox, Bolick, Jones, Boris
Middle Row: Davis, Burdick, Major, Hobert
Front Row: Lieutenant (jg) Sutton, Ensign Schmitt, Ensign Clark

This Machine Kills Fascists

Wartime pilots came in all shapes and sizes—mentally as well as physically. For some it was just a different kind of job, one they wanted to do well. Others simply hoped to survive. Then there were those who saw flying and fighting as a calling and felt fear mostly as an afterthought. The writer James Salter, once a fighter pilot in Korea, said that for such men combat "was not duty, it was desire."[358]

When Commander E. O. Rigsbee finalized the VPB-117 roster back in San Diego, he numbered the crews one through eighteen. As commanding officer, he obviously led crew number one, and Harold McDonald, his executive officer, had crew number two. After that, it's unclear whether seniority, experience, or other factors determined where crews ranked in the pecking order.

But had they, in hindsight, been ranked by the number of enemy planes shot down, Sheldon Sutton's Crew 18—the last on the roster—would have, in fact, been first. And not just in the squadron but among all Liberator crews in the entire navy.

At the beginning, though, the crew's biggest threat was the weather. On Tinian they bombed a phosphate plant more than twelve hundred miles from the base, flew home through a storm that drained their fuel, managed to find the base in the dark after fifteen hours, and landed with only a few minutes of fuel left in their tanks. Later, on a two-plane trip to Iwo Jima with Harold Stang's crew, they were bracketed by five Zeros that fired a few shots and then stayed out of gun range.

But it was on Tacloban where Sutton and his men really made their mark. On their first flight, they sank a Japanese ship running close to a sheltering cliff on the shoreline—attacking it low and fast, thirty feet off the water. Bow gunner Bill Bolick was firing and copilot J. W. Clark was telling Sutton, "You'd better pull up a little!" A few seconds later, they made a violent right turn, banking away just in time to avoid the cliff. Later they skip-bombed a ship near Mindoro, leaving it burning and sinking with its crew jumping into the water.

The next mission found them first for takeoff in the morning, followed by an almost immediate sighting of a large enemy convoy. They were so close it was hard to believe the ships were Japanese, so Sheldon announced over the intercom that he would challenge with flashes from an Aldis lamp used to signal friendly forces. One of the crew immediately answered, "Yes, Mr. Sutton, and they are challenging you right back with five-inch guns!" Bursting shells bracketed the plane, but it wasn't hit, and the convoy was later sunk by bombing from a squadron of marine fighters.

So far they'd not had any encounters with Japanese planes. But that changed on December 12. Coming home from their search sector, they saw a small ship and went into a skip-bombing run twenty-five feet off the water. At the same time, crewmen spotted an enemy fighter called a Tony heading down the coast of Mindoro. With its low wing and bullet nose it resembled a German Messerschmitt or an American Mustang, and it was equally formidable. It was also much faster than the Liberator, but the enemy pilot apparently hadn't seen Sutton's plane climbing toward him from behind.

The Japanese pilot, looking for something along the coast, went lower. Now well above the fighter, Sheldon knew he could dive and get within gun range. But as they fired their first bursts, still slightly too far away, the tracer bullets alerted the enemy, and he dove for the water. The Americans followed, and then the pilot of the Tony made a literally fatal mistake. He pulled up into a steep climb, which gave the bomber's nose and top turrets a slower, larger target. The fighter did a wingover and tried to ram the Liberator, but he barely missed and crashed into the sea. So violent was the impact that no trace of plane or pilot could be seen.

The next day, Sheldon was summoned to see Admiral Frank D. Wagner, Commander Aircraft, Seventh Fleet. Wagner wanted to impress on the pilot that his plane and crew were essential to the overall effort in the Philippines. The squadron's first priority had to be search and reconnaissance, so the navy would know where the enemy was and wasn't. Taking risks to chase planes or bomb ships got in the way of that mission. Sutton said he understood but that he and his crew had to defend themselves. The admiral agreed, shared some scarce ice cream with Sheldon, and sent him back to base in a jeep.

Clearly Wagner meant what he said, because he soon issued an order forbidding squadron planes to carry bombs. So Sheldon turned his eyes to the sky, rather than the sea, for targets. On Christmas Eve 1944, his crew was given the sector that included the coasts of Mindoro, Luzon, and Formosa, which meant they would be within range of Japanese fighters the entire time. And sure enough, near Formosa they came across a Japanese floatplane used mostly for antisubmarine searches.

It had a two-man crew, the pilot and a rear-facing machine gunner. Their problem was, the Liberator's guns had a longer range than theirs. So when Sutton's crew began firing, the Japanese tried to become a mobile, maneuvering target, like a rabbit running from a hunter's rifle. But they were soon cut down.

Not long after, they spotted another antisub plane with a pilot and rear-facing gunner, this one a biplane. The chase found the biplane and the bomber trying to outthink and outfly each other while down on the deck just yards above the water. But again, the Japanese plane lost the battle.

That made three confirmed kills for Sheldon and his men. They saw no more Japanese planes that month, but their last mission in December proved at least as dangerous as some of their encounters with the enemy. On a flight to the Indochina coastline, their number four engine abruptly lost power, sending the plane into a spin to the right. Quickly adjusting power on the other side, they feathered the prop on the crippled engine and began to consider their options.

They were more than a thousand miles from Tacloban, a good portion of that distance through Japanese airspace. Inside enemy-controlled

Indochina there was a clandestine, friendly crash-landing strip. But just getting there meant flying the whole way through enemy territory. And even if they made it, there was the problem of getting out again—likely by hiking, again through hostile terrain. Sheldon asked each member of the crew for his preference. In the end, he decided to head for home and hope for the best.

They lightened the plane by tossing all the extra gun barrels, armor plating, and heavy equipment overboard. Sheldon chose the best altitude and power settings to minimize their fuel consumption. And for four hours, as they neared Mindoro, things were going pretty well. They even restarted the crippled engine, which ran rough but helped. But an hour later the number one engine quit and had to be feathered, and number two was losing power. They were still two hundred miles from base, in skies patrolled by the enemy. But at last Tacloban came into view. Back, safe, home again.

On patrol early in the new year, they found a Japanese convoy that included eight destroyers and more than twice as many support ships. As before, the warships fired at them but missed. On the way home across the South China Sea, they spotted a Japanese Jake floatplane about five miles away, off the coast of Luzon, and three thousand feet below. Sutton dove toward it, and the Jake dove too, trying evasive maneuvers to lose the Liberator. They both reached the coast and were locked together as they now raced across the island—the Jake twenty-five feet above the ground, Sheldon slightly higher, driving the floatplane into a high, narrow valley.

The Japanese plane was now like a desperado caught in a box canyon. The sides of the valley were too steep to pull up, as was a hill directly ahead. On his tail, and slightly above, was the Liberator. So the Japanese pilot flew on, full speed, right into the side of the hill. There was a large explosion and fire; Sheldon pulled back on the yoke and barely cleared the hill himself. His gunners had not fired a shot.

Not long after, again off the coast, they spotted another Jake, heading in the opposite direction. Sheldon turned to follow; the Jake dove toward the water and increased his speed. The Liberator dove as well, chased for ten minutes, and finally got within range. The Jake fired back with its rear gun; the firing continued until the planes were only one hundred feet apart. The Jake began to burn and splashed into the water, leaving a trail of smoke and flame.[359]

By now, though, darkness was coming fast, and they were low on fuel, so they headed for a newly built dirt strip on Mindoro, captured from the Japanese less than three weeks earlier and lit only with oil fires. As they approached, the tower told Sutton that enemy planes were in the area and the lights would be turned off as soon as he landed. But they doused the oil pots while the Liberator was still two hundred feet in the air. Sutton and crew landed with a thud, jumped from the plane, and ran for cover. Antiaircraft fire filled the sky, and when the all clear sounded, Sheldon and young radioman Doug Burdick saw that they had hidden under a fuel truck.

When they returned to Mindoro the next morning, the admiral summoned Sutton again. Maybe Sheldon thought Wagner wanted to congratulate him on becoming an ace with his fourth and fifth kills the day before. Instead, he reminded Sutton that he had promised not to chase airplanes either and asked him to explain himself. "Well, Admiral," he replied, "we both know that the best defense is a good offense." He got a laugh, another dish of ice cream, and another jeep ride back to base, this time with Wagner behind the wheel.

The next mission took them back to Cam Ranh Bay and Cap St. Jacques, where they found another large Japanese convoy, including a cruiser, three destroyers, and almost twenty other ships. As usual they were flying low, and the big ships fired into the water just ahead of them, hoping the plane would crash into the geysers they created. Dodging the waterspouts, they spotted a Japanese floatplane headed in their direction. This time the enemy pilot was skilled, weaving up and down and side to side while diving down to fifty feet above the water. But the Liberator had bigger guns with a longer range, and downing the Jake took only a few bursts. It was their sixth kill.

Their following two flights were aborted because of mechanical problems, followed by a trip to Hong Kong harbor. Three days later, they were sent to Okinawa, about halfway between Formosa and the Japanese mainland. Again, once they got close to their destination, they flew down on the deck to avoid detection. Heading south along the coast, they spotted a Japanese plane above and ahead of them. It was a Kate, a torpedo bomber like the ones that had attacked Pearl Harbor and later helped sink the aircraft carriers *Lexington* and *Hornet*. Stalking from below and behind, unseen by the enemy pilot, they fired. The plane fell, trailing heavy smoke until it crashed into the ocean. Their seventh and final kill set a navy record for multiengine planes that still stands.[360]

Their next mission was between Formosa and the Chinese coast. They saw no ships and encountered no enemy planes. But they lost one engine five hundred miles from the nearest U.S. airfield, so they diverted to an emergency dirt strip on the island of Luzon. Before they got there, a second engine faltered, but they were able to land. The strip was out in the boonies, and they couldn't contact Tacloban. Getting parts and making repairs took several days, after which they flew back to the base.

When they got there, the bad news was that other pilots had appropriated Sutton's mattress, his radio, and all his spare food—figuring he must have been shot down somewhere. The good news was that relief crews would begin to arrive in a few days and, by virtue of his record, Sheldon would be one of the first heading home. After island hopping backward across the Pacific, he reached California early in February.[361]

Jan Carter was a big man: six feet, four inches, 230 pounds. A good athlete, he excelled at basketball and football in high school in Oklahoma. He wanted to be an engineer and was offered a scholarship to play football at Purdue. But the University of Arkansas pursued him too, and it was closer to home.

He was in his senior year and had been drafted by the Pittsburgh Steelers when the Japanese attacked Pearl Harbor in December 1941. At the end of the semester Jan volunteered for the navy. To pass the physical, he had to lose thirty pounds, so he went on a crash diet. He looked terrible, his brother remembered, skin and bones. But he made the weight, signed the papers, applied for flight training, and ate his way back into fighting trim.[362]

He never did like his given name, Jan—thought it sounded too feminine. But in the 1940s several movies—and then a popular radio serial, sponsored by Acme Paints—featured the exploits of Nick Carter, Master Detective. So he became "Nick" to everyone in the squadron.[363]

Like Sheldon Sutton and my dad, he flew in VB-102 on Guadalcanal as a copilot in 1943. Also like them, he then got assigned to VPB-117 in 1944, training in San Diego and at Kaneohe before reaching Tinian and the front in early October. His crew's first patrols were relatively uneventful, although one trip found them very low on fuel and afraid they'd have to ditch in the water, before making it back after twelve hours.[364] Their first contact with the enemy came on October 27 on a flight near Iwo Jima. Because of a large enemy presence in the area, the squadron normally sent two planes to that sector. But on this day, Carter's wingman had to turn back because of mechanical problems.

After spotting two Japanese destroyers, they were within a hundred miles of Iwo Jima when an enemy Kate torpedo plane crossed in front of and below them. They dove and gave chase; the Kate went down to the water and started weaving. Nick tried to cut him off, but the floatplane was more maneuverable and got beyond the Liberator's gun range. But then he made a climbing left turn, and Carter turned tightly with him, bringing the Japanese back within range. The bow guns knocked off pieces of the tail and center section, white smoke streaming from the wing root and fuselage. It was last seen trying to limp home, but the Liberator didn't have enough fuel to chase and still make it back to Tinian. The Kate became a probable.

The rest of their flights from Tinian were mostly uneventful, with the exception of a two-plane mission to Iwo Jima with Sheldon Sutton, where five Japanese Zeros feigned attacks on the Liberators before machine-gun fire forced them to stay out of range. But the move to Tacloban upped the ante considerably. On their second patrol, toward Luzon, they spotted and reported a formation of Japanese transports protected by a dozen Zeros. Coming back to base late that same day, they were in a holding pattern because another Liberator had blown a tire and was blocking the runway.

Then, just at dusk, the air-raid siren sounded, and the sky lit up with tracers and searchlights. Several of the Japanese transports they'd seen earlier were right behind the Americans in the landing pattern. Their pilots spoke English, and the planes were loaded with suicide troops who planned to land and blow up the parked American planes with hand grenades. When Nick hit the runway, Commander Rigsbee pulled up in his jeep and told them to get to an air-raid shelter because "the whole strip might blow up." American antiaircraft gunners shot the enemy planes down in flames.[365]

The next day copilot Jack Crawford left the crew and was eventually replaced by my dad's original copilot, Lloyd Bloomquist. On December 10, Nick substituted for plane commander "Dusty" Rhodes on Crew 15. During the homeward leg of their search, a Japanese Judy dive bomber suddenly broke below the clouds and passed within one hundred feet of the Liberator's bow. Gunners opened fire. Carter turned and followed their target, which pulled up into the clouds and then reappeared, spinning. Again it went into the cloud and again it fell, this time headed for earth. Just at that moment, a Japanese Zero dropped out of the clouds overhead, saw the bomber, and scurried back into the cover.

And the excitement for the day wasn't over. Twenty minutes later, two Hamps, variants of the Zero, attacked the Americans in clear skies at one thousand feet. One came within thirty feet of the Liberator as Nick's gunners fired back. Then they noticed three more Hamps, high and behind. The bomber dove for the water and leveled off at fifty feet. Two fighters made a run on the starboard side and then passed below the Lib and just above the waves. Next, two Hamps tried attacking from behind, but tail gunner Armour Burgan put 150 rounds into the engine of one, which immediately started smoking. The crew reported a large splash but didn't actually see it hit the water. They later listed it as a probable. The final Hamps left when two navy Corsair fighters arrived. It had been a hectic few minutes, with five enemy planes buzzing around them like angry bees. Yet, although the plane had a few bullet holes, everyone inside was unscathed.

The next couple of weeks were relatively quiet. Then, on December 28, out of the corner of his eye Nick saw a Japanese Topsy transport, two miles away and a thousand feet above them. He turned right and began to slowly gain altitude, apparently undetected by the enemy pilot. Now above and behind his quarry, Carter dove as the bow and top gunners fired, but their rounds fell behind and below the target. Alerted, the Topsy turned hard right and headed for the water with the Liberator on its tail. They leveled off fifty feet above the waves. Four times the transport turned hard to the left, temporarily losing the bomber as it flew past. Finally they got back on the Topsy's tail and fired, setting the starboard wing root on fire. It went into a long, slow glide, hit the water as if it were making a normal landing, and then cartwheeled and burned. There were no survivors.[366]

Two days later, they went out again, north of Luzon near Batan Island. A little over three years earlier, on the same day the Japanese bombed Pearl Harbor, it had become the first American territory invaded and occupied by the enemy. This time, though, the tables were turned. Heading north at one thousand feet, they spotted a Jake below, going in the opposite direction. Nick dove to chase. His top and bow turrets fired, flames engulfed the enemy's wing, and the plane hit the water, exploded, and burned.

They turned north and resumed their patrol. Less than fifteen minutes later, they spotted a Val torpedo plane, five miles away and five hundred feet above, again headed in the opposite direction. They closed from behind on the enemy, who apparently hadn't seen them. They fired when they were within a hundred feet. The Val's wing began to burn, parts of the canopy and tail section were torn away, and then the plane itself exploded right in front of them. They flew through the debris, untouched. What was left of the Val hit the water, "leaving only a small smoking spot on the surface." Two for two on the day, and neither enemy plane had fired a single round in their direction.[367]

Maybe because he'd been so successful sneaking up on the enemy, about a week later Nick decided he'd try to catch "Washing Machine Charlie" unawares. This was a Japanese light bomber that showed up over Tacloban on many evenings. His job wasn't to destroy so much as to harass and keep the Americans on alert all night. Coming back from a mission, Carter circled at dusk and spotted a twin-float monoplane where it shouldn't be. It was a Jake, he decided, so he dove and opened fire. Just then, he realized it was an army ambulance plane instead! He tried reaching them on the radio, but they weren't answering. Instead, they dove for the water and headed straight for the safety of the airstrip. Nick and the crew later theorized that an army pilot had maybe taken a nurse out for a joyride and strayed a little too far from base. He was lucky, but so were Carter and his crew. They related the incident to the squadron's debriefing officer, but no one from the army ever complained, and no official report was ever filed.

A month later, they moved to Mindoro and on their second mission from the new base had their most harrowing day yet. It started out well. On patrol near the Indochina coast, they spotted three Japanese cargo ships. Above them, presumably to provide cover, was a Japanese Jake seaplane that immediately left the ships and headed for shore, juking back and forth just above the hilly jungle terrain. Nick gave chase and got within a hundred feet before firing. Fifty-caliber rounds hit the fuselage, the cockpit, the wing roots, and the engine. It was over in seconds. The Jake crashed into the trees and burned. It was the crew's fifth confirmed kill. Nick Carter was an ace.

But what to do about those ships? The crew talked it over and decided to attack the largest one. On a masthead run, dropping bombs and strafing all the while, they did serious damage. But all three ships put up antiaircraft fire as well. It riddled the plane and hit five of the men inside.

Now the fight was not for glory or country but for survival. The men patched each other up as best they could. Their best bet was to try landing at a dirt field on northern Mindoro. But they weren't as sure about the plane, and they were nine hundred miles from base. The engines were still running, but Japanese guns had severed all their hydraulic lines. That meant they'd have a hard time lowering their flaps or using the brakes on landing. So after they hit the ground, the riddled bomber just kept rolling. Planes were parked on both sides of the runway, all the way down, so they couldn't "ground loop" to slow themselves. By now they were being chased by an ambulance, which pulled up just as they ran off the end of the runway and into a drainage ditch. The injured were taken off and rushed to a field hospital. Everyone survived, mostly with minor wounds. The plane was a total loss.[368]

Lloyd Bloomquist had been hit during the flight, and his injuries would keep him from flying, so John Bullock became Nick's copilot. Three days later, on their regular schedule, they went out again, helping track a

Japanese naval task force for thirteen hours in rough weather. The rest of the month was fairly quiet.

In March, they poked their nose into Cam Ranh Bay, coming in two hundred feet off the water, strafing a string of Jakes tied to buoys, and managing to wend their way through the flak as they left the way they came. The rest of the month and all through April, flying mostly to the China coast, they encountered no Japanese ships or planes.

And then it was over. They were relieved early in May, after more than a year of training and fighting together. Some from the crew would keep in touch or meet up after the war. Some would come together at squadron reunions forty or fifty years later. And some would never see each other again.[369]

Art Elder was from Texas, and he had a bit of the gunslinger about him. Never showed fear, never backed down, and seemed to believe he'd always come out on top.

He got his pilot's license while he was still in high school. A few years later, he volunteered for Britain's Royal Air Force, trained, and was accepted. He was headed to England when Pearl Harbor happened, so he decided to fly and fight for Uncle Sam. His first tour was with VP-54, a "Black Cat" squadron on Guadalcanal in 1943. They flew mostly at night, in PBY Catalina flying boats painted black, scouting and attacking Japanese ships and bases. One of their tricks was to take along empty beer bottles, which made a high-pitched sound like a bomb when dropped from the plane. After a few such false alarms, when the enemy thought they'd caught on to the tactic and were no longer worried, the PBYs would then deliver the real thing. They also helped rescue dozens of downed fliers and sailors.[370]

After being relieved, Art spent some time with a photo reconnaissance squadron before getting what he really wanted, a chance to fly B-24s as a plane commander with VPB-117. But he still needed a crew. Turned out one had been training but recently lost its pilot, who had checked himself into the hospital. Only one member had combat experience—plane captain and head enlisted man Ed Elliott had served a tour in Alaska. But the rest were willing and able.

So they readied the plane, took some test flights, and on January 3, 1944, left for Kaneohe with one extra passenger—a golden cocker spaniel named Windy smuggled aboard by Elder.[371] After a month in Hawaii and another week or so hopscotching across the Pacific and into the Philippines, they arrived at Mindoro on February 13 and flew their first mission three days later.

It took them to Cap St. Jacques, on the coast of Indochina where the Mekong River empties into the South China Sea. They arrived at daybreak and found a Japanese cargo ship more than three hundred feet long in the harbor. They made a masthead run, dropping five-hundred-pound bombs, while gunners on the ship and the plane fired back and forth. The bombs scored a direct hit amidships; the freighter exploded, burned to destruction, and sank up to the gunwales. On the way out of the harbor, they strafed two oceangoing tugs, which also burned and sank, as well as a launch with more than fifty people aboard, many of whom were killed. They also saw what looked like an airfield under construction.[372]

On their next mission three days later, they found a similar freighter in Cam Ranh Bay. As they came in low from behind a nearby hill, their bombs released prematurely, but they repeatedly strafed it and another, smaller cargo ship. They also fired on a smaller gunboat. Again, they received machine-gun fire in return but were not hit.[373]

Next they went south to Borneo and Sarawak, bombing a railroad bridge and strafing an airfield.[374] After a couple of relatively quiet flights, on March 1 Elder decided to see whether the airfield they'd noticed earlier at Cap St. Jacques had been finished. They came in at treetop level, strafed the construction equipment, and dropped bombs with delayed fuses on the runway, leaving big craters. Then Elder saw a large, camouflaged ship close to shore in the harbor. He strafed and dropped one bomb, a near miss against the side of the ship. When he came back for a second run, he saw fires and a small explosion, and then, just after he passed over the ship, there was a huge roar. Black smoke poured into the sky, and the freighter burned to destruction.[375]

A couple of days later, they helped track an enemy task force in the South China Sea. On their following flight, again to French Indochina, they strafed railroad trains, bridges, and tracks. This time the enemy gunners did some serious damage to the plane, but no one was hurt.[376] Next they joined Tom Mulvihill and Dan Moore to attack Japanese radio stations on the Paracel Islands south of the Chinese mainland.[377]

After they had sunk and damaged some small ships on the following two flights and the plane had sustained more than a dozen holes,[378] they were scheduled for a solo mission at dusk to attack a convoy that had been spotted in the harbor at Cap St. Jacques. But mechanical trouble meant they arrived after dark and couldn't see well enough to do much damage.[379]

On March 19, they went up the eastern coast of Indochina to Tourane, where they damaged and sank some barges before spotting an airfield a short distance inland. Coming in low, they saw two fighters ready to take off after them. Instead, the Liberator's gunners destroyed them on the ground. They also shot up a barracks, a hangar, fuel dumps, trucks, and some locomotives. The Japanese fought back with antiaircraft and small arms, again scoring several hits on the Liberator.[380]

On their regular schedule, three days later, they attacked and exploded a locomotive in Borneo and then went looking to see what damage they could do to a nearby airfield. Coming in at treetop level, under low clouds, they saw a Japanese torpedo plane just taking off. Elder turned sharply and pulled alongside the Kate while the bow, top, and starboard waist gunners fired away. The pilot never even got his wheels up before the plane made a slow right turn and crashed into the ground. Then Elder went back, strafing the field and a parked twin-engine Betty bomber before attacking more small cargo ships nearby. They took fire themselves, this time in the nose turret. But, as before, no one was hurt.[381]

The next trip brought them back to the Mekong Delta, and when they didn't find anything there, Elder decided to fly upriver toward Saigon. He soon came upon three large Japanese cargo ships. One bomb took care of the first; another dropped between the other two sank them both. He then attacked several smaller ships with four runs, using only machine guns. Again, they dodged antiaircraft fire, getting two holes in one wing.

After all that, they left the harbor and began to head for home when they saw a Jake seaplane five miles away. Chasing from below and behind, they got to within a half mile before the Japanese pilot spotted them. He turned away, but too late. The Liberator gunners opened up, and the Jake caught fire and crash-landed; the pilot somehow managed to get out of the plane and began to run away, but the top turret cut him down.[382]

Their next flight took them back to Tourane, where they strafed and damaged one parked plane at an airfield, went back for a second run and damaged two more, and then made a third pass and set another afire. By now, though, the Japanese antiaircraft gunners had gotten into place, and when Elder came back the fourth time they opened up. They set the number three engine on fire and put holes in the port wing. Ed Elliott cut fuel to the damaged engine and feathered the prop. They dumped everything heavy—guns, ammo, the radar dome in the belly—so the plane could climb on its remaining engines. They radioed VPB-117 pilot Ralph Castleton, flying one sector over, who joined up with Elder for the rest of the trip back to base.[383]

Three days later, they flew up the Indochina coast, shot up a freight train, and moved on to an enemy airstrip where they set two parked fighters on fire, as well as dump trucks, steamrollers, and four buildings.[384] On their next mission they went back to the same neighborhood, damaged more railroad engines and tracks, and sank a three-hundred-foot Japanese freighter anchored in a small cove.[385]

Then, on April 6, in the same sector, they strafed some small cargo ships and barges. But again, heavy fire riddled the plane. The hydraulics were out, so the gun turrets and the wing flaps didn't work; the brakes and the radio were shot. Luckily, they had transferred all the fuel to the wing tanks and purged the extra bomb bay tanks, or the plane would have exploded. They flew home in the dark, signaled the tower with an Aldis lamp because they had no radio, and got down in one piece. In his memoir, Ed Elliott remembered, "The flight surgeon met us at the plane and got out bottles of whiskey from his jeep and handed the booze to whoever wanted them. I said yes to mine, as our nerves were getting frayed about this time."[386]

On April 9, they went to Borneo, attacked some small cargo ships, and set a torpedo bomber afire at an airstrip.[387] Their next mission was on Friday, April 13. Looking back, Ed Elliott wrote,

The ground crews and some of the flight crews had been talking about when we were going to get it, as we were always going into the heavy action and coming back safely. . . . Tokyo Rose even reported us shot down one time on her broadcast. On this day, our luck ran out.

They went to Cam Ranh Bay in Indochina, looking for Japanese planes that had been harassing American subs along the coast. As they came in through a pass in the hills they'd used before, a Jake floatplane passed them from behind so quickly they couldn't train the guns on it. The Jake apparently didn't see them.

When they got to the target, they found no planes, so they turned down the coast and went into the north end of Cam Ranh Bay, fifty feet off the water, doing more than three hundred miles an hour. Then, as Ed Elliott remembered,

> Every gun in the area let us have it. As I turned around the loudest "BANG" I have ever heard slammed us. Two 40 mil. shells hit us just behind me where Scott the radioman and Boyd our second mech were standing. . . . They were hit very bad. Scott lost his legs and died, Boyd got hit in one leg and chest.

Ed was hit too, in the head. Blood poured into his eyes, but he went forward and told the pilots that men had been hurt. Copilot John O'Dougherty gave him first aid and then went aft to help the others. It was a long flight back to base, and the ambulances were waiting for them. They were able to stitch up Ed pretty quickly, but Boyd stayed in the army field hospital for intensive care before being shipped home to the States.[388]

The rest of the crew didn't fly for a while, except over to Guam to bring back an ice-cream machine and other cargo for the squadron. Then, on April 25, Ed was released from the hospital. He hitchhiked back to base and heard that his crew was out again on a mission. A little later, he was told they were coming back with casualties.[389]

They'd again gone up the Mekong River in French Indochina, but this time they were met by three Japanese fighters, Oscars. One turned into the Liberator and made a head-on run. The bow and top gunners opened fire, and the Oscar started smoking, but the pilot still scored hits along the top of the fuselage—knocking O'Dougherty out of his seat, killing top turret gunner James Taylor instantly, and wounding four other crewmen with flying glass.

But it wasn't finished. The Japanese pilot kept coming on, either to ram the Liberator or because he'd been hit himself. The Oscar passed five feet overhead and continued to dive toward the ground. The other two fighters made some halfhearted runs but didn't press. Elder took the bomber down to twenty feet off the deck and headed for home. The Japanese followed for another thirty miles and then turned away.[390]

Their nose wheel had a flat tire, so they had to land at a nearby dirt field. Admiral Frank Wagner was there. He went back to base with the crew, sat in Art's tent, and talked with him a while. Art was sad, shaken. Wagner was "fatherly," he remembered.[391] Most squadron crews flew fifty missions or more before being relieved. Art's had flown twenty missions together, encountering the enemy on all but three flights, with two men killed and six others wounded. The admiral said he was sending them all back to the States. They'd done enough.

Two days later, the squadron buried James Taylor on Mindoro. Officers carried his casket to the grave. Ed Elliott found Taylor's favorite ruby ring in his belongings and sent it back to his family in Humboldt, Tennessee.[392]

Art Elder went home and married his sweetheart, Lois, on June 10, 1945. When he returned from his honeymoon, the navy told him he had to go to Chicago for a broadcast of *The First Line*, a weekly radio drama, sponsored by Wrigley's Spearmint gum. It highlighted the American war effort and had decided to do an episode about Art and his crew. Most of it featured zippy dialogue between an "old hand" and a "new guy" in the squadron, with a scripted reenactment of Art's exploits. But the producers also wanted Art himself to appear live. So he did and read lines like the following:

Everyone has been mighty nice to us since we came home. That is, those of us who could come home. We left three of our boys out there in the hospital. That was rugged duty and we had our share of casualties, maybe more than our share, because we always seemed to be able to find something to shoot at, and someone to shoot back.[393]

When he got there, the Wrigley people told Art they couldn't pay him for the broadcast, but they did have a "generous per diem" account. Would $200 a day be enough? Since annual salary for lieutenants back then was about $2,500 a year, that seemed fair.[394] And of course, even though he'd flown from San Diego on a navy transport, they gave him the price of a ticket on American Airlines, plus a suite at the Ambassador West Hotel for four days.

Later Secretary of the Navy James Forrestal presented Art with the Navy Cross for his courage in pressing home the attack against the enemy on the crew's final mission to Saigon.

Woody Guthrie, America's bard of hard times, hated the Dust Bowl, the Depression, and dictators. The guitar on which he wrote songs like "This Land Is Your Land" bore a sign: "This Machine Kills Fascists." If Tom Hyland had thought of it, he might have lettered the same thing on the nose of his PB4Y-1. Because, for him, being a navy pilot was more than how he escaped a hardscrabble childhood of his own; it was a way to personally fight the forces that threatened millions more.[395]

Besides, he was very good at it.

Raised in Denver, he was the oldest of seven children. His father was a bricklayer who often had trouble finding work, especially once the Depression hit. The resulting poverty was grinding—the family threatened with eviction, living without light or heat, often hungry. But his mother was intelligent and ambitious. She saved money to buy an encyclopedia on installment, and Tom devoured it all, *A* through *Z*.[396]

He earned a scholarship to a Catholic high school where he was a standout, academically and athletically. One 1934 news clipping about his exploits began, "Tom Hyland, rangy Cathedral back, thrilled 3,000 frenzied fans yesterday at Merchants Park when he led the championship-bound Bluejays to a 19–6 victory over Regis High."[397]

Still, he couldn't outrun privation. Once, walking home from school during a blizzard, having had almost nothing to eat for more than a day, Tom passed out on the sidewalk and was covered with snow. He survived only because someone later tripped over him.[398] But he went on to become Cathedral High's student body president and captain of the debate team, which won a national championship. When he finished school, he was offered scholarships to Notre Dame and Columbia. The priests at Cathedral were rooting for Notre Dame, but at the last minute he chose Columbia and deferred his entrance for a year to help support the family. After the year was up, he packed a bag and hitchhiked all the way to New York City.

He worked odd jobs and tutored children to pay expenses. He played sports and loved the academic atmosphere. A philosophy major and budding Marxist, he was an acolyte of Professor John Herman Randall, who wrote *The Making of the Modern Mind*. But after two years Tom went back to Denver to help his family, expecting to return and finish later.[399]

He first got a job as a bricklayer and then fell in love with (literally) the girl next door. The only trouble was that she was a freshman in high school, and he was halfway through college. Plus, she was a Protestant. They were secretly married by a justice of the peace in 1941. Tom by then was working as an auditor in a bank, but he could see that war was coming and joined the navy before Pearl Harbor. Becoming a pilot would make him an officer, with better pay and privileges. Plus, as soon as he flew for the first time, he knew that's what he was meant to do.[400]

His introduction to the war came on Guadalcanal with VP-54, where he met Art Elder. Near the end of his hitch, his mother wrote and asked him not to volunteer for another tour. He answered,

> I won't hear any more of this worrying. It's stupid. For the hundredth time, I like this business and when this trip is over I plan to come out again. All I want is a new aircraft so I can do more damage.[401]

He got his wish with VPB-117.

Tom and his crew arrived at Tacloban in January 1945, but their first action reports don't show up until February, when they'd moved to Mindoro. On a flight to the Indochina coast, they spotted a Japanese cargo ship almost two hundred feet long. Tom set up for a masthead run, but the ship turned broadside to make itself a tougher target and the first bombs fell short. His gunners, though, cut down enemy crewmen trying to man the ship's antiaircraft weapons.

Then Tom turned to make a second run, again just one hundred feet above the water. This time the bomb exploded under the stern, rocking the ship end over end. It began leaking oil and steaming in an uncontrolled circle. A couple dozen Japanese sailors jumped overboard, all of whom were strafed and killed by the Liberator's crew.[402]

Their next flight took them back to Indochina, where they spotted a twin-engine Japanese Betty bomber one thousand feet above, headed in the opposite direction. Tom turned and climbed, getting below and behind the Betty, and his gunners fired, hitting the cockpit and the fuselage. The Japanese ran for the cover of antiaircraft batteries in the nearby harbor, and Tom broke off the chase.

Less than an hour later, this time near Cam Ranh Bay, they spotted three Japanese Jake floatplanes about two hundred feet off the water. They were flying in a row, separated from each other by maybe two miles. Tom lined up for a head-on run on the first plane; bow gunner Walter Bryant and top turret gunner Albert McCoy fired from about 750 feet away and immediately knocked out the Jake's engine. The plane fell to the water, bounced once, took some more fire from the Liberator, fell back into the water, and was strafed one last time.

Then Tom turned his attention to the second Jake, again with a head-on run and again destroying its engine. The Jake turned toward shore, and Tom chased, his gunners stitching the fuselage and killing the floatplane's rear gunner. It skimmed the water, crashed, and burned just off a beach. The third Jake broke away and headed for Cam Ranh Bay before the Americans could give chase.

But the fireworks weren't quite finished. Ten minutes later, two Japanese Oscar fighters showed up, maybe contacted by the Jakes. They came straight in, from both the right and the left side of the Liberator two hundred feet above the ocean. Tom first turned to attack the fighter coming from the left, which gave the fighter on his right a chance to score some hits on the prop for the number two engine and in the tail section. Tom turned away from the shore and headed out to sea. The Oscars followed for a time but were kept at a safe distance by the tail gunner until the bomber disappeared into the clouds. All in all, a good day's work.[403]

Exactly one week later, they were again near Cam Ranh Bay, again fighting with Jakes and an Oscar. First came the Jakes, two of them, a thousand feet or so above and headed in the opposite direction. They hadn't seen the Liberator, so Tom turned, climbed, and came at the rear Jake from its port side. Gunners in the bow and the top turret, along with John Fuller in the waist hatch and Tom Trottier in the tail, all scored hits—killing the Jake's rear gunner and sending the smoking floatplane diving toward the water. But at the last second the pilot leveled off and headed toward shore.

Meanwhile, the first Jake had turned toward home as well. Tom gave chase and caught him seven miles inland. Gunners hit the starboard wing tanks; the floatplane flamed and fell burning into the ground. Later, on the same flight, they were attacked by an Oscar fighter plane. He climbed four thousand feet above them and dropped a fragmentation bomb, which exploded about one hundred yards behind. A second bomb exploded only fifteen yards away, rocking the Lib but doing no damage. Then the fighter came down to make several strafing runs, but Tom's gunners kept him at bay. They broke away and finished their patrol.[404]

Five days after that, they were working with the navy's pro-submarine patrols looking for enemy shipping off the Indochina coast when Tom spotted two twin-engine, twin-tailed bombers. They were dead ahead, eight miles away, and the Liberator closed the distance without being spotted. Because American B-25 bombers also had two engines and twin tails, Tom got close enough to make sure these belonged to the enemy.

The Nells were flying a two-plane formation called an echelon, with the second plane to the left of and slightly behind the leader. Neither saw the Americans until it was too late. Tom's gunners took aim on the trailing Nell first, hitting the port engine and setting it on fire. The attack alerted the plane in front, which fired one short burst before the Liberator shot out its engine as well. They plunged into the ocean together, still flaming, still in formation.[405]

Tom Hyland had become VPB-117's fifth and final ace.

Things were relatively quiet for a few weeks, but eventually trouble was likely to find Tom—or vice versa. On March 30, they were assigned to fly toward Hainan Island off the coast of China and help track a Japanese convoy, including two cruisers and two destroyers, that had been spotted a day earlier trying to escape to the safety of the Japanese home islands. When they got there, the convoy couldn't be found, so Tom checked along the coast and ran into a plane from a sister squadron, VPB-119. They said they had discovered the convoy, fifteen or so ships in all, holed up in a harbor on the southern coast of Hainan. Tom went over to take a look and radioed their position to army B-25s, which had the job of bombing the ships.

Then he saw two Japanese Frank fighters dropping phosphorous bombs on the other navy plane. They immediately turned and came after Tom, who climbed to one thousand feet and then dove to meet the attack. The fighters came in firing their guns, almost head-on, breaking away at the last instant and flying just under Tom's left wing. At that point they were joined by two more Franks. Now it was four against one, and the Japanese decided to try a double-team approach.

Two fighters feigned an attack on the Liberator's left side, and when Tom turned to meet it, the other two Franks came in, again head-on. They pulled up and attacked a second time, from above and on the bomber's right side. At point-blank range, they shot out the number one engine and riddled three fuel cells. Tom's waist and tail gunners hit back as the fighters flashed past. One of the Franks showed damage in the fuselage, and the other was trailing black smoke as it fell toward the water.

But now the Liberator was in even worse shape. Tom couldn't feather the prop on the engine that had been destroyed, so it would be a drag all the way home. Plus, the holes in the fuel cells meant precious gas was leaking away every minute. Tom ordered the crew to toss out everything that wasn't essential and started figuring out what to do next. At that point, the other two Franks decided to get into the act. They attacked from the rear; Tom's tail and waist gunners opened up at point-blank range and scored some hits on the lead plane. That seemed to discourage them, and they turned back toward their base.

At about the same time, the Liberator from the other squadron came and flew just behind Tom, skidding back and forth, acting as cover in case of another attack. And VPB-117's Dan Moore, who'd been assigned to relieve Tom on his patrol assignment that day, radioed that he was on his way. Tom decided to make for Triton Reef in the Paracel Islands, south and east of their position.[406] Getting there would take some time. And because they couldn't feather the damaged prop, Tom and copilot Ken Minnock had to take turns standing on the right rudder pedal to keep the plane flying straight. Each would brace himself against the seat and press down until his leg began jumping up and down like a jackhammer; then the other would take over.

Tom and Ken discussed what to do next and then got all the crew-members on the intercom at the same time. Tom said they had two options. There were parachutes on the plane, and anyone who wanted to jump as they approached their destination could do so. The crew asked what the pilots planned to do. Tom said he and Ken were going to ride the plane in. Every man said, "We'll go with you."

Triton Reef was a sandy atoll about two hundred yards long, and they arrived at the same time as Dan Moore. Their battered Liberator was almost out of fuel, but what was left could still ignite upon landing. Tom came in as low and slow as possible, wheels up. They hit softly and began to skim across the sand. The metal made a crunching noise, and they started to slow and eventually stopped. The gas fumes were thick. Everyone got out as quickly as they could. Ken Minnock tried to exit through the hatch on the right side of the cockpit, but the damaged engine was on fire. Then he reached for the top hatch, and by the time he squeezed through, he was the last man out. They all went running toward the water as fast as they could. They waded and waited in the ocean, but the plane never burned. And no one in the crew was injured. One had a small scratch on the back of his hand.[407]

Earlier, the navy had radioed that it would send a big flying boat, a PBM Mariner, to evacuate the crew if and when they made it to the reef. Dan Moore was circling overhead and watched the landing. He wrote a note, weighed it down, and dropped it out the cockpit window as he made a low pass over the sand. It read,

> Tom:
> If <u>none</u> are seriously wounded, <u>wave arms </u>when I come in low again. If wounded, stand upright and arms to side. I have notified base. This playmate says his load is too big to pick you up but will orbit as long as possible. I have contacted other Army rescue planes and they are trying to get loose to come and pick you up. I am getting low on gas and have to leave after the next pass. Believe you will be picked up before nightfall. Hope so, anyway. <u>Damn</u> nice landing.
> Dan

The "playmate" he referred to was the navy flying boat, which was balking at a rescue because its pilot feared that the four-to-six-foot seas would make it too hard to get airborne again with a heavy load. But Moore decided to encourage him by raising the Mariner on the radio and telling its pilot, "You either pick those men up or we'll shoot you down." All arrived back at base that night, safe and sound.[408]

After all that in the first three months of 1945, the rest of Tom's tour might have seemed rather tame by his standards. Japanese ships and planes became frustratingly hard to find. On a flight in April, they came across some small cargo ships at anchor off the coast near Cap St. Jacques. Tom tried five times to get his bombs to release, but they hung up each time. So he decided to drop one of his extra bomb bay fuel tanks on the ships, figuring he could come back and set it afire with his guns. But he missed and got a few holes in his fuselage for his trouble.[409]

Most of the time, though, he began heading inland. One likely source of targets was the Japanese railway, which ran for five hundred miles between Saigon and Tourane, on the coast of the South China Sea. From early April through mid-June, they destroyed five locomotives, two roundhouses, more than a dozen boxcars, a Zero fighter being carried on a flatcar, fifteen passenger cars, and an unknown number of Japanese soldiers who ran from them during one attack.[410]

Sometime in July they were strafing targets in Haiphong Harbor, in northern Indochina, when antiaircraft fire took out one of their engines. Rather than try to make it all the way back to base, more than one thousand miles over open water, they headed north toward an airstrip in Nanning, China, that had recently been liberated from the Japanese. The runway was full of bomb craters, but they managed to land safely, and Tom contacted U.S. forces, who agreed to send a replacement engine, fuel, and ammo.

Tom and the other two officers hitched a ride on an air force transport to visit Chunking, at the time the capital of Nationalist China. The crew stayed behind to guard the plane and to supervise the installation of the new engine and the workers filling the holes in the runway. But they also managed to make it into town for some Nanning night life.[411] On the last day of July, they all climbed back into the plane and headed toward Mindoro. Along the way they spotted a convoy of large Japanese junks carrying troops. They strafed and damaged the ships, killing an estimated forty soldiers.[412]

It was Tom's last combat act. And two weeks later, on the night Japan surrendered, Tom Hyland cried. He did not want the war to end.[413]

One of Those Days

The arc of living memory spans less than two centuries, from the stories our grandparents told about growing up to the ones our grandchildren will tell about us. And in that time, so much gets lost. Casual facts, random remembrance. Moments that glimmered like fireflies in the summer of someone's life and then went dark forever.

So it was good when, in 1995, one of Bill Quinn's many daughters sat him down before a video camera and asked him to tell his story. They were in his favorite place, the kitchen of the family home in Northern California, and it was his favorite time, just before dawn.

Scratching the head of the dog asleep on his lap, he talked about growing up in Southern California and one Sunday drive with his father. Eight-year-old Bill asked whether they could turn into Alhambra Airport, where they pulled up next to a hangar. Did he want to see an airplane up close? Oh, yes. The two walked inside, and there was a biplane, gleaming silver with bright red paint. A mechanic was working nearby. He came over, answered their questions about the plane, and then lifted Bill up and put him in the pilot's seat. He couldn't even see over the instrument panel, but it didn't matter. It was one of those days, he told his daughter, that changes your life.

Another came a few years later. His father, an accountant with a big firm who played squash at the University Club and had movie studios for clients, took a fall at home, broke his neck, and died. The family's fortunes fell with him. Soon Bill was working for twenty-five cents an hour at a wrought iron factory and helping out at a local airport. He was tall, a good athlete, and a coach arranged a scholarship to a big Catholic high school where he played football and ran track.

After graduation he worked the night shift in an airplane factory, spending his days studying at a local junior college and learning how to fly in its Civilian Pilot Training program.[414] And there was a lovely girl, Mary. They'd known each other in grade school, and their mothers decided they should meet again—prophetically enough, at a wedding.[415] Before long Bill was burning up the Pasadena Freeway, California's first, to see her.[416] When he got his pilot's license, he immediately rented a two-seater plane for $6 an hour and took her flying. She loved that too.[417]

By now it was the summer of 1941, and war looked more and more likely. At the airplane factory he had noticed that the navy inspectors seemed a lot tougher than the army ones. So in September Bill signed up for the navy's flight program, getting his wings and his commission a year later. His first posting was to a naval air station in Washington State. But soon they sent him off to war in the Aleutian Islands, where the foul weather and the fog killed more pilots than the Japanese did.[418] He came back, much to Mary's relief, and married her in Pasadena two days after Christmas 1943. A few months later, he reported to VPB-117.[419]

His time with the squadron lasted more than a year, seven months of that in combat. He and his crew sank several ships and shot down four Japanese planes, one short of making Bill an ace. One victim tried to hide in a fog bank, but his tail stuck up through the clouds like the fin of a shark in the water. They chased him past two enemy ships and into a small bay, where shore guns hit one of the Liberator's engines before the wounded victim flew into the side of a hill.[420]

Another time, off the coast of Borneo, three Japanese fighters made runs on his plane. The bow turret jammed, Bill dove down to fifty feet off the water, and they fought off the attacks.[421] Crew chief Dave Palmer, in the top turret that day, said that when he returned home to Vermont months later, his mother told him she had been sweeping the floor one morning when she had a vision of him standing in the doorway, saying, "I'm all right, Mom." That same day, radarman Rod Donnelly's father came down to breakfast on his family farm in Oregon and told his wife he dreamed something bad had happened to their son. Moments later, Rod's brother came into the kitchen and said he had a dream about Rod too, but he was all right. Bill's crewmen compared the stories with entries in their flight logs, accounting for different time zones and the international dateline, and discovered that both premonitions had occurred at the very same time they were being attacked by the fighters.[422]

The whole crew made it home, and Bill stayed in the navy another twenty-four years, flying transports through two more wars. He and Mary had five girls in a row, then a son and one more daughter. The family was always moving; the kids were born in California, Kansas, Alaska, Texas, Maine, and Maryland. Wherever they were, Bill took college courses when he could and got his degree from George Washington University in 1963. He retired as a commander in 1967. He spent a few more years working for the Federal Aviation Administration and then as a flight instructor.

On a checkout flight, one of his pilots asked whether Bill would like to work on his farm in Northern California. It sounded intriguing, so for another decade he tended to the machinery in almond and walnut orchards. He and Mary bought a few acres, enough for a goat, some dogs, a house, a swimming pool—and a landing strip for their Cessna. They used it mostly to visit the family, which eventually included twenty grandchildren and eleven great-grandchildren. In 2009, fourteen years after he told his life story on videotape, Bill died.[423]

Of course, you can stack up facts like alphabet blocks and still not know someone. So here are some other things about Bill.

His brother-in-law described him as "the most honorable man I ever met."[424] Near the end of his tour with the squadron, he said he felt almost sorry for the Japanese "because they were outmanned and outgunned and they still kept coming out there."[425] It also seemed to him that, by supplying chaplains to the military, the Catholic Church had condoned the war. Bill saw the fighting and killing as his duty but believed religion shouldn't actively support it. He came home and asked several priests about it, but their explanations didn't make much sense. So he left the church. A military man all his life, he admired true conscientious objectors.[426]

He loved opera, especially Puccini. And he read constantly, often in the early morning in his kitchen. There was always a stack of library books in the house. Classics like Steinbeck and almost anything about flying. His favorites were *The Spirit of St. Louis*, Charles Lindbergh's account of the first transatlantic flight, and *A Hostage to Fortune*, the autobiography of author and aviator Ernest Gann.

He liked to whistle. And he would talk about almost anything. In conversation he could be disarmingly thoughtful, making you see a whole different side of an issue—think Jimmy Stewart in *Harvey*, one of his favorite films.

For decades he and Mary hosted everyone at the house for the Fourth of July. All the kids and grandkids came, more than fifty camping in a tent city on the lawn. He pulled the same trick year after year, standing by the edge of the family pool and announcing that he was "looking for bugs," until someone pushed Big Papa in.[427]

And he never got over the wonder of flying. His den at home was plastered with news clippings and pictures of airplanes. Models hung from the ceiling.[428] He talked Mary into getting her pilot's license too, and they flew together. One granddaughter remembered a night flight through a thunderstorm, she in the back seat with her book and her flashlight and her blanket, feeling completely happy and safe.

In his seventies Bill even took a few lessons and got checked out in his son's ultralight plane, basically a big kite with a little motor. Coming in for a landing on his first solo, a gust of wind caught him; he skidded off the runway and into a ditch. Running to help, his son shouted, "Are you all right? Is anything hurt?" Bill yelled back, "Just my pride."[429]

When he and Mary were in their early eighties, they sold the Cessna. And a couple of years later, they moved to a retirement community. Not too long after, Mary started noticing that Bill was forgetting things. He would call the hardware store several times and ask about the same thing. The lapses became more frequent, his confusion more obvious.[430]

There were tests, meetings with the doctor. In the end, the diagnosis wasn't a real surprise. One of his daughters drove up to see him shortly after, debating whether she should mention it and wondering how he would react. Bill brought it up himself, right away. "You know that A word?" he asked her. "Alzheimer's?" she guessed. "Yeah," he said. "Well, I got it. I know I got it. And it's terrible."

But the disease never broke his spirit; he remained the man his family had always known. More and more often, though, he could be found meandering through the house in the middle of the night, living out a story as it unfolded in his head—disjointed but very vivid, like a waking dream. If you were with him, he would describe what was happening, circling back again to the same themes, the details changing a bit each time. You had to listen closely, almost translate his accounts into what you thought he might be trying to get across. Usually it still didn't exactly make sense, except to him.[431]

Rarely at these times did he seem anxious. Mostly he was amazed and delighted. And he moved easily between our world and his. Another time, hearing her father wandering in the wee hours after a party that celebrated his eighty-seventh birthday, one of his daughters sat with him in the kitchen. First they talked about what was happening in his head. He had been walking through a submarine. He came upon some kind of engine that made no noise. He was supposed to be looking for someone to relieve him on watch but wasn't sure where the bunks were. His daughter told him there were some bunk beds just down the hall. After a pause, he asked where they were. At the house of another daughter, she told him. He was surprised and pleased. So they reminisced about the party earlier in the day, with all the family. They talked about how he'd been feeling older lately and how he hoped "it" wouldn't be too long. He thought it would be "pretty nice" on the other side. A moment later he fell silent. His daughter let it linger and then asked what he was thinking.

"I was thinking about how to think," he said.
"How that's going?" she asked.
"Not too well," Bill said. Then he, and she, laughed.[432]

And Bill carried on. In all the moves the family made over the years, he had always gone ahead to get things ready. In some ways now, for him and for his children, it felt like that. He was going on ahead, sending back stories and reports.

There was one other constant. During his life Bill spent thousands of hours in the air. In those last years, he flew mostly in his mind. And toward the end especially, flying and dying became synonymous for him. As usual, it took some translating at first. He told one of his children to make sure they "get everyone to the airport on time."[433] He asked another, with urgency in his voice, "Can't you hear the engines?" Another time, waking in the middle of the night, he described how "the plane is waiting for us. There should be lots of engine noise, but it's absolutely silent."[434] They put their heads together and agreed that he was talking about dying. The references became more frequent. For him it wasn't a euphemism or an allegory. He was ready to take off. He wanted to make sure everyone would be there.

And so it was. One late night in March 2009—heading for his plane—Bill fell in the hallway at the retirement home and broke his hip. Pneumonia set in—"the Old Man's Friend," some veteran nurses still call it. The kids and grandkids gathered at the hospital, taking turns looking after him. He would rally sometimes. Once he woke up and announced, "I'm in charge of this human airplane machine."

He took the final turn for the worse on March 21, 2009. His son and daughter called Mary, who had gone home earlier. They put the phone on the pillow where Bill could hear, and she whispered prayers in his ear. In the moment that he died, a helicopter lifted off from the hospital roof. It was the first day of spring.

Days later at the graveside, "Taps" sounded clear above the chirping birds and the passing cars. An honor guard and a folded flag for Mary. More stories from his children and grandchildren. Flowers and handfuls of dirt dropped into the hole.

A few horsetail clouds in a china blue sky. A perfect day for flying.[435]

The Vacant Air

In May and June 1945, Henry Luce, founder and editor of *Time* and *Life* magazines, made a tour of the Pacific theater, which he recalled in a book that he was writing at the time of his death years later.

> I spent a morning at Cavite in the Philippines with Admiral Frank Wagner in front of huge maps. Admiral Wagner was in charge of air search-and-patrol of all the East Asian seas and coasts. He showed me that in all those millions of square miles there was literally not a single target worth the powder to blow it up; there were only junks and mostly small ones at that.[436]

But still, they flew. And still, the enemy fought.

There is lost as in unfound, vanished. Without a trace. And there is lost as in bereft, heartsick. Unmoored by grief. On June 14, 1945, Jerry Dougan and his mother were both lost somewhere in Indochina.

The story is frustratingly partial, like scraps from a letter or a photo torn in two. Dougan had been with the squadron less than two months. He was quiet, the men said, easy to get along with. Helped tutor his radioman in algebra.[437] Liked playing volleyball.[438] He and his fiancée were planning their wedding in October.[439]

Jerry and his crew had flown maybe ten missions. They never found any Japanese warships but did manage to sink a few coastal freighters and shoot up some locomotives and boxcars on the inland rail lines.[440]

Then they drew the sector including Ha Tien on the Indochina coast, near the border between what is now Vietnam and Cambodia. It was a well-defended port, one of the few hot spots left. Around 2 p.m. a squadron plane in the next sector radioed Jerry, who was south of Saigon headed for Ha Tien. Dougan said they were using a bit more fuel than usual, but otherwise all was well.

It was the last anyone heard.

But if Jerry Dougan left few traces behind, the record of his mother's anguish is well documented. It's called an individual deceased personnel file, with reports and correspondence about service members who died during World War II. Jerry's file runs to more than 250 pages, much of it letters from his mother, Viola, to anyone who might listen.

From the first she was convinced her son had survived and was captured or hiding somewhere in Indochina. Six weeks after the Japanese surrendered, she wrote the wife of a crewman,

> I am not calm and patient at all. I do believe our boys are safe and will return—I see no reason to believe otherwise from all our information to date, and I well know that God would never be confused by man's confusion.[441]

But in the months and then the years that followed, confusion was common. For one thing Indochina was still at war, with the French fighting the Vietnamese for control of the countryside—making ground searches almost impossible. Then there was the bureaucracy. The army had been given responsibility for finding missing men, even those from another branch of the service. At various times the War Department, the U.S. Navy, the Quartermaster General, and the American Graves Registration Service all were involved. And just to make things more complicated, finding downed fliers in the Indochina sector had been assigned to the British, not the Americans.

None of which deterred Viola Dougan. Nor did the letter from Secretary of the Navy James Forrestal, dated a year and a day after the crew was reported missing, declaring them all officially "deceased." She scoured newspapers far and wide for articles about Indochina and missing servicemen. She wrote officials quoted in them as well as their bosses and anyone else who might have influence.

She prodded; she pleaded. She wrote to the quartermaster general in 1947,

> It is specific information we seek. The Senate Committee on Armed Services has been active on our behalf, as has Senator [Robert] Taft. . . . We realize the conditions now existing in French Indochina, but we are well aware that our sons were sent into that isolated, forsaken area and the length of time they have been abandoned to their own resources scars our very souls.

There were foul-ups and false hopes. First she was told the area south of Saigon had been searched; then she was told it hadn't. She exchanged letters with a Vietnamese man who claimed to have seen survivors of a bomber crash near Saigon executed by natives; he turned out to be a fraud. Another report said a bomber may have crashed on an island in the Mekong Delta on June 14, 1945; it was later disproven.

It's impossible to know what she truly thought or hoped. The war had ended years earlier; almost all the families of missing men had moved on. But Viola Dougan did not declare peace. She was divorced from Jerry's father and had lost her only child. She was a schoolteacher in Ohio who had spent her summers earning a master's degree from Columbia University in New York. She was used to getting answers, used to following through.[442] And giving up meant giving in, finally, to the grief that waited to engulf her. So the handwritten letters continued through 1948, 1949: "Our prayers and faith are constant. A just God hears, and I believe He will see justice done. The waiting is agony beyond expression."[443]

Then, in early March 1950, the U.S. Consulate in Saigon received a letter from Vo van Ho, first provincial inspector at Ha Tien during the war. He was responding to an ad in Vietnamese newspapers asking for information about missing American planes from World War II.

Sir:

On Thursday, June 14 1945 about 1600 hours was shot down in the Gulf of Siam about 5 kilometers from the chief town of the Province of Ha Tien (south Viet-nam) an American plane.

Several days later there was recovered at Hon Chong (25 kilometers from the place where the plane was shot down) the body of an aviator named Harrold. This body was buried in front of the school of Hon Chong. They recovered also a leather jacket belonging to Paul Dougan.

Several other bodies were recovered the same day on the islands in front of Hon Chong.[444]

Ha Tien had been Dougan's destination, and the time of the attack, 4 p.m., would have been about right. But the letter didn't say what type of American plane. And the names weren't quite correct. Jerry's full name was Jerry Penrose Dougan, not Paul, as was on the leather jacket. And there was no crewman with the last name Harrold; closest was the tail gunner, Woodrow Harold Stewart. Still, the discrepancies might be explained by the language barrier or by memories slightly clouded in the five years since the crash.

That same week, a wire service story appeared in American newspapers, including the *Cleveland Plain Dealer*. It described how a search team had recently recovered the body of an American pilot held prisoner for three years before being executed by Vietnamese rebels. Viola Dougan read the story and immediately wrote the chief of naval operations: "The enclosed clipping verifies our constant, firm belief that my son and his crew are surviving somewhere in that war-torn area, awaiting the aid and rescue so long overdue."[445]

The recovered body of the pilot was not that of Jerry Dougan or one of his crew; neither the description nor the dental records matched. More promising was the report from Ha Tien. But here, too, following up was considered impossible. The team that found the earlier pilot's grave had included a gunboat and a detachment from the French Foreign Legion; yet it still had to fight its way in and out of the recovery site.[446] It was the same problem at Ha Tien; a Graves Registration officer cabled his commander, "Not—repeat, not—safe to enter at present due to political situation there."[447]

So once again, nothing had changed. Except instead of another form letter, she got a telephone call from a Captain Joe Vogl in the quartermaster general's office. He filled her in on the reports from Indochina and the problems in searching for missing fliers. She was appreciative but adamant:

> From my conversation with Mrs. Dougan it is quite evident that she does not believe her son is dead. She insists that unless proof is furnished her by the Navy Department that her son did die as a result of an air crash, the family will not look upon their son as dead but rather as a prisoner of communist forces in French Indochina.[448]

But she took heart from Vogl's personal interest. He promised to keep her up to date and a month later called again, reading her the official report that explained why they believed her son's plane could not have crashed near Saigon that day. He told her he was being posted to Europe but would get in touch with her again when he returned later that year.

Vogl's hitch in Europe lasted longer than he expected, and he was then transferred out of the quartermaster general's office. So another year passed. Viola Dougan wrote him again:

> Please don't fade away along with all the other half-hearted efforts to locate our beloved sons. We were so encouraged by your interest and apparent skillful determined effort.[449]

Three months later, the Board of Review of the American Graves Registration Service convened to consider the case of Jerry Dougan and his crew. They went through the history of the various searches and the problems stemming from the fighting in the area. They conveyed their conclusions in a letter mailed to Viola Dougan in November 1951:

After careful consideration of the length of time that has elapsed since the disappearance of your son's plane, the past attempts to recover remains from this area and the present conditions of hostilities and political unrest, the Department of the Army has been forced to conclude that the remains of your son are not recoverable.

In the first week of December, Joe Vogl, now a major on a cross-country trip to his new posting in Asia, stopped at Viola Dougan's home in Cleveland Heights to personally explain the board's decision. But she was staying with her sister in Northern California for several months. When he learned this, he made arrangements to see her there in early February 1952.

He did not have to go. In the formal letter sent two months earlier, the government had done its duty. But to be still among the missing, especially after so long a time, means there is no knock on the door, no face and no uniform, nothing personal in the respect paid to those you love. Joe Vogl might have felt that Jerry's mother had earned at least that.

According to his later report, the visit lasted five hours. Five hours. And somewhere during that time, something in Viola Dougan gave way. Maybe she was just tired of hoping. Of not knowing. Of fighting the odds and the bureaucracy. Of denying something part of her had known since she first got the telegram more than six years earlier.

Almost surely there were tears. Maybe Joe Vogl offered her his handkerchief. Maybe he sat in silence while she buried her head in her hands. Maybe she showed him pictures of Jerry as a boy. Maybe she made him lunch and they talked for a time of other things. Maybe when he stood at last to leave, she rose and gave him a hug. Maybe he hugged her back, his hat in his hand.

Or maybe they just shook hands at the door, and when it closed, she leaned her back against it, as if to somehow keep out all that had happened.

Mrs. Dougan expressed her sincere appreciation for the information furnished and said she is now resigned, since the Army has done everything possible to recover the remains without success, that they are not recoverable. However, she expressed a hope that perhaps in the future something may turn up which will indicate her son's burial place.[450]

It was the last page in the file.

Viola Dougan taught school for more than forty years, and when she retired, she went to live with her sister in California. She died there in 1976. She was eighty-four.

There is something different about men who go missing in airplanes. Jerry Dougan's was not the only such crew in the squadron. It took months or even years to unravel the facts behind the others. But only he and his men remained disappeared.

We want what his mother wanted. We want a story, maybe even if it's made up. We want an ending, maybe even if there is none. Instead, it's as if they're still up there, in the vacant air. And we're still here, waiting.

Fire on the Water

Farther down the long list of war's unanswerable questions, here's another: How do you mourn or miss someone you never knew?

In the fall of 1942, Mary Mercer was a senior at the University of Iowa, daughter of a state senator and a sweetheart of Sigma Chi. Her cousin had married a sorority sister, and one weekend he arranged a blind date for Mary with a cadet from the navy's new pilot training program, which seemed to have taken over the campus. All she knew about her expected escort was his name.

But the first thing the tall fellow in his dress uniform said was "I'm not John Glenn." He quickly explained that Glenn had backed out at the last minute because he was "practically engaged" and didn't feel right about going out with someone else. "So I volunteered to take his place. My name is Stan Sayre." Mary wasn't upset; it would be almost twenty years before her intended date became the iconic astronaut. Besides, she had an almost immediate feeling. Fate looked a lot more like the grinning guy in front of her.

He was from Indiana—hazel eyes, dark hair, an easy way about him. His father, an Episcopal minister, had died when he was still a boy. His mother was an accomplished musician. Stan took after them both. He was devout, serious about his faith. He played the piano by ear, learned the trumpet, and had a strong singing voice. His mother had hoped he would become a preacher like his father, but he chose to study business instead, eventually getting his MBA from the University of Michigan. He volunteered for the navy right after graduation and was sent straight to Iowa City.

If you were young in that autumn after Pearl Harbor, everything seemed accelerated, intensified—like living in a time-lapse movie. Within weeks, Stan and Mary knew. They took long strolls across the campus. Sometimes they went for dinner and dancing at the Mayflower Inn, a Victorian mansion that had been converted to a supper club on the banks of the Iowa River. He called her "Purty" and sang her favorite songs. They held hands, made plans.

Winter came, and Stan was transferred to Kansas. Mary visited there and met his mother. The wedding date was set. He went on to Corpus Christi and earned his wings. She went back to school and graduated on Easter Sunday 1943. They were married on Flag Day; a picture shows them cutting the cake, both dressed in shining white and smiling.

They honeymooned in Hollywood, Florida, while he went to navigation school, and then to Kansas again and on to San Diego. They took the ferry to parties at the Officers Club on Coronado Island and lived in Ocean Beach. Every morning he left for the base, and every evening he returned—calling her name and singing his way up the sidewalk.

Stan's first tour as a copilot took him to the Marshall Islands with VB-108, the first Liberator squadron in the central Pacific. He wrote Mary frequently but never spoke about the danger or the missions.[451]

About the time Stan Sayre returned from the Pacific, Marcellus Faustin Brownlee was walking down the aisle with his high school sweetheart, Dorothy Ann Vogel, in Arcadia, Wisconsin, population 1,830. Unlike Stan and Mary, they had known each other as long as they could remember. She was "Dort" and he was "Sally," a corruption of his first name coined by his four older sisters. In high school Dort had been a cheerleader. Sally was a top student and quarterback on the football team, which went undefeated, untied, and unscored upon his senior year.[452] After graduation she went to nursing school in LaCrosse. He left for Madison and the state university. They would marry after college.

Pearl Harbor came in the middle of Sally's sophomore year. He volunteered for the Army Air Force but failed the physical because of a hernia. He went to the doctor in Arcadia, had it repaired, and signed up for navy flight school. The training took him all over the country, and he wrote frequent, funny letters home.

> We had liberty Saturday so to make sure we wouldn't enjoy it, they went about getting us all tired out Saturday morning. We went on a hike. We marched out of here and just got going good when they gave the command, "Double Time," so we started to run. I think the officer forgot how to get us back to Quick Time (that's normal step) because we kept going on the run for over a mile. Then every once in a while we'd walk, but we ran most of the time. We went on a circular route and got back too quick. We got right up to the entrance, the officer looked at his watch, said "About Face" and we started running back up the road. We got about a half mile up the road, stopped, did another "About Face" and ran all the way back. We looked like a freight train switching, or a one-sided game of tug of war. Believe it or not, by that time most of us were sweating a little bit.
>
> I had wrestling last week, and boy was that a deal. The first couple of days were all right while they taught us fundamentals, but the last two were different. I'm a sucker, though. I got in front of a guy, got my arms around his neck and my legs around his waist. Do you know what he did? I don't. He stood up, and from there on it's got me puzzled. He either slammed me on the floor or picked the floor up and hit me on the back of the head with it. I haven't been the same since.[453]

Sally survived, got his wings, and married Dort on September 16, 1944. A picture shows him in his dress blues, her arm entwined with his, the train of her wedding dress pooled at her feet.

Stan and Sally, Mary and Dort met in San Diego in the spring of 1945. Promoted to plane commander, Stan trained Sally as his copilot/navigator, and by the time they reached Mindoro in early June, they were good friends. Both had lost their fathers as boys. Both were churchgoers. Stan, in fact, often rousted buddies from their beds for Sunday services. You couldn't really resist him; he was, one friend recalled, "the glue that held things together."[454]

Sally was the same—well liked, easy to be around. Both wrote home faithfully. Sally to Dort, June 15, 1945:

> You're just too wonderful, so how can I help but miss you? That's all I do. I guess you know, tomorrow we'll have been married nine months. . . . I can remember how I looked forward to coming home when I was out at the base during the day. I even missed you then, so you can imagine how I feel now.

The following flight took them to the Indochina coast, where they went inland, attacked some railroad cars, and damaged a bridge.[455] The morning after, Sally wrote two more letters, and two days later he wrote three. The third, written on a rainy night in a leaking tent, ended this way:

> I know you don't want me to stay up too late. Just wait till I get back, though; I'll keep you awake all night. Boy, what fun. Mean, aren't I? Already I'm fixin' for a hard life for you. Maybe I'll just stay awake and watch you sleep. I don't want to miss a minute of it when I'm with you. I guess I sound lonesome, but the truth of the matter is, I am. I miss you, darling, more than you know. I guess I'll be lonesome all the time till I'm with you again.
> I love you,
> Sal[456]

Stan Sayre wrote loving letters too. But the only one that survived is more serious. Feeling their separation more keenly this second time around, Mary had written and asked why God would let so many die. "Why is life worth living, just to be killed in a war?" Stan didn't pass it off as a mood or mere anxiety; he took her question seriously. His answer drew heavily on his faith:

Wars, which are the creation of sinful man, can never interfere with God's purpose in this world. God is metaphysically responsible. Man is morally responsible. . . .

We must always fight the good fight and keep the faith. Wars are as old as the most ancient history, yet there has been progress! Look at the position of the Church today; look at the great strides of medicine, education and invention. Despite all man's sinful ways, progress has been made, which is proof of the purpose of God in this life.[457]

The next day, June 22, Stan and Sally were scheduled for a special mission: a three-plane strike to Ha Tien on the coast in the Gulf of Siam. Normally, squadron planes flew alone, but just a week earlier a Blue Raiders crew flying that sector had disappeared without even a distress call.[458] So this time they would send more firepower and try to do some real damage.

To get there and back—and to carry enough fuel, ammo, and bombs— they would have to seriously overload the planes. According to the manual, maximum takeoff weight for a PB4Y-1 was about fifty-six thousand pounds. The squadron had often flown them with sixty-five or sixty-seven thousand pounds. Sometimes even sixty-nine thousand pounds. The three planes that day each weighed seventy-three thousand pounds. No matter what awaited them in Ha Tien, getting into the air might well be the most dangerous part of the trip.[459]

When Stan and Sally got to the flight line well before dawn, the plane they were supposed to fly had mechanical problems. They settled for a backup. John Iler, who would later become a member of the navy's first all-jet squadron, piloted the third bomber that day, last in line for takeoff. At one end, the McGuire Field runway reached to the ocean's edge. The other end was close to camp and some palm trees. In a light following wind, Iler opted to take off toward the water, figuring that if he got even a few feet off the ground, he could nurse the plane up to altitude from there. Stan Sayre and the third pilot, Walt Greene, headed in the opposite direction, into a light wind, and wallowed into the air. Waiting for clearance,

Iler heard the tower operator call Stan and say, "Did you know you nicked a tree on takeoff?" In a calm voice, Sayre said no, but they'd check it out. A minute or two later, rolling down the runway himself, Iler again heard the tower: "Fire on the water!"[460]

The clinical details come from a letter that squadron commanding officer Roger Crowley sent to Dort Brownlee:

> At about four-thirty on the morning of June 22nd, your husband's plane took off on a routine patrol mission. As the plane left the runway it was so low the left wing struck a tree; however, the plane continued in flight and appeared to be under control. The plane was observed gaining altitude to approximately five hundred feet as it headed out to sea. Suddenly, and for no explainable reason the plane went out of control and crashed into the sea about nine miles offshore. Crash boats were immediately dispatched to the scene in the hope of recovering survivors, however, none were found by reason of the fact that the plane exploded and burned upon striking the water.[461]

Inside the plane, the men probably struggled from the start. The pilots would have been glued to the gauges and the controls, the crew told to look for damage. They were in the air maybe three minutes, and five hundred feet was considered the minimum "safe" altitude; from there you had a brief chance to react if things went wrong. So when they got that high, the crew must have felt a little relieved. And then—maybe an engine failure left them without enough power. Maybe a problem with the damaged wing, or the controls, threw them into a spin. Maybe fumes from the extra fuel tanks in the bomb bay exploded.

Surely Stan Sayre had said a hurried prayer.

The *whump* when the plane hit the water was the sound of a door slamming. It's easy to imagine a future where Stan and Mary go back to Iowa City, him following her father into politics and becoming deacon of their Episcopal church. Or Sally Brownlee being president of the bank in Arcadia, maybe helping out as a volunteer football coach at the high school. The two families living within a few hundred miles, car trips with the kids, Stan and Sally propping their feet on a porch railing, remembering that summer in the South China Sea.

Instead, it all sank in two thousand feet of water, and time, like the ocean, closed over them.[462]

Twenty minutes after the crash, the rescue boats arrived; they found shreds of debris and Sally Brownlee's body—the only one recovered.[463] Six hours later, the two remaining planes arrived at Ha Tien harbor. They came in fifty feet off the water and were met by nine Japanese fighters, two of which made runs and one of which was hit. The bombers sank and damaged half a dozen ships and left as quickly as they came. By sunset they were back at base.[464]

The next morning, the squadron buried Sally Brownlee in a monsoon rain. John Iler, one of the pallbearers, slipped in the mud and stepped onto a recent grave, sinking up to his hips before the casket beneath stopped his fall.[465]

Four days later, Dort Brownlee got the telegram:

SINCEREST SYMPATHY IS EXTENDED TO YOU IN YOUR GREAT LOSS. WHEN FURTHER DETAILS ARE RECEIVED YOU WILL BE INFORMED.

Mary Sayre was still in bed when the doorbell rang at her parents' home in Iowa City. She heard her father talk quietly with two navy officers and waited until they left before coming down the stairs.[466]

That weekend Mary wrote Dort,

I know there is nothing I can say to console you if you did receive the same report I did, but I wanted you to know that I was thinking of you. Stan always said never to give up hope, so I can't until I hear more of the details but I'm not too optimistic. Please write real soon and let me know how you are.[467]

The next Monday, two days before Independence Day, they held a memorial service for Sally in Arcadia. The American Legion fired a salute, and someone played "Taps."[468]

And more than two months later, on September 20, 1945, Dort gave birth to James Faustin Brownlee, naming him after Sally's father. Six days after that, Ed Sayre was born in Iowa City. Mary named him for Stan's brother.

Nursing their sons through long winter nights, steadying their first steps in the summer that followed, Mary and Dort struggled and survived. Gradually memory became more a comfort, less a curse. All around, the war was well and truly over. And in time, like millions more, they made their private peace with the past.

Dort Brownlee remarried in 1947, to John Koetting. During the war he'd flown army transports over "The Hump" in Burma; afterward, he went back to school, becoming a teacher and later principal of Arcadia High. Dort promised Sally's mother that his son would always keep the Brownlee name.[469]

Mary Sayre remarried in 1948, to John Dawson, a college professor. They had known each other in high school; their families were friends. They lived first in Oklahoma and later in California, where John taught and worked.[470]

And what of their boys?

For most sons, a father is a fixed point they steer toward or from. But a father lost before his boy is born is only an inkling—a meteor, not a star. When Sally Brownlee's body finally came all the way home from the Philippines in 1948, there was a service in the Arcadia Armory. Three-year-old Jim saw the flag-draped coffin. After high school Jim joined the air force, where he learned a lot about computers. He later ran the computerized circulation system for a large newspaper chain. His mother died of cancer in 1966.[471]

Ed Sayre believed John Dawson was his natural father until age seven, when Mary thought he was old enough to understand. After high school he went back to Iowa City and got a degree in psychology at the University of Iowa. At the urging of a girlfriend, he joined the university's graduate program in creative writing; he soon knew he didn't want to teach writing. He's worked as an executive for an insurance company, a deep-sea fishing guide in Baja California, and an investment advisor, among other things. He never married.[472]

Jim Brownlee has all the family mementoes of his father—his letters, his navy records, Sally's dog tags, the flag from his coffin, pictures of his grave and monument in Arcadia's Memorial Park. Jim's researched a little on his own about his father's past, but not too much. Just curious, he says, not trying to fill some emotional void.[473]

I visited Ed Sayre in Iowa City, where he lived. He said that while in the writing program there years ago, he knew of James Tate, who taught poetry and whose first collection had just won a prestigious award. The book was called *The Lost Pilot*, and the title poem was dedicated to the author's father, a bomber pilot who disappeared over Europe when his son was five months old.

Ed thought he might have tried to write something about his own father back then. But only once, and he never kept what he wrote. Later he asked the government for Stan's service records, but they'd been destroyed in a fire. He doesn't dwell on the subject—he told me he can't make up memories he doesn't have.[474]

Yet blood, like a river, finds its own course in time. So there is this: Like his father, Ed Sayre has loved music all his life. Classical first, and then jazz starting in his teens. He played in bands and made a living at it for a time. And when he visited his mother, into her nineties, she said she always heard him coming up the sidewalk singing—just like Stan.[475]

And there is this: Jim Brownlee has two sons, the youngest of whom has a son of his own. When the boy was born, at the suggestion of his son's wife, they named him after his great-grandfather. In 2009, for the first time in decades, Jim went back to Wisconsin for a family reunion. There he found his Aunt Dorothy, Sally's only surviving sister. "Dodo," as she was called, was ninety-two.

They sat together. She asked about his family. Jim showed her pictures, including a high school photo of his older son placed next to a picture of Sally at the same age. They might well have been twins.

He told her he had a grandson too and put another snapshot in her hand. Dodo smiled. "Turn it over," Jim said. On the back he'd written the boy's name: Marcellus Faustin Brownlee.

She was silent for maybe a minute. Then Dodo wiped her eyes and whispered, "Thank you."[476]

Like a Prayer

The old men knew that in war, choice and chance are always entangled, impossible to separate or make sense of. Why that sector, that day? Why bank right, not left? Why him, not me? A cat's cradle of questions that cannot be unraveled in this life. So for decades they told themselves what they told others who asked: "Just luck, I guess." In the summer of 1945, good luck and bad luck both brought Joe Lowder to a hill above a bay where, in shock and in shambles, he somehow managed to perform an act of surpassing kindness.

He shouldn't even have been there. His dream of becoming a pilot had been denied. His orders had said he would be a stateside instructor, not a combat crewman. His post in the plane had been taken by a buddy at precisely the wrong (or right) moment. Yet it made perfect sense that flying would help decide his fate. Joe had grown up next to an airport—really, more like a flat pasture wedged between two hills in Bluefield, West Virginia. His family's house was on the glide path to the runway, so close that from his porch he could hear instructors bringing students in to land ("Right rudder. Right rudder!!").

Soon he was hanging out with the pilots, offering to wash their planes, checking for holes by running his hands over the fabric-covered fuselage the way a trainer strokes a thoroughbred's back. Sometimes they took him up, and before long he had learned how to fly himself. One pilot, a Canadian World War I ace named Bill Duff, literally took Joe under his wing. Bill taught him aerobatics, emergency procedures, and aircraft maintenance. He let him help assemble a plane from scratch. He drilled him on everything he would need to know to pass his pilot's exam. And at age sixteen, the minimum, Joe became one of the youngest licensed pilots in America.[477]

Then hard times brought everything back to earth. His father's insurance business failed, and the family moved from Bluefield to the big city of Charleston. Joe was the new kid on the block, so to introduce him around, the boy next door took him to the local lake. There he saw a tall girl in a blue bathing suit, drying her strawberry-blonde hair with a towel. He asked who she was. "That's Gwen Kinsey," his neighbor said. "But you'd better leave her alone. She can beat you at anything you name."

Gwen was smart, he explained, a top student. She started reading the *Encyclopedia Britannica* at the age of five. Her father worked at Union Carbide Company. She had won a state tennis championship and was a strong swimmer. Turned out she was a tomboy too. A week later, as the neighborhood guys met for a game of flag football, there she was again, this time wearing blue jeans. Joe's friend said, "When we choose sides we have to pick Gwen first, or we're gonna get beat." After that Joe would see her riding her bike, and they chatted a few times, but he felt she was, in all ways, out of his league.

Joe soon discovered that classes in Charleston were a lot harder than back in Bluefield, but he found success as an end on the Charleston High football team. At the close of the season, the team had a banquet and dance, but Joe said he wasn't going. "Why not?" asked a teammate. "Because I can't dance. I don't want people to laugh at me." His buddy said not to worry. "My girlfriend knows someone who can teach you." Two days later, they walked up to a house, and when the front door opened, Gwen was standing there. Joe's friend wished him luck and left.

She took him inside and told him she was sure he could learn to dance. Remembering it to me a lifetime later, Joe still stammered as he had that afternoon. "Well, ma'am, I don't . . . I'm not sure . . . I just think." She went to the kitchen, brought him a glass of orange juice, and told him to relax. "Whatever I do with my feet, you just do with yours. OK?" He swallowed his juice, stood up, and faced her in the middle of the floor. She seemed suddenly very close. He could smell her hair. But he still managed to concentrate on his feet and picked up the steps pretty quickly. Gwen was impressed. Then she said, "And by the way, I'm going with you as your date. When we dance, I'll lead you. But it will look like you're leading me."

The deal was done; the date was set. The night of the dance things were going smoothly when Gwen went to the orchestra leader and asked him to play a Latin number. She came back and said to Joe, "All you have to do is pay attention to me. We've practiced spins. Just go with the music." He nodded, "Yes, ma'am." The next four minutes were straight out of a Fred Astaire movie. The music swayed; Gwen and Joe swirled; half the couples stopped dancing and formed a circle to watch. It was the high point, the closest thing Joe had found to flying.

But once the party was over, he didn't have an excuse to visit Gwen. And he was too shy to just ask her out. So she again came to the rescue. Walking home one Saturday, he heard a bike coming up the sidewalk behind him. Gwen hopped off and said, "Mind if I walk with you?" Sure, he said, and with his best attempt at nonchalance, "How have you been?" Fine. She had seen him at school, but he always seemed to have his head in a book. He told her he had to because he was having trouble passing his classes. "I know," she said, "so here's what we're going to do." She pulled a yellow tablet out of her bike basket. "When you go to school Monday I want you to write down *everything* the teachers tell you. And if they say something is important, I want you to underline it. Then bring it to me." She taught him how to study, how to take a test. They were still a good team—Joe's grades got better, and he graduated in the spring of 1940.

By then they were actually dating, but they hadn't passed the kissing stage and hadn't made any plans beyond the immediate future. Gwen graduated in 1941 and put off college for a year, going to work at the phone company instead. For Joe, college wasn't in the cards; family came first. His father had spent World War I in France, running a field hospital just behind the front lines. He'd seen carnage he could never forget and had been gassed himself. That meant he couldn't do any kind of physical labor, and for whatever reason, he never got his insurance business going again. So, as much of the country began to break free from the Depression, debt still surrounded the Lowders. Joe went to work to help pay the bills.

He first tried to get back into aviation, working as an apprentice mechanic and ground crew at Wertz Field in Charleston. But the money wasn't enough. A pilot who worked at Carbide got him a job in the company's Prestone division, which had a huge contract supplying antifreeze for Spitfires in the Battle of Britain and tanks taking on Erwin Rommel in North Africa. Joe worked the midnight shift, twelve hours, seven days a week, loading boxcars. The lifting made him very strong; he could climb a thirty-foot rope using only his arms and hold cinder blocks straight out from the sides of his body. Their jobs made it harder for him and Gwen to see each other, but they still got together in the evenings when they could. In the fall of 1941, she left for college in Ohio. A few months later, and within weeks of Pearl Harbor, Joe went to a navy recruiter, showed him his pilot's license, and said he wanted to get checked out in fighters. He was told he'd have to go to boot camp, take tests, and go through more than a year of training with no guarantee that he'd ever get to fly.

He decided there must be a better way, so he went back to boxcars for the time being. With Gwen away at school, he found new outlets, learning gymnastics at the local YMCA and joining a boxing club. He became good enough to win the amateur light heavyweight championship of West Virginia—never defeated, never even knocked down. However, his heart wasn't really in it. He won all his bouts on points because he refused to hit his opponents in the head. He didn't want to see anyone punch drunk or seriously hurt.

But he never got flying out of his system. So in the fall of 1942, Joe applied for the navy's V-12 program: two years of training and college classes and, if you made it, a guaranteed commission as a naval aviator. He threw himself into it and did well. By the end of his first year at the University of Louisville, he had been named a cadet company commander. Then one Friday afternoon he was called to the office of the program's new executive officer (XO), who had arrived less than a week earlier. Joe had never met him, but as soon as he saluted, the XO jumped up, leaned forward across his desk, and began screaming. The XO said he had sent Joe a note ordering him to place a fellow cadet on report for being AWOL. Joe said he thought the unsigned note was a prank by a buddy, and besides, the man in question had spent the whole weekend with Joe, studying for a project they were working on. The XO called him a liar, told him he'd make him an example, and then literally got in his face. Joe, sure the XO was going to hit him, in a boxing reflex, put his hands up to protect himself. Things got worse from there. The XO screamed; Joe forgot his military manners and lost his temper too. The argument escalated until Joe said, "I hope they never send you to sea, because you'll get the ship sunk." Then, without even a salute, he left the room.

Four steps down the hall, he couldn't believe his mistake. He'd never had a bad temper. Why did he rise to the bait like that? What kind of punishment would he get? All the next day, head in his hands, he sat on his bed in the barracks and waited for word. It came early Sunday morning: He would be thrown out of the V-12 program, busted down to seaman second class, and shipped to Great Lakes Naval Training Center outside Chicago for boot camp. That day.

After a sleepless train ride, Joe arrived at 7 a.m. on Monday morning, a chill wind blowing off Lake Michigan. He stood with his seabag at parade rest, the only man in uniform amid a sea of raw recruits wearing civilian clothes. Up walked a chief petty officer, who told the men to form four lines. He spotted Joe and said, "Hey, Mac, front and center." Joe stepped forward and said, "Lowder reporting, sir!" The chief said, so only Joe could hear, "I don't give a damn why you're here. But do you think you can move these men a half mile to the barracks yonder?" On the trip to Chicago Joe had promised himself that he would never again question military authority; it would all be by the book from there on. He chirped, "Yes, sir!" The chief said, "I'll see you there," and left. Joe looked over the two hundred recruits, split them into smaller groups, and gave them their first lessons in how to march. Within an hour they were moving in formation toward the barracks, and when they got there, he had them halt, face right in unison, and stand at parade rest, still in their civvies. They looked good, and Joe was proud of them.

The chief watched all this and said, "Lowder, that's a job well done. I need an acting chief petty officer to run this barracks here, and I don't think I need to look any more. You interested?" Forty-eight hours earlier, he had been stripped of his rank and self-respect. Now both were going to be at least partially restored. His barracks became the best at Great

Lakes, won more awards, and had highest marks on the tests. He settled in, learning not just to tolerate but also to appreciate military life. He wanted to be good at it. Then, a few months later, he saw a notice on a bulletin board, headlined "Air Crews Wanted." Factories were building planes faster than the navy could find men to fly them, and Joe jumped at the chance. Within two days he was on his way to Memphis for six months of training in everything from radar to Morse code. Then more school, this time in gunnery, in Jacksonville, Florida. He learned to strip and reassemble a .50-caliber machine gun, blindfolded, in thirty-four seconds. His vision was 20/10; he could read the trademark in the corner of the eye chart. Again he excelled, with the highest scores on the firing range, and again, he had his own reasons. He didn't want to shoot another human being. So the boxer who wouldn't hit an opponent in the head practiced until he knew he could knock out an engine or another vital part of the enemy's plane instead of aiming for the cockpit. He would keep his crew safe, but he did not want to think himself a killer.

In all this time, more than two years, he and Gwen hardly saw each other. She was in college; he was in training. But they wrote, and the letters became more and more serious. Ten days before Christmas in 1944, Joe got a quick leave and rode the bus from Jacksonville to Ohio, where Gwen was still in school. By the time he arrived, he had only hours before he had to catch another bus back to Florida. Joe had his speech ready. He told Gwen that it looked like the war was winding down; he'd been told he wouldn't be sent overseas and would stay in Florida as an instructor. He said they knew how they felt about each other, and there was no reason they shouldn't get married the first chance they got. It took her about a second to say yes, which was good because now Joe had to hustle back to catch the bus. He kissed her good-bye, turned up the collar on his peacoat, and walked out into the middle of a midwestern blizzard. The bus, it turned out, was forty minutes late. He stamped his feet; he rubbed his hands; he worried that he had missed it and would end up AWOL. Finally the bus's headlights sliced through the snow-flakes. The driver stopped and said, "Where are you headed?" Joe told him Florida. "Well, you've got the right bus. It'll just take us a while to get there."

Sort of like Joe and Gwen. For so long their future had seemed locked up, out of reach. Now the tumblers started falling into place. Christmas came and went. Joe made plans to move to his new base, and their new home, near Miami. In late February, he sent a one-sentence telegram: "I'm coming home to marry you." He forgot to tell her when. But the navy wasn't going to make this easy. He'd been granted leave to get married, but when he went to pick up the papers, he also found his orders had changed. Instead of Miami, he was being sent all the way across the country, to San Diego. He would be an instructor in the Privateer, the updated and improved Liberator being phased in by the navy. That sounded OK too, but it complicated things. California meant more time traveling, which gave them less time in Charleston for the wedding.

When Joe finally arrived on a Friday afternoon, they had only the weekend. They dashed to the courthouse and got their license just before the clerk's office closed. They sent the announcement and Gwen's picture to the Saturday newspaper. Joe pressed his only dress uniform. They were married in front of family and friends on Sunday evening, March 11, 1945. There was no time for a reception; as soon as the ceremony ended, Joe went to the foyer, picked up his seabag and Gwen's suitcase, and hailed a cab to the train station.

The overnight trip took them to Lafayette, Indiana. A friend of Joe's who lived there said he had a car and was driving to San Diego anyway, so the three could go together. His friend's name was George Palmer, and his car was an Auburn Boattail Speedster, one of the great glamour roadsters built during the Depression. It wasn't brand new, but it was bright red. It had chrome exhaust pipes that snaked from holes in the long, hinged hood and a front bumper that drooped in the middle like a starlet's pouty mouth.[478] To make the coast on time, they would have to drive nonstop, so they strapped their luggage on back, crossed into Illinois, and picked up Route 66.

South of Saint Louis the weather warmed up, and the top went down. They drove and slept in shifts. Joe remembered waking somewhere in the high desert, stars tossed across a blanket of sky. His new wife was at the wheel, her cheeks blushed by the wind, her face glowing in the dashboard lights. George was saying, "Gwen, you let it get under eighty again!"

They made San Diego with no time to spare; Joe reported fifteen minutes before he would have been declared AWOL.

He was anxious to start his new assignment, but within a week the navy had changed its mind again. Instead of instructing crews who would fly the new Privateer, he would help deliver a plane to a base in the Pacific. The next day, another switch—Joe was told he'd been picked for a replacement combat crew. The plane commander needed a good gunner and had found Joe's shooting scores in the files. He was the last crewman chosen.

In forty-eight hours their life together had gone from a long honeymoon in California to a separation that would last weeks or more to orders that would take Joe half a world away and put him in danger for the duration. For two frantic weeks he spent his days doing shakedown flights with the new plane and his nights savoring every possible moment with Gwen. Then he was gone.

The crew spent six weeks in Hawaii, practicing and getting to know each other better. The plane commander was Bob Hepting from Nebraska, quiet and considerate. He could give any order or answer any question without making you feel stupid. He had served an earlier tour with a "Black Cat" squadron, flying PBYs. So had copilot and navigator Ralph Messick, who also didn't feel the need to throw his weight around. The junior officer was Ensign Donald Gross; it was his first time out, and he was more concerned with rank and protocol.

Some of the enlisted men, like radioman Leonard Fisher, had been on previous combat tours. But for most, this was their first experience. They were from New York and New Orleans, Chicago and Saint Louis, small towns in Texas and Florida. Mechanic Bill Core's parents had been captured by the Japanese in the Philippines and put in an internment camp. At one point he had tried to become a pilot, but there weren't enough openings. Bombardier John Knauss was tall and thin and joked a lot, always with a straight face. Youngest in the crew was Les Gottberg, barely seventeen. He'd lied about his birthday to get into the navy, and by the time they found out, he'd been through gunnery school and reached the legal age for enlistment. So they let him stay.[479] Joe's experience as a pilot and his knowledge with radio and radar were a help, but his skill as a gunner drew the most praise. Before long, Lieutenant Hepting had made a rule: "Whenever we're in combat, Lowder is in the bow."

From Oahu they made the hopscotch flights west, reaching Mindoro in the first week of June. No sooner had they arrived than they lost their brand-new plane. A crew with more seniority in the squadron claimed it; Hepting and company would fly a battered old Liberator. Their first chance to do some damage came on June 27, when they attacked and knocked out a railroad bridge while looking for targets north of Tourane. Four days later, as they were waiting in line for takeoff on their next mission, a jeep came alongside the plane, and a messenger passed a note up to Hepting. Reconnaissance showed that a bridge north of Cam Ranh Bay, destroyed earlier, had been rebuilt. Hepting and company were told to bomb it again.

Cam Ranh Bay, on the Indochina coast, was still solidly in Japanese hands. The hills around it were heavily fortified, so it wasn't going to be a "normal" mission. But there was time to prepare; the target was more than eight hundred miles from Mindoro, four hours at least.

A little over halfway through the flight, Joe took a break from the bow turret, giving his seat to chubby-cheeked radioman John Palm, and went aft where the waist gunners had made sandwiches for lunch. To pass the time while he ate, he looked out the open hatches at the flat-bottomed clouds rising like chimneys all the way to the horizon. Then Joe saw something unusual: a pale strip at the edge of his vision that was smoother and longer than the bottom of a cloud. "It looks like a coastline," he said to himself, "but we're still way too far out." Soon, though, he was convinced and called the flight deck on the intercom. Hepting had the crew drop three smoke bombs; each hit the water with a puff and immediately started streaming tendrils of white westward.

Oh, no. They had been pushed ahead by a gale-force tailwind. Joe had indeed seen Indochina, now only minutes away. Normally, a hundred miles out they would have dropped just above the water to avoid enemy radar. Now the Japanese knew they were coming. Hepting called for battle stations and put the plane in a tight descending spiral, falling fast from nine thousand feet. Joe bolted for the bow, using all his strength to hold on to the bomb bay catwalk while they spun toward the water. Then he crawled toward his turret in the nose. Hepting stopped him. They might see fighters any minute; there wasn't time to make the switch with Palm.

With no gun to man, Joe decided to act as a lookout and stuck his head in a window that bubbled out from the forward fuselage. In a journal written decades after the fact, he could still recall exactly what he saw:

> The engine nacelles were so close to the water I would swear they were riding on the wavetops. Shortly, the coast came into view, this time as a green line. We pulled up, clearing the trees, and turned north.

To make the plane a tougher target, Hepting had decided to run the gauntlet of guns flying as low and fast as he could. But it was a little like trying to shoot an arrow through a thicket; you were bound to hit something.

> Ahead I saw the mouth of Cam Rahn Bay. Then several ships came into view. . . . At mast height, throttles wide open, we weaved across the bay and pointed toward the beach. Just above the tree tops about two miles ahead was the superstructure of a large railroad bridge, our target. Two red lights came on, indicating the bomb bay doors had opened.

Joe glanced back toward the bomb bay; then he turned to the window again.

> I could not believe what I saw. Number four engine was one ball of white fire. "No, No, No!" I kept yelling. There had been no warning. The fire just suddenly appeared. I turned away, not daring to believe it, then looked again. It was very terrifying. I was staring at the end.

Joe began moving toward the rear of the plane where he had stowed his parachute. On the windblown catwalk, he passed another crewman headed forward. Both looked down at green jungle rushing upward. When he reached the aft station, his chute wasn't there; someone had borrowed it to sleep on. Didn't matter—there were only seconds left. Gunners Les "Coot" Gottberg and Pete Hourcade stood by the open hatch, staring at the stream of fire from the engine. A shrieking sound as Joe turned toward the bomb bay, grabbed a rack, and pulled his legs up. Darkness.

Then, just as suddenly, light. Clouds and blue sky. He was lying on top of bombs in what was left of the fuselage. He wiped water from his eyes only to realize it was gasoline. He stood, saw he was on a beach, and then a *whump!* knocked him down again. The fuel tanks had exploded behind him. He knew fire would follow, and he tried to outrun it to the water. He almost made it before the flames caught him. He stumbled the last few steps and dove under. When he could hold his breath no longer, he found himself in waist-deep water, alone.

> My only thought was that my wife was going to receive one of those dreaded telegrams reading "Missing In Action" and it would make her feel bad. I tried to send her a mental apology for the hurt I would cause. A wave of loneliness engulfed me, and I felt every mile of the 11,000 that separated me from home. I turned toward the beach and saw the wreckage. The scene jarred me back to the present. The destruction was unbelievable. Nothing seemed to be left standing. Yellow-red flames licked the bottom of an enormous column of black smoke that spread back over a swath in the jungle made when the bomber hit at better than 200 miles an hour. I wondered if, indeed, I might be dead.

He didn't wonder for long, because when he took two steps toward the beach, pain dropped him to his knees and then pitched him face first into the water. Joe struggled to control his emotions and clear his head. He had to get out of there; the smoke from the crash was a beacon for anyone searching. He looked around and saw no one from the crew. He tried moving again and slowly angled toward the beach about two hundred yards from the wreck. His skin was seared. To relieve the pain from the saltwater and sand on his burns, he managed to pull off what remained of his gear and his clothes.

I shoved off again. I had not traveled far, as I could still hear the occasional faint cracks of 50 caliber shells going off. Ahead I saw the form of someone approaching. I was hoping to find a native, borrow a boat, and shove out to sea where our subs were on patrol and I could get picked up.

Not so, as a man dressed in Bermuda shorts, neat shirt, and knee socks walked up to me. For a few moments, we just looked at each other. Finally, thinking one of us should speak up, I gestured with my hands like a plane coming in then blowing up, then pointed at myself and said, "American."

He responded with a quick nod, saying something that certainly was not English, and waved to someone off on the side. Immediately six or seven soldiers encircled me with rifles and pistols at the ready. The man was a Jap marine, and I had just become a POW.

They took him to a house in the hills with a beautiful view of the bay and left him standing in the foyer. He was worried; the Japanese had a bad reputation when it came to POWs, and they were said to be especially hard on fliers. No one spoke to Joe, offered him water, or asked about his injuries. After about an hour, another group of soldiers arrived, bringing with them waist gunner Coot Gottberg and tail gunner Irving Stark.

So others had survived! Joe felt a little less alone but afraid for his fellow crewmen and sorry they hadn't somehow managed to escape. Later, they were able to compare notes about the crash. When the engine caught fire, they were fifty feet above a jungle, a quarter mile from the bay. Hepting banked the plane right, maybe trying for a forced landing in the water. But they either hit a tree or dug a wing, and everything came apart.

Stark, the tail gunner, had been in the turret when the plane hit the water. The turret broke free from the fuselage and went skipping across the bay like a stone. After it stopped in a few feet of water, Stark opened the door and walked out. Not a scratch. At first he was in shock, walking in circles on the beach. Then he saw the fuselage in flames and went to see whether he could help anyone. After the war he told navy investigators what he found:

Stark went back to the plane after he had recovered somewhat and saw two officers. One called him. He pulled him out but the officer was so badly burned he couldn't recognize him. He believes the voice was that of D. R. Gross, Ensign. His leg was broken. Stark did not recognize the other officer lying on the ground near the plane. Both his person and his clothing were on fire. Stark put out the fire on this officer.

Everyone in the front of the plane died. Coot had been thrown through the rear hatch during the crash. He didn't remember anything until he was wading in the water and saw Stark nearby. They sat down together on the beach and were quickly captured. Coot must have tumbled across the water because his back and shoulders were sprained and dislocated. He also probably had a concussion because every time he stood up, he quickly fainted.

Within fifteen minutes another group of soldiers arrived, carrying a man strapped to a door as if on a stretcher.

It was Pete Hourcade, clad only in his dungaree pants. The soldiers set the door down and cut him loose. He immediately got to his feet and aimlessly started wandering about. The soldiers tried to herd him within a small circle. When he turned toward me I saw he was terribly burned, his head was enormously swollen, and half his face had been sheared off. Blessedly, he was totally out of it. I was mustered into watching him and to keep him put.

The Japanese took the four fliers to a fresh garbage pit they had dug, shoulder high and about six feet square. They motioned for the men to climb in and posted a guard nearby, sitting under a palm tree. By now Joe himself was in bad shape. His eyes felt like they were filled with dust and sand, and pain arced through his body every time he moved. Later, he would learn he'd lost his right eye, suffered a skull fracture and a broken ankle, and sustained more than a dozen puncture wounds and burns on his face, neck, back, hands, and legs.

Worst off was Pete Hourcade. He was a big, handsome kid whose parents had come from France to New Orleans, where they ran a dairy. Pictures show him with slicked-back hair and soulful eyes. He liked girls and good times, loved to sing and dance; he had won jitterbug contests back home. He volunteered for the navy right after graduating from Warren Easton Boys High School.[480] But he was not the same boy now. His buddies couldn't understand how Pete was still alive; yet he seemed unaware of his predicament. He sang. He laughed. He spoke with people who weren't there. Listening to him, Joe realized that Pete was back home in New Orleans. And he desperately wanted him to stay there, away from the pit and the pain and everything that would surely follow.

So Joe stood next to him and spoke softly into his good ear: "Stay there, Pete. Don't you come back here. Stay there." This went on through the afternoon. Pete gradually weakened, but he kept singing to himself. And Joe kept repeating, like a chant, like a prayer, "Stay there, Pete." The sun fell behind a hill, shadows spread across the bay, and guards came to get the four from the pit. Coot and Stark left first. Despite his injuries, Joe pulled himself out and reached to help Pete. But he couldn't pull him up, and Pete was almost unconscious, too weak to move. A guard watched for a moment and then ordered Joe to keep going. After he'd taken five steps, he looked over his shoulder just as Pete was bayoneted through the chest, the blade coming out his back.

Joe's first thought was "That was a mercy killing." His second thought was "They can do the same thing to me anytime they want." The remaining three were taken back to the house and questioned by three men, one wearing civilian clothes who spoke English. They wanted to know the frequency of the plane's radar; they asked them over and over to spell their mothers' names. It lasted until 2 a.m.

The next day they brought Joe back again. His eyes were swollen, he was having trouble seeing, the burnt skin was peeling off the back of his hands, and there was still no mention of a doctor. The interrogator, who was sitting on the porch, asked Joe whether he wanted some water and then sent a young boy to get it. As the boy with the water was walking back up the porch, a loud gong sounded nearby. The civilian dropped his papers, the boy dropped the water, and both ran off, motioning for Joe to follow. Joe ran after them into the backyard, where he saw Coot, Stark, and some Japanese pile into an air-raid shelter dug out of the hillside. It had an opening in the front, and when he reached it, Joe saw there was no more room. One of the Japanese pushed him away and closed the door.

So Joe stood alone in the yard. And he realized the plane the Japanese had spotted might well be from the squadron, looking for them. Anyone flying the same sector the next day would be keeping a sharp eye on the coastline. They might have seen that the bridge hadn't been hit; they might have spotted the wreckage. "Somebody's coming," Joe said out loud. Just then he heard engines and knew immediately it was a B-24. Only one plane.

But his elation immediately turned to panic. If he knew the squadron would search for them, so did the Japanese, and they would be waiting. He looked up again, and there it was in plain view, at five thousand feet, paralleling the coast: a camouflage blue bomber. Joe looked down the hill to the ships and the guns in the bay. Then, trying to warn the plane away, he ran to a clearing and began shouting, "Get up! Get up!" He knew they couldn't hear him, but slowly the noise and the outline of the plane began to fade. Relieved, Joe slumped. Then he realized he was alone and unguarded. He wanted to make a break, but he had no clothes, his body was wracked with pain, and he was having trouble seeing. If he had been in shape, he would have run in an instant. But he knew he would never get far, so he stood and waited for his captors to find him.

That night Joe, Coot, and Stark were put in a boxcar on a train and sent south. The next morning they were in a small town farther down the coast, kept in what seemed like a large food-storage locker. From there they were taken in the back of a truck to Saigon and put in a former French Foreign Legion barracks. They stayed there for six weeks, and when the Japanese surrendered in August, their captors simply walked away. Joe and the others had been moved into a main POW camp in a neighborhood of railyards and warehouses near the Saigon River. Still no one came to liberate them. Meanwhile, fighting between the Vietnamese and the French had broken out. They could hear small arms fire and were afraid to show themselves in the street; Vietnamese couldn't tell French from British or Americans and were shooting every Westerner on sight.

On September 6, the Allies finally stepped in to rescue the American, British, Dutch, and Australian prisoners still in Saigon. They came with troops and transport planes, picked up the men, and flew them to Calcutta. Joe was there two weeks. They patched him up as best they could and gave him postcards to fill out for his parents and Gwen. For more than two months, she hadn't known whether he was alive or dead. All he could manage to write was "See you soon."

From India they brought him to the States. Joe landed in Miami in late September and finally was able to communicate with Gwen. But he had to stay in Florida for treatment: eye surgery, burn therapy, physical rehabilitation. Finally, he boarded a train to Charleston.

It was a long ride, and all the way he worried that he was just a "remnant" of the man Gwen married. What would she see in him now? As the train pulled into the station, he was more nervous than he ever had been or ever would be again. Yet, late in his long life, when he told me about that day, he couldn't recall a thing about their meeting. Not what Gwen wore, not what she said. He just remembered standing there, he and she. But we do know that Joe and Gwen were married another fifty-two years. So we can make an educated assumption and give them back the moment that memory erased.

As the train pulls in, Joe sees Gwen first, through the window. He steps gingerly onto the platform, trying not to seem thin, diminished. She's looking in the wrong direction, a car or so behind. Then she turns. She doesn't run; she walks slowly, arms open. He doesn't know whether to go to her or wait. He forgets to put down his satchel, so when she envelops him, his hug is awkward, one-handed. She laughs. He drops his bag, lays his right cheek on her left shoulder, and frames her face in his one good eye. Only then, and at last, Joe cries.

It was a Wednesday. The day before Thanksgiving 1945.

Going Home

Some memories rise like a fish in a dark lake, then disappear again, and we're left to wonder: Did that really happen? When I was maybe three years old, I rode a tricycle down some flagstone steps outside my grandparents' house, cut my head open, and had to be taken to the hospital for stitches. I'm pretty sure the story is true, but I don't remember anything from that day or for a long time after. Except this: my dad walking into the hospital room, his double-breasted coat unbuttoned, hair slicked back, a nervous grin splitting his face.

I must have been very glad to see him.

Do you recall the "Dirty Linen Boys," the five pilots who raised their hands in San Diego and said they would prefer not to fly in Commander E. O. Rigsbee's squadron? One was Brad Brooks, a California native who had already served two tours in the Aleutians. The other four had all been together on a previous combat tour. Royce Timmons transferred to another assignment stateside and stayed in the navy for twenty years.[481] Nick Carter and Sheldon Sutton went on to become aces.

The fifth was my father.

He came from Mississippi. His mother's people were once-wealthy landowners, she herself a music teacher and a southern belle in the soft-but-steely mold. From her he learned the piano, the violin, and the duties of the oldest son. One of them was to find his father, an affable pharmacist descended from physicians and alcoholics, on those many nights he went wherever the liquor led. From him, Dad learned the uses of charm and to drink at home.

Together with his younger brother, they lived in a white house on a hill. Like many, they were rich in the 1920s and broke in the 1930s. At age eight, Dad had his own car. At age ten, he walked two miles to school. At age fifteen he graduated from high school and won a scholarship to the local junior college. After that he wanted an education in life, so he got a job selling cars, taught himself guitar, and played in dance bands. He also acquired a nickname ("Kit") and fell in love with airplanes. His navy records show he had a private pilot's license when he enlisted, likely through the Civilian Pilot Training program. And he told of flying on contract for the rural electric company, skimming treetops after storms, looking for downed power poles.

He joined up six weeks after Pearl Harbor—maybe out of duty or patriotism, maybe for the adventure, maybe just to get away. At E-base in New Orleans, he met Nick Carter and Sheldon Sutton, and they spent the rest of the war together—through Pensacola, with its colonial architecture and blinding summer sun; to Oahu and VB-102, the first navy squadron to fly B-24s; and on to Guadalcanal for six months—as copilots. Dad brought a seabag and a violin case. Many evenings they built fires to keep back the bugs while he sat on a log and played.[482] The weather was hot and wet, day and night. The flying was difficult and dangerous. The squadron lost three dozen men.

When the rest were relieved in November 1943, the way home went through San Francisco. Years later, talking about a trip to the top of the Mark Hopkins, Dad said there was no feeling like coming home from the war, putting on your dress whites, heading out to a swank place, and, when the elevator doors opened, realizing that everyone in the room was looking at you. When I went to my first squadron reunion and met Sheldon Sutton, I told him the story. He said, "I was with him, and there's a reason your dad remembered so well. That was the night he met your mother."[483]

Catherine Merle Harrison was nineteen years old, a sophomore at Mills College in Oakland, a Catholic girls' school. The family story said that back home in Chicago, she had fallen in love with an Irish lawyer and her parents did not approve, so they sent her as far away as possible. Which is why she was standing there when the elevator opened—tall, beautiful, with a wide smile. Everyone called her Kay.

Within a week, Sheldon said, they decided to get married. Both went home to visit their families over Christmas and met up again in San Diego when Dad was ordered to VPB-117. Kay's parents were not happy; much worse than a respectable, if older, Chicago lawyer was this mysterious flyboy—from Mississippi, and not even a Catholic. Her mother came out to meet the prospective groom, went back to her hotel room, and cried. But Kay was willful and in love. They were married in February 1944. A college friend of hers was maid of honor; Nick Carter stood as best man.

They settled into a rented house, made friends, went to parties, and took short trips. A blurry photo from Lake Arrowhead shows Dad and three pilots in a rowboat, reenacting the scene of Washington crossing the Delaware. On the back, Kay wrote, "The Four Buffoons on the boat landing. You should have seen the facial expressions!"

A few more shots from those times survived, along with Kay's notes. Nick Carter with his wife and baby: "Those wonderful Carters Three!" Dad in his dress blues, hands behind his back, standing in front of a house: "Kit, looking just a little grim. Maybe he was thinking of the coming months, 'somewhere in the South Pacific.' August 13, 1944."

That evening he took off for Hawaii and went back to war. The big difference on this trip was the move from copilot to plane commander. He took the responsibility seriously. One of his men remembered that, before their first flight from Tinian, Dad gathered the crew together under the plane. He said, "We're going to do everything that's asked of us. And we're going to do it as well as we possibly can. But I want you all to know, I have a brand-new wife. I love her, and she loves me. And we're all going home."[484]

That first mission they flew into a typhoon and almost didn't make it back. On the second flight, they nearly ran out of gas. On the third, they lost an engine 750 miles out. December and January, flying from Leyte, was the worst. Some in the squadron said the Dirty Linen Boys kept getting the dangerous sectors more often, places like Cam Ranh Bay on the Indochina coast or Formosa. Gung ho guys like Nick and Sheldon reveled in it. Dad, I'm pretty sure, did not. But he went where they sent him, and he did have his moments.[485]

Coming back from Formosa one day, a collapsed fuel cell forced him to make an emergency landing on Luzon, close to the front-line fighting in the Battle of Lingayen Gulf. They set down on a grass field at dusk, in the midst of a firefight between marines and the Japanese. It went on all night, muzzle flashes lighting up the dark, the fighting ebbing and flowing. With what gas they had left, they kept one engine idling and manned the machine guns in the turrets, just in case. Toward dawn the noise started to die down, and at daylight the marines told them the perimeter was secure. Now, how to get home? They filled part of the wing tanks from fifty-five-gallon fuel drums the army brought. A half-track pulled the plane out of the mud, and the men pushed it to the top of a shallow rise. They revved the engines and aimed for the ruts gouged in the grass during their landing the night before. At the last instant Dad hit full flaps, and the plane lifted maybe five feet in the air. John Bullock was his copilot that day:

> Seventy knots is not flying speed, but the plane was hanging on the props and the wheels were on the way up as we left the ground, so there was no stopping now. Finally the airspeed reached 76 knots and we were getting to where the plane was holding its own. I looked at Kit and he started to smile as we swung around and flew over where we had just been.[486]

Another time, flying from Mindoro, Tom Hyland went to the Indochina coast and, finding no enemy opposition, got on the radio and dared the Japanese to come out and fight. "We'll be back tomorrow," he said, "and if you have any guts you will be too." Dad drew the same sector the next day. Some army fighters decided to tag along, out of sight, to see what would happen. The note in his logbook for February 25, 1945, says, "Cam Ranh Bay. Jumped by 7 fighters. Bait for P-38s." In the log of his plane captain, R. C. Strickland, the entry for that day says simply "Remember." By the time I met R. C., he couldn't.

Around camp, Dad moved slowly and didn't seem to get upset. Nick Carter, who gave everyone nicknames, called him "Old Shiftless." A tall guy with small hands and feet, long legs and fingers, and tiny, almost girlish ankles, he didn't walk so much as skim, arms swinging, gliding him forward. His bearing was not military. Didn't spit *or* polish. Hats that navy officers wore with formal uniforms had crisp crowns and peaks; Dad's was always scrunched and wrinkled, as if he'd maybe done it on purpose.

He read a lot. The few pictures from that tour show him, usually half dressed, almost always smiling. There's one of him and his men, taken in front of a bomber called the *Shady Lady*, probably on Mindoro. On the back, he lists everyone's names and then adds a note to Kay:

A motley looking crew, isn't it darling? Its boss doesn't help the picture any.
Kit

This was spring, and by then both the planes and the men were tired. Four times in March alone, Dad's log shows that mechanical problems forced him to make an emergency landing immediately after takeoff, with a full load of fuel and bombs. At this point, over two tours, he'd been in a war zone more than thirteen months and flown almost 120 combat missions. Art Elder once told me that some pilots who were assigned "hot sectors" along the Indochina coast would sometimes fly just offshore and reconnoiter with their binoculars rather than head further inland and risk finding the enemy up close.[487] Only later did I wonder whether he was trying to tell me something about Dad. If so, it doesn't matter. At that point I suspect my father was focused, more than anything, on simple survival for him and his crew. His last fitness report from squadron CO Roger Crowley said as much: "Lieutenant Kittrell has performed his regular duties as a Patrol Plane Commander in a satisfactory manner. He is a competent Patrol Plane Pilot, but is not too aggressive."[488]

Dad wasn't offended, because the day the report was filed—May 15, 1945—he was on a plane leaving Mindoro. Five flights and a week aboard a troop ship later, he made San Francisco again. Stuck there for another two weeks, he finally caught TWA to Chicago. The last entry in his log is a single word: "Home!"

Like most, he didn't talk about his time "out there." Only once did his mother ask about the war, and he said simply, "I hope I live long enough to forget it." He didn't, and he never flew a plane again. But as soon as Japan surrendered and he was released from active duty, he headed back south to pick up life where he left it.

Dad and Kay moved to Indianola, Mississippi, and he went back to selling cars. It was a small town, very southern, and surely very strange to her. Pregnant almost immediately, she returned to Chicago to deliver my older sister, Cathy, in 1946. I was born in February 1948, in Mississippi.

I was older than Dad ever was before I saw two pages in my mother's handwriting on stationery from Weber Chevrolet Company, Indianola, Mississippi:

> Last Will and Testament of Catherine Harrison Kittrell
>
> I, Catherine Harrison Kittrell, being of sound mind and dis-position, leave all my property and belongings, real and other-wise, to my children, Catherine Mary Sue Kittrell and Edward Joseph Kittrell. I also request that custody of the children, espe-cially of Catherine, be given to my parents, Mr. and Mrs. Joseph R. Harrison of 942 Lake Shore Drive, Chicago, Ill. (Whitehall 6839) and my brother Joseph R. Harrison, Jr.—all three of whom I consider executors of my will. . . .
>
> May it please the court to grant my wishes, especially regard-ing custody of my children, in the event of my death. There are no witnesses to this will but I beg the court to consider that I do not have time to secure them, as I am leaving on a trip to Biloxi in a few minutes and there is no one here to witness. But I myself am a witness before God to its authenticity.
>
> Signed,
> Catherine Harrison Kittrell
> October 24, 1948[489]

What happened? Why a will, so hastily written, without witnesses and, seemingly, without Dad's knowledge? Was she afraid? Was she upset? The language is appropriate legalese. Who told her what words to use? Why give custody to her family instead of her husband? And why not "especially" me, too, Mother? There are many possible, painful answers. The most likely is that, when it came to custody, she didn't want her children raised in the South. And as for why a will at all, she might have sensed something no one else could.

A little over two months later, she was diagnosed with cancer: lymphoblastoma. And she was pregnant again. Dad asked her to please take radiation, at the time about the only treatment doctors offered. Kay refused, because of the child she carried. Her parents became almost hysterical, taking her to experimental treatment centers where they found quacks, not cures. At some point she went back to Chicago and took my sister with her. Dad, who still had to work, stayed part of the time in Mississippi with me. Doctors waited as long as they could before taking the baby early, at seven months. My sister Rita died two days later. By then the cancer had spread to Kay's stomach and liver, her bones and her brain. She died in late August 1949, about the time she should have delivered her second daughter. She was twenty-five years old.[490]

Dad never spoke of her, period. So I know almost nothing—how her voice sounded, her favorite song, her best friend. While researching this book, I sent letters to every surviving member of her class at Mills, more than one hundred women. I explained about the book and about her. I said I'd be grateful for anything they could share, no matter how small. I got many lovely replies: "Your story is very touching. And I hope you have, by now, gotten answers to your many questions."[491] But nobody recalled her.

I have her eyes. I was her baby. And she has always been, for me, a well in which light never reaches the bottom. Calling out and hearing only echoes.

After Kay died, Dad, my sister, and I lived with her parents in Chicago. Our grandparents doted on us but didn't bother to hide their distaste for Dad. They deeply resented his taking her away, as if that had somehow caused the cancer. The tension was evident, even to a small child.

They talked Dad into interviewing for management jobs with companies their friends worked for, but it was just not him. He started selling cars again and, after some time, began seeing Kay's first cousin, Lorraine Jung. She was engaged at the time, whip smart, teaching college history and finishing her PhD thesis. She never turned it in, and she never taught again. Instead, she and Dad married in 1952. Shortly before he died, I asked why. She said, "Because he was the most interesting man I ever met. And because you and your sister needed a mother, badly."

So that's who she became: Mom. She and Dad had three more girls, and she taught all five of us to think and to speak for ourselves. She always assumed we'd all be spectacular at whatever we wanted to do. After I was grown and a father myself, I started riding a bike to work in good weather, just for exercise. Mom was watching the Olympics with one of my sisters when the bicycle racing came on.

"Edward could do that," she said.

"Mom, these are the Olympics," my sister laughed. "These guys train for years and years. They're the best in the world."

She said, "I know, but he could do that if he wanted."

It was the same for all of us. She didn't care what honors we might or might not win. Those were other people's opinions. What counted was what you believed about yourself.

It was a good strategy, because before long she knew we would need all of that, and more. We had moved to the beach house in Indiana, and I remember adults coming over, loud talking, glasses we weren't supposed to drink from. Men in the squadron said Dad did not have a drinking problem when they knew him. But sometime after the war, it started. You could blame it on genetics—his father, his physician uncle, other relatives. You could blame it on his troubled family life growing up. Or on the stress of two combat tours. Or on losing his first wife. All those things are true. Also true is that you can always find reasons, and none of them really matter.

After a year or so, a Chevrolet dealership in a small Illinois town came up for sale. Dad heard about it and bought the business—buildings, cars, parts, everything—for $3,000 down, $20,000 total. He'd realized his only real ambition since he'd been a teenager: a dealership of his own, with his name on the building.

It was the heyday of the American automobile, and Dad reveled in it. He liked driving brand-new cars; his always had every gadget and were painted yellow or purple or turquoise. Every fall, he kept the next year's models hidden until the day of the official unveiling in the showroom, complete with free apple cider and donuts. He liked people too. He once told me to "take folks as you find them, not as you want them to be." Maybe the best advice I ever got. He read widely and could discuss the Cold War and the price of corn with equal ease.

Because he liked cars and he liked people, he saw himself not so much a salesman as a matchmaker, pairing customers with the sedans and station wagons and convertibles he knew would make them happy. To him it was both an art and a business. His salesmen always brought wavering customers to Dad to close a deal. I remember an old farmer leaving one such session and walking back to the showroom, where his wife waited on a couch. "Well, what happened?" she asked. "I'm not exactly sure," he said, "but I think we just bought a car."

At home, he and Mom always were an odd pairing. Dad was never in a hurry. He spoke slowly too; the drawl had disappeared sometime after the move from Mississippi, but sentences still trickled rather than tumbled from his mouth. He kept most opinions to himself. Mom, however, never minded telling you what she thought, even if you didn't ask. She was short and stocky, moved quickly, and never doubted a decision once she made it. That was true even about her marriage. There was shouting sometimes; more than once she filled a suitcase. But I don't think she ever seriously considered leaving. What would we do without her? And vice versa?

The drinking continued downhill but rarely in public; instead, he stayed home and poured Hiram Walker, ice, no water. Mom tried different strategies; none worked. As a teenager I confronted him several times: Why was he killing himself like this? Didn't he care about his kids? He sat across the kitchen table, staring at his hands. He probably was thinking that I didn't have to go out, find him in some bar, and drag him home, as he had done for his own father. What did I have to complain about? But what he said was "I don't have a problem." That was that.

By the time I left for college, I knew it would never get better, and I would never live there again. I felt guilty and sad for my sisters and for Mom. But I couldn't wait to pack the car and pull away.

Five years later, I was married myself, and before long we had a boy of our own. Dad was thrilled; the Kittrells would live on. Two years later, our second son was born. We lived outside Chicago, three hours from

Geneseo, and visited often. The boys remember the goofy chaos of that house: the incredible clutter, Grandpa walking around in his underwear, Grandma teaching them how to play poker. "Ante up, boys."

In late 1978, Dad began complaining of back pain but never bothered to see a doctor. By the time he did, the prostate cancer had spread. Maybe he fell back on some of what he learned in the squadron, because the disease seemed to summon something in him. "We're all going home." The drinking slacked off; the pain medication probably helped. He often seemed oddly at ease.

I remember the Fourth of July 1980. My sister and her husband lived on a couple of acres outside town, and it had become a tradition to have family fireworks there. Mom even got a commercial permit so we could shoot off the really big ones. Dad sat in a folding chair on the lawn, his face reflecting explosions that maybe reminded him of ack-ack. He died quietly the first week of December. For a long time after he was gone, Mom sat by the bed, patting his arm.

And if he were here now, what would I say? What would I want to know?

The heart, like the eye, is drawn to absence, the missing picket in the fence. But I would not ask him to fill in the blanks. Not about his own father. Not about that day with the fighters over Cam Ranh Bay. Not even about my mother, who she was and what had happened.

I would want it to be easy. I would ask what it was like to be a boy in a dance band, watching grown women glide by all evening.

I would ask about campfire concerts in the jungle, notes from his violin rising like smoke, like prayers.

I would ask about celestial navigation—staring at cold sparks from some cosmic fire and finding his way home across a thousand miles of dark ocean.

I would ask what was his favorite car ever and why.

I would ask whether he remembered sunsets on the lake and swimming to the sandbar. With me.

In my office are three daily reminders of Dad. One is the silk survival map from his flight case, now framed on my wall. On the left-hand side, in bright green, you see Borneo, the Indochina coast, the Philippines. But much is totally blank ocean. It reminds me how little I know, even now, of his life. Tinian, Leyte, Mindoro; Mississippi, my mother, bourbon glowing in a glass. They are pinpoints, splotches in an otherwise empty sea.

The second reminder is a photo, taken the day he married Mom. He has squatted down, and I am standing next to him. He's smiling, wearing a suit with a carnation in his lapel. I am four years old, in a little open-collared suit of my own. Just out of the frame, his left hand holds my right. My other arm is wrapped around his neck, and I'm smiling too.

I loved him, then and still.

The third memento is also a picture. Mom kept the dealership going for a dozen years after Dad died, and there is a photo taken not long before she sold it. The building with the big "KITTRELL" sign is in the background. Parked in front is a classic '57 Chevy that someone traded in. I'm smiling, leaning on the front fender; inside the car are all three of my sons, mugging for the camera. They have since grown into thoroughly admirable men—husbands, fathers, and friends. Dad would be proud.

When they were little and we visited Geneseo, once the boys were in bed, Dad would get out a beat-up old Gibson electric guitar that he bought used from a sailor around the time I was born. I had gone to college in the 1960s, and being a semiprofessional singer was a great way to meet girls, so naturally I took it up. Folk songs, the blues—those were Dad's favorites, mine too. So once the house was quiet, he would refill a mug with whiskey and ice, hand me the Gibson, and ask me to sing. He liked the sad ones best, like "St. James Infirmary."

I'd go on as long as he liked, but usually after an hour or so we'd have to help him to bed. It got to be a ritual, one I didn't always look forward to.

After Dad died, I inherited the Gibson, but for more than twenty-five years it stayed in a case at the back of a closet. Then I pulled it out and took it to a guitar restorer. He said he could make it look like new, perfect. I said that wouldn't feel right. He said he could research exactly when it had been made. I said I didn't need to know the history.

I just wanted to hold it, to hear it. To play songs I loved once and learned to love again.

If They Could Speak

They are almost all gone now, and they haunt me. Especially, sometimes, the ones you haven't met yet.

In the book prepared for the squadron's first reunion in 1983, there is a photo of a handsome officer in his thirties standing in front of a tent, pencil in his pocket, pipe in his mouth, smile on his lips. The caption reads, "Lt. Cmdr. R. M. Faxon of Groton, Harvard, Boston, VPB-117, and the West of Tokyo Officers Club."[492]

They got it nearly right. He prepped at Milton Academy, not Groton, and lived in Quincy, not Boston. But Bob Faxon, or "Fax," was just what the caption implied—old school, blue blood. His ancestors had been in Massachusetts for more than three hundred years; he ran his family's real estate business and the community fund for decades after the war.[493] Yet the smile in the picture said more than anything. He was a gentle man and made friends easily. As communications officer, he knew almost everyone in the outfit. And he was there for the worst of it, to and through V-J Day.

The picture eventually led me to his daughters. They shared memories and his letters to their mother—funny and loving, full of tidbits about daily life. From Mindoro, dated June 19, 1945:

> It always gives me a kick to go down to the strip in the early morning while the stars are still out and watch the planes roar off at dawn. This morning the sunrise was out of this world. The sun came up from behind the mountains in a typical Maxfield Parrish "sunburst"—golden rays stretched out till they blended with the

pink of the sky on each side. At the foot of the strip a small bit of rainbow was sticking right up, and above it were red, white and blue clouds.[494]

He didn't say that he often went down to the strip at dusk as well, to wait for the planes coming home. Just five days earlier, Jerry Dougan's crew had disappeared on its mission to Ha Tien. I think of Fax staring into the dark, with still no word. Three days after he wrote the letter, Stan Sayre's crew crashed after takeoff. Fax arranged for Sally Brownlee's burial. And barely a week later, Bob Hepting and Joe Lowder and their crew never came back from Cam Ranh Bay.

There is little about all this in his letters, but once in a while it came out. On July 30, 1945:

In the afternoon I was about to write, when a message came that one of our planes was returning to base with two wounded aboard. You sort of lose the train of thought. Last Sunday I was checking up on arrangements for memorial services for one of our crews. I had gone down to the office [and] a young Red Cross girl worker was there looking for her brother who had promised to come and see her in Manila. She told me his name, and he was a member of the missing crew.

The services were not to be held till 4:30 in the afternoon so I took her over to the Army hospital so that the nurses could put her up for the night and kind of look after her. She had been in the Jap concentration camp in Manila for three years. She was a bit thin, but a very good sport. I picked her up in time for the services.[495]

After he finished the letter, he learned that one of the two wounded men mentioned in the earlier radio message—Frederick Thomas, a waist gunner in Conrad Leonard's crew—had died. A single shell from a Japanese machine gun had left him lying on the deck between the guns, his entrails in his hands.[496] He became the sixty-eighth and final member of VPB-117 killed in the line of duty.[497] Bob Faxon did not have to write the families of those fliers; that was the commanding officer's job. But he handled just about everything else. And it all took a toll.

When he finally came home, he was still a sweet, loving husband and father. But he had trouble adjusting. "He couldn't take it all in," one of his daughters said. He had a nervous breakdown. Took electroshock treatments on and off. Drank too much after dinner. Today, he would be diagnosed with posttraumatic stress disorder. But back then, there was no such thing. So he soldiered on—president of the board of the local hospital, director of the Chamber of Commerce and the Quincy Savings Bank, member of the Harvard Club and the Historical Society. An accomplished sailor, happiest out on the water.[498]

When Fax died in 1978 at the age of sixty-nine, the mayor of Quincy said the whole town was "saddened by the death of this wonderful man. It's a terrible loss. He was truly a gentleman, a very calming influence." At the mayor's request, flags in Quincy flew at half-staff.[499]

Armour Burgan was raised in Michigan's Upper Peninsula, small-town copper country near Lake Superior. He left high school in his senior year to join the navy and ended up as tail gunner in Nick Carter's crew. He was handsome, quiet. Did his job, never complained. But a few weeks after he returned home, his mother called Carter's crew chief, Joe Papp. She asked, "What happened to you boys out there?"[500]

Armour was "acting funny." He "wasn't himself." He took off with his motorcycle and a friend, working in Alaska for a time. But when he came back, he was worse. Finally, he was admitted to a Veterans Administration (VA) hospital in Tomah, Wisconsin. They gave him shock treatments, like they did with Fax, after which he was "very quiet" when the family visited. This went on for a couple of years, until his father thought Armour seemed better. He asked to have his son discharged, but the doctors refused. Armour's father went home, came back with a lawyer, and returned with his son.[501]

Armour worked in his father's gas station. Had several lady friends but never married. Loved to hunt and to fish for lake trout. He was quiet and kind. Literally wouldn't hurt a fly: whenever Armour found one in his house, he would catch it in his hands and set it free outside.[502]

As he got older, he began having problems with his legs. Eventually the VA doctors told him they would likely have to amputate. Armour said he didn't want that to happen, but nobody saw what was coming. In February 2008, he backed his pickup into a turnaround on a wooded, dead-end road—so it wouldn't be in anyone's way or block the snowplow when it came—took his deer rifle from the back, and shot himself in the head. He was buried with military honors.[503]

Don Golden was older than most in the squadron. He'd earned his master's degree in math, taught college, and joined a flying club before the navy hired him to help cadets unravel the intricacies of trigonometry and navigation. Then he got a draft notice of his own. But his commanding officer didn't want to lose him, so he made Don a lieutenant junior grade within a week.[504]

Later, E. O. Rigsbee commandeered Don as one of the first members of VPB-117. In the squadron he quickly became known as "the Professor" because of his teaching background. He had an air about him: wore a pith helmet, smoked cigarettes through a holder clenched in his teeth. Don became Harold McDonald's navigator and always kept two position fixes during flights. The first was what he told his pilot, the second was their actual position—which was always closer to home base, "to keep on the safe side."[505]

Within the squadron as a whole, he was probably best remembered for setting up officers clubs in the combat zone. His first, on Tinian, was well received. But when Rigsbee asked him to repeat the feat on Tacloban, it was perhaps Don's finest hour. During those early dangerous weeks in the Philippines, when they were still living aboard the *Currituck* and enduring almost nightly bombing raids, he spent his spare time in a launch visiting navy ships in the crowded harbor. The ships had liquor, and he had cash from the squadron's coffers. He also asked pilots, during checkout flights after their planes had been repaired, to visit other islands and pick up more "supplies."

He commandeered a Quonset hut, had a bar built, and got some tables. Nothing fancy, no decorations—they didn't need that. But his master-stroke may have been the name. As a navigator Don knew his longitude, so he christened his creation the "West of Tokyo Officers Club." Had a sign made up. Printed membership cards—men I met decades later still had theirs.

The grand opening was Christmas Day 1944. Don had gone to another island and brought back six WAVEs to "add a little color" to the festivities. Then he brought marines in to guard them. The club was an instant success. It was soon making a profit of $6,000 a month and became one of the largest in the Pacific.[506]

When he wasn't flying missions or managing the club, Don also, in the words of a fellow officer, "taught mathematics to the ensigns in the squadron along the lines of probability and chance."[507] Every month he sent money home to his mother, and once she wrote back saying, "I looked it up, and you're sending me a lot more than the Navy is paying you." By the time he left he'd netted an extra $4,000 playing cards.[508]

Don came back, met his wife, Betty, and returned to Phoenix. He taught at first; then he became personnel manager for the Phoenix Union High School District for many years. He and Betty had two daughters and enjoyed golf and going to the racetrack. Just for fun, he graded geometry papers for an online high school until he was ninety-two. Don died on May 4, 2012—ten days shy of his 101st birthday.[509]

Brad Brooks never said much. Never got excited. If you were looking for someone to play him in a wartime movie, you would have placed your first call to Gary Cooper. He was a pilot's pilot; before the war he was an instructor in the PBY flying boats at Pensacola. And after Pearl Harbor he'd been sent to the Aleutians. During his first tour, in June 1942, the Japanese landed on the American island of Kiska and Brooks's squadron, VP-41, was ordered to "bomb the enemy out" of there. Because they flew agonizingly slow and lightly armed PBYs, they approached from behind cloud cover, flying single file. Once over the harbor they dove into the open, dropped their bombs, and tried to pull back up into the clouds as quickly as possible. Flak was murderous. This went on for three days and became known as the "Kiska Blitz." The tactic was insane but effective.[510] Brooks won a Distinguished Flying Cross.[511]

On his second tour, he was executive officer of VB-136 and flew PV-1 Venturas—fast, erratic twin-engine bombers with a reputation as pilot killers. Once, low on fuel, he decided to land at an alternate field, where he had never been. As was often the case in the Aleutians, the ceiling was zero. On final approach, with no strip in sight and almost out of gas, the port engine began to miss. PVs couldn't fly on just one. What else could go wrong? Brooks looked at his copilot and said, "Bet the food's lousy too."

In VPB-117 Brooks named his plane *Sweet Marie*, after his wife. One of his copilots was Greg Roberson, barely five feet tall and known as Robie or, inevitably, Shorty. The other was Jack Sager, a baby-faced ensign from Detroit who still called his wife his "girl" and whose favorite curse word was "Nurtz!" Brooks himself quickly earned a reputation as a first-rate flier and a very cool customer. Almost too cool. Most pilots shared a certain fatalism. They'd seen friends fly into mountains or fall into the ocean. They knew that an average PB4Y squadron lost one-tenth of its planes every month. For some, brash talk helped defend against the dread that could pop up anytime like flak, punching holes in your resolve.

During such bull sessions Brooks said nothing, as usual. But in the air, he seemed truly impervious to fear. He routinely asked his copilots to tell him when they thought he was taking stupid chances. Coming from some plane commanders, that request might have made men question his judgment. Coming from Brooks, it fostered a contagious confidence. The crew knew he would listen to them if they were worried. And they knew Brooks would always find a way.[512]

Take December 8. Rounding the southern tip of Luzon two hundred feet off the water, Brooks came literally face-to-face with a Japanese destroyer. Shells flew; the Liberator's engines yowled; Brooks's legs and arms jabbed at the controls, taking evasive action. Somehow avoiding a hit, he dropped down to one hundred feet and entered a nearby inlet, now with six Zeros on his tail. Off to their right, enemy antiaircraft batteries fired at navy carrier planes attacking Japanese ships in the harbor. The melee helped shake the Zeros, and Brooks took advantage to set a course for home, jogging in the overcast around mountains on the island of Masbate. On the approach to Tacloban in a ferocious rainstorm, seeing the field through the windshield was impossible; only one tiny space at the bottom was clear. So Brooks bent forward with his chin above his knees, like a jockey, and rode *Sweet Marie* home.[513]

Two days later, they went out again. This search sector was further south, stretching into the China Sea between the Philippines and Indochina. Over open ocean halfway through the flight, the crew spotted a Topsy, the Japanese version of a DC-2 transport plane. It was at six thousand feet and didn't see the Liberator below and behind. Brooks dropped his bombs to lighten the load, added power, and began climbing. It took twenty minutes and was like stalking a deer downwind. The quarry never had a clue. Brooks closed to within two hundred feet, the bow and the deck turrets set the Topsy on fire, and it crashed into the sea.

Four hours later on the homeward leg, Brooks and the crew were two hours from Tacloban when a Dinah, a Japanese twin-engine reconnaissance plane and interceptor, crossed directly in front of their bow two hundred yards away. This one was even easier than the Topsy. Less than one hundred rounds set an engine and wing on fire. The Dinah stuttered and fell one thousand feet, crashing into a native hut. Two for two on the day, without a shot fired in their direction.

That was about to change. Almost immediately after the Dinah went down, someone spotted five Zeros high, at two o'clock. Two broke off from the formation and lined up on the Liberator, head-on. Some American fliers believed that all the good Japanese pilots had been killed by this point in the war; those left were all scared or green, or both. These two were neither. The first Zero came straight in. It knocked out both inboard engines, wrecked the turning track on the top turret, and shot out the right rudder controls. The crew fought back and set the Zero on fire. But with only two engines and no top turret, the PB4Y1 was now helpless, like a half-conscious sailor who's lost a bar fight but is somehow still standing.

The second Zero destroyed another engine and splintered the pilot's compartment with 20-mm cannon shells. The wind rushed in; shrapnel and Bakelite and plexiglass swirled. Brooks, Roberson, and crew chief Sheldon Hooper were all seriously wounded. Robie called out for ditching stations; Brooks tried to gain control over a plane that now had no flaps, no right rudder, and was falling fast.[514] Everyone in the crew headed aft except

Jack Sager. He didn't have his earphones on, so he hadn't heard Robie's order. His first warning came when he looked out the navigator's window and saw they were only twenty feet off the water. He immediately jumped up on the plotting table, put his back to the bulkhead separating him from the pilots, and loosened the emergency escape hatch over his head.

Robie and Brooks kept flying all the way down. The Liberator's outline on the water grew larger and larger until the plane crashed into its shadow at 120 knots. The tail touched first, almost gently. A second later there was a tremendous wrench, the bow bored below the waves, the stern split off just behind the bomb bay, and everything started sinking. The next thing Jack Sager knew, he was ten feet underwater, trying to claw his way through the escape hatch. His pants were caught on something; he couldn't get loose. He reached for his wife's picture in his pocket, one last look. Then he thought, "What the hell am I doing? I have to get out of here!" Somehow he wriggled free and made it to the surface.

There he found six others who had been thrown clear on impact. Missing was mechanic Melvin Long, who was last seen trying to work the life raft free; gunner Jim Tedrowe; and radioman Vergil Bolton, who was only on the flight because regular crewman Jim Nelson was sick that morning. Together with Robie and Brooks, they went down with the plane, which sank in maybe three minutes. Thanks to Long, though, the rest had a raft. They swam to it and began to climb or pull each other in. Then they looked up and saw the Zero still there.[515]

The Buddhist concept of karma says all our actions, good or bad, have consequences. In American, "what goes around comes around." On patrol near Iwo Jima in October, Brad Brooks had come across a raft full of Japanese crewmen from a downed plane. Throughout the war in the Pacific, both sides often strafed survivors in the water. But Brooks gave the Japanese a pass that day. It was an unusual enough decision to rate an on-air thank-you from Tokyo Rose. Now, six weeks later and almost two thousand miles away, here were the survivors of Brooks's own crew—hurt, soaked, scared, bobbing on a yellow rubber bull's-eye as the Zero circled above them. The pilot dropped down near the water and came on. Killing them all would take less than a minute. He buzzed the raft, banked, and flew on.[516]

The seven were still in serious trouble, though. Hooper, the crew chief, was hurt worst, with a bad wound in his right arm and shoulder. Almost everyone else except Sager had serious injuries from the battle or the crash or both. Night was coming on when a lone Filipino in an outrigger sailboat came abreast and threw them a line. He towed them through the dark for eight hours, reaching the small island of Molocaboc about midnight. The islanders dressed the crew's wounds as best they could, fed them, and let them sleep for a few hours. Next day, in two boats manned by Filipinos, they sailed again for several hours to Bantayan Island, where there were doctors. Seven doctors, in fact, all of whom had fled Manila when the Japanese invaded. The crew was given a hero's welcome, quartered in the home of the mayor, and given the best possible care. The doctors worried most about Hooper's arm, fearing he might lose it if he didn't get to a hospital.

After two days, a message was sent to the squadron through the guerilla network. When they got no reply and after waiting another week, Sager, bombardier Miles Sullivan, and a marine pilot also stranded on the island decided to rescue themselves. Borrowing an outrigger sailboat, Sager navigated their way to Leyte in seventeen hours. Near the end the wind and their spirits sagged; the last fifteen miles took five hours. Approaching an army command post in the dark, they were nearly shot out of the water by gunners expecting a Japanese attack that night. From there they hitched rides on landing craft and a PT boat back to Tacloban. Two days later, on Christmas, a PBY flew to Bantayan and brought back the rest.

Sheldon Hooper was sent to a hospital ship where doctors told him they could save his arm. Jack Sager was summoned for congratulations from Admiral Frank D. Wagner.[517] Brad Brooks was awarded the Navy Cross posthumously. The citation said that, despite being seriously wounded, he ditched "with such superb skill that the lives of the majority of his crew were saved. His actions on this occasion showed the highest degree of professional skill, heroic courage under fire and determined devotion to duty."[518] The remains of his plane and his men lie under forty feet of water in Concepcion Bay east of Panay Island, 11-15N, 123-06E.

Bud Buchheim grew up on a small farm in South Dakota, and on the day he left to go to college, the first ever to do so in his family, he filled a pint jar with dirt from his father's fields to remind him of where he came from.[519] In his sophomore year he was hog-tied by calculus, and a navy recruiter pounced. He soon got his first airplane ride and in June 1944 earned his Wings of Gold at Pensacola.

He arrived on Mindoro in late April 1945 as copilot/navigator in Walt Greene's crew. Their scariest mission came in July as part of a two-plane strike to Ha Tien harbor, where they sank three Japanese merchant ships.[520] He also was a good friend of Jerry Dougan, who had disappeared on a flight to the same place a month earlier, and lived in the tent next to his. Bud had to sort through Jerry's things and send them home to his mother. He said he later regretted not delivering them personally.

The GI Bill let Bud finish his college degree and go on to a Lutheran seminary. He spent eighteen years in his first parish, later became a bishop, and then taught at a seminary before retiring. I've visited him and his wife, Dona, and we correspond frequently. In one of our early emails, talking about Jerry Dougan and his crew, he wrote, "I think about that quite a bit. Those of us who survived really don't know why. We know that it wasn't because we were the nicest or the bravest. . . . It's too bad we can't hear from them. If they could speak, what do you think they might say?"[521]

Reverend Buchheim is ninety-six years old, and when we correspond, he always signs off, "Peace, Bud."

Hawaii was still America, but barely, and it was the most exotic place many of the men of VPB-117 had ever seen. Sharks in the shallow water at the end of the runway, like the crocodile waiting for Captain Hook.[522] Cliff-hanging bus rides over the Pali into Honolulu.[523] Men lined up outside whorehouses at 9 a.m. on a Wednesday morning.

And then there was John Bourchier. He was an exotic himself, a guy other guys tell stories about. He left home at age eighteen and joined the navy. Starting as an ordinary seaman on the aircraft carrier USS *Saratoga*, he later applied for flight training. In 1938, he became a naval aviation pilot, an enlisted man with wings. Since then he'd flown everything the navy owned, served two combat tours in the Pacific, received his officer's commission in January 1944, and spent the previous six months at Kaneohe as the test pilot for all Liberators. When VPB-117 came for its final six weeks of training, Rigsbee had him transferred to the squadron as its nineteenth pilot.

During his decade in the navy he'd been everywhere: Guantanamo, Newfoundland, Iceland, Norfolk, Bermuda, New Caledonia, Fiji, Espiritu Santo, and, often, Oahu.[524] He was said to have been the West Coast navy boxing champ.[525] But the best story, the one that made Bourchier a legend, was about the madam.

The sale of sex wholesale was maybe the most exotic thing of all about Hawaii. Before the war, brothels had served soldiers, sailors, and local plantation workers. They were relatively low key and generally tolerated by the authorities. But the tidal wave of troops and the coming of martial law turned what had been a cottage industry into big business. The military believed a regulated trade would help morale and keep venereal disease rates low. The island's elite went along with the plan, as long as the whores and their customers were kept away from better neighborhoods.

The epicenter was Hotel Street in Chinatown. And because blackout rules prevented nighttime visits, business was done in the daytime. Seven days a week, morning until night, men stood on the sidewalks. After waiting sometimes for hours, they reached the stairs leading to the second floor of the brothel. At the top they paid the standard fee, $3 for a three-minute encounter, and were led to the "bullring"—three interconnected rooms. In the first a man undressed; in the second he met with the prostitute; in the third he put his clothes back on. It was all very efficient and very profitable. During the war, many prostitutes made $40,000 a year, twenty times what the average woman earned. The madams for whom they worked cleared $150,000 (some twice that much).[526]

But John Bourchier—tall, thin, disarmingly handsome—wasn't one to stand in line, especially for a woman. He knew Oahu as well as he knew the navy. And by the time the squadron arrived, he was the live-in lover of a madam who owned one of the island's biggest brothels. Just scuttlebutt at first, the story was soon confirmed.[527] A squadron officer told me about the time he hitched a ride from Kaneohe into Honolulu with Bourchier, who took him to meet the madam at her expensive home in the hills overlooking Waikiki. Years later, the guest could remember few details, including the lady's name or what she looked like. He just recalled standing on the veranda, soaking it in. The breeze was fresh, the view impressive. The hostess was gracious. The talk was small. The visit was short.[528]

As it turned out, those weeks were the high-water mark for whoredom in Honolulu. By the summer of 1944, with the threat of another Japanese attack nil, civilian authorities began chipping away at the strictures of martial law. One of their first acts was to reassert control over the vice district. On September 21, 1944, the governor ordered all the regulated brothels closed. It was the end of an era. A week later, the squadron left for the front. The madam gave Bourchier a gold Rolex to remember her by.[529]

Out in the war zone, he continued to find and fascinate women. One young flier remembered being startled by a noise as he arrived for a 3 a.m. preflight check on his plane. Bourchier was inside with a young lady, to whom he had promised to show the "golden rivet."[530] He also earned a reputation as an excellent pilot, smooth and rarely rattled. Over Indochina he shot up a Japanese fighter that then tried to ram him, missing the Liberator by less than fifty feet before crashing in flames into the ocean.[531] He rotated home sometime in May 1945, and that's the last anyone saw of him.

The stories didn't stop though. He was said to have flown in the Berlin airlift. He left the navy sometime in the early 1950s. He was married four or five times—no one was quite sure—and fathered five children. He worked for a time selling insurance. In his fifties he owned a motorcycle and took up skydiving. Which brings us to the final story, and this time there were witnesses.

In February 1975, at age fifty-nine, Bourchier made his fifty-ninth jump near Pittsburgh. He left the plane at twelve thousand feet, and at three thousand feet, as planned, he pulled the rip cord. The main chute didn't deploy, and he reached behind his back trying to get it open. The motion caused him to barrel roll, losing altitude and precious seconds. At one thousand feet, he stopped spinning and faced the ground. He yanked the rip cord for the reserve attached to his chest but forgot to pull the chute from its pack; it never opened either. At that point, it might not have mattered anyway.

This man who lived fast all his life hit the ground at 130 miles per hour. The impact partially buried him. And, in a final burst of irony that probably wouldn't have surprised him, at that instant his parachute opened. The silk bloomed a few feet above the ground, before settling over him like a shroud.[532]

Marshall Beals was a bombardier, which meant his station in the plane was below and in front of the pilots, just behind the nose gunner. On one long flight, he looked out a small window and saw through a break in the clouds the last remaining Japanese battleship task force, trying to use monsoon weather to escape to the safety of Tokyo Bay. Planes from the squadron tracked them for four days but were forbidden to attack. The army sent its own bombers, which failed to sink the Japanese.[533]

To help while away the long missions in cramped quarters, he kept a small library of paperback books on a shelf he made himself. Marshall came back home and worked for many years as a tool designer at the Rock Island Arsenal in Illinois, where he grew up. After he retired, when religious groups came to his door, he would listen politely for a while and then say, "I found God in the belly of a B-24 bomber in the South Pacific, and that was the best church I ever went to."[534] He lived to be ninety and was buried with military honors in the Rock Island National Cemetery on Arsenal Island.[535]

Ralph Castleton was a devout Mormon and an enthusiastic flier. He'd gotten his pilot's license while he was still at Utah State, which is also where he met Emelyn Reading at a sorority dance. By then he'd already graduated and joined the navy, stationed in Corpus Christi. That's where he proposed to her, on the beach beneath a beautiful moon. They were married on her twentieth birthday in May 1943.

Their first home was a room behind a garage. Ralph was an instructor but joined VPB-117 when it was originally organized in San Diego. Remembering those months, Emelyn said, "We were all very young, and very much in love. And everything happened so fast." Then he was gone.[536]

Ralph served as the squadron's executive officer under Tom Mulvihill and, later, Roger Crowley. He also flew more than fifty combat missions, including one to Hong Kong harbor looking for a Japanese battleship that wasn't there. On the trip back, they were almost out of fuel, and enemy antiaircraft gunners in Manila nearly brought them down. Coming into Tacloban they were maybe thirty feet off the ground when a battle-damaged fighter jumped in front of them. Ralph pulled up, went around, and told the crew to go to the bomb bay. "If I open the doors," he said, "bail out because if we run out of gas, we'll crash." They made it down, and seconds after they landed all four engines quit.[537]

His bow gunner on that flight and all the others was Gil Ragland, born and raised in the Texas panhandle. He'd joined the navy when he was nineteen; married his sweetheart, Pauline, in 1944 in San Diego; and left for the front five months later. On one mission, the top of his turret was blown off by a Japanese fighter. To get him out, they opened the back door of the turret, and a two-hundred-mile-per-hour wind blew him back into the plane. Another time, flying up the Saigon River, they had to stay just eight feet above the water to avoid enemy gunners onshore.[538]

Ralph Castleton returned in 1945, got a degree from Stanford University, and lived and worked in California for many years as an executive for several different companies. He and Emelyn remained active in the Mormon Church. He died in 2011.[539] Gil Ragland came home and farmed for more than sixty years, raising cotton and cows. All his life he loved to dance, and he kept it up well into his eighties.[540] He died in 2012, aged eighty-eight.[541]

But earlier, on the fiftieth anniversary of the end of World War II, for a middle school project in Kansas someone asked members of the squadron to write about their experiences. Gil sent his reply to a young man named Jamie, talking about how the squadron was formed, where they flew, and what they did. And he closed his letter this way:

> I learned that war is fear, war is homesickness, war is sadness, war
> is hunger, war is horror, war is anger, war is tears, and war is hell.
>   But, as I kneel and feel the warm sun on my back, and handle
> some of the fertile soil on my farm, or as I watch my two-year-old

grandson try to wear one of my old boots, or watch my beautiful granddaughter run toward me with arms outstretched, I know my effort was worth it.

But, Jamie, I left a bit of my soul in the South Pacific.[542]

Jack Parker was born and raised on Florida's Gulf Coast, near Clearwater. A picture of him at twelve years old shows a big smile, with maybe a hint of mischief around the eyes. He weighed only 140 pounds in high school but was a good athlete. And he had a way of finding fun. His father's 1928 Model A Ford had long since seen better days, hadn't run in several years, and was parked in the side yard at the family's house. One day after his dad left for work, Jack convinced three friends to help him resurrect the jalopy. They got the engine running, sawed off the roof, painted the body bright red, and installed whitewall tires. Then they went out and bought four derby hats, cigars, white shirts, and black ties. They pulled up in front of the house as his father was arriving home from work, and his younger brother, Buddy, remembered it as the happiest he ever saw Jack.[543]

Then Pearl Harbor happened. Jack was sixteen and wanted to join the navy right away, but it took some time before his father finally gave permission. When he went to sign up, the navy told him that "Jack" was a nickname, so he became "John Robeson Parker" on his enlistment form. By early January 1945 he'd found his way to VPB-117, based at Tacloban. A machinist's mate, a gunner, and a substitute for squadron crewmen who were sick or wounded, he had flown four missions—once strafing a cargo ship and another time encountering a Japanese fighter that only made one run before turning away.[544]

On January 28, he replaced a gunner in Robert White's crew who had been hurt on an earlier flight. That day they drew the Formosa sector, almost always a hot spot. And shortly before noon they found two Japanese cargo ships off the coast. Dropping down to a few hundred feet and making a bombing run, they sank the first, with Jack at the starboard waist gun. Then they turned and went back for the second ship. But this time, they were the ones on the receiving end. First one and then a second engine was hit by return fire. Crippled and falling fast, the Liberator hit the water and broke apart.[545]

Four crew members, including the pilot and one copilot, were never seen again. The other seven were plucked from the ocean by the Japanese navy, taken to local headquarters, and interrogated by the Kenpeitai, military police famous for their brutality.[546] One crewman injured in the crash died a few days later. Because he was an officer, navigator John Bertrang was sent to a prison camp on the Japanese mainland. The five remaining crewmen were taken to the Taihoku prison on Formosa.

We know almost nothing about most of their time there in the winter and spring of 1945. How, and how often, they were interrogated. Whether they were tortured. Whether they were separated or kept together. What they ate, what they wore. How, and if, they managed to keep their spirits up. No records survived, and the men were not allowed to write letters home.

But we do know what happened next, because the Japanese kept meticulous accounts of a "war tribunal" convened at the prison in late May 1945. All told, fourteen American army and navy airmen were charged with "indiscriminate bombing or strafing"—in short, attacking civilian rather than military targets. All were tried on the same day, May 21, in groups according to their units or squadrons. The "testimony" of the crew from VPB-117 consisted of transcripts from interrogations conducted nearly two months earlier, in March, in which the men appear to suggest that they knew the ships they attacked were not armed.

For instance, this is supposedly Jack Parker explaining how they strafed the ships:

> We saw four Japanese cargo ships, which we attacked. The time I think was about 2:00 in the afternoon. Whether these ships were connected with the military or not I cannot say. . . . After the second attack the commanding officer said that we would make a forced landing. I then noticed for the first time that the motor was damaged and we fell into the sea.

A minute or so later, the prosecutor circles back to the question of whether their targets were military, and Jack replies,

Up to now, whenever we sighted a small Japanese ship, we attacked it at a close distance. Consequently I can say that we have up to now attacked ordinary civilians and non-military objectives.

And here is what ordnance man Delbert Carter allegedly told his interrogators when they asked how the Liberator's engines failed:

I do not know. I thought that we might have been hit by an anti-aircraft shell, but at the time I did not notice any bursting of shells in the air. The ships we attacked were small civilian vessels so [I] cannot imagine that the damage was caused by them. I therefore think that something just happened to the motor and [it] went dead.

It was like that with the others as well, and no further evidence was presented. When the prosecutor finished reading from the transcripts, the presiding judge asked the men whether they had anything to say "regarding the inhuman acts" they had committed. None replied. The main points of the indictment were read to them, and they were offered a chance to speak in their own defense. Their response was silence. The prosecutor then recommended the death penalty, and the judge asked the five whether they had any last comments. Again, they said nothing.[547]

Eight days later, the death sentence was handed down. And at 6 a.m. on June 19, 1945, the five Blue Raiders—along with nine other American airmen—were taken outside and lined up in front of a shallow ditch.[548] The bark of the officer's order, the report of more than a dozen rifles, the thud of the falling bodies—it all took only a few seconds.

After which, somehow, time did not stand still.

Less than two months later, Japan surrendered. The need to sort out all that had happened with prisoners of war meant that Jack's family wasn't officially notified of his death until October. In early December, after he'd finally returned home himself, navigator John Bertrang wrote to Jack's parents:

I didn't know John well, but when the skipper gave him to us I knew we could depend on him. And we certainly could—he stuck with us all the way down. After the crash I swam with him until we were picked up by the Japs. That's the last I ever saw of him or any of the boys. . . . I certainly offer you my heartfelt sympathies and all I can say is, I'm mighty proud to have known John Parker.[549]

Several months later, they learned that the bodies of Jack and the rest had been cremated and an urn containing his ashes would be shipped home.[550] Then, in July 1946, just over a year after the executions, a U.S. Military Commission convened in Shanghai, China. It heard testimony that records used as evidence in the trial of Jack and the other American airmen had been falsified. The interpreter who was present during the interrogations, as well as others who recorded the statements, said that none of the fliers ever admitted to bombing or strafing civilian ships or targets. The commission also found that there was little or no other evidence of illegal bombing; that the prisoners were denied defense lawyers, as well as the chance to have witnesses or evidence presented on their behalf; and that most of the proceedings were not translated for them. Two Japanese officers, including the chief prosecutor, were condemned to death, two more to life in prison, and four others to terms ranging from twenty to forty years.[551]

In December of that year, Jack's ashes finally arrived, and in March 1947, a military funeral was held at Clearwater Cemetery, complete with a twenty-one-gun salute.[552]

But, as many an old soldier knows, time doesn't always heal all wounds. More than forty years after Jack was buried, when the U.S. Congress passed a bill apologizing to Japanese American citizens who were interned during the war, John Bertrang sent a letter to his hometown newspaper in Indianapolis. He wrote,

I, too, was held in a prison camp during the war, only it was in Japan. My confinement was also due to "racial prejudice and war hysteria." Most of my confinement was in the POW camp of

Ofuna, Japan, which was an "unregistered camp" and one of the most nefarious and notorious in the history of the war.

For those not familiar with the term, an "unregistered camp" was one in which the identities of the prisoners were not released to the Red Cross, as required by the Geneva Convention as well as by the bounds of human decency. As a result, the prisoners in Ofuna were considered expendable by the Japanese. Whether we lived or died was of little consequence to them.

I also believe that a couple of differences exist between Ofuna and the camps in which the detainees were confined. In Ofuna we received daily beatings with a club approximately the size of a baseball bat. We were fed two small cups of barley and hot water daily.

We received absolutely no medical attention or supplies. We were held in solitary confinement for months. We were forced to work at indescribable jobs, such as cleaning out outdoor toilets and spreading excrement over gardens.

My clothing consisted of one shirt and one pair of pants of light material and one pair of thongs. I lived in a cell seven feet by eight feet, with no bed, a straw mat on the floor and one small window in a building similar to a chicken coop.

The building was unheated, and Ofuna has the same approximate temperature as Washington, DC, as they are very near the same medians. The winter of 1944–45 in Japan was one of the coldest on record.

Our free time was spent trying to kill the lice that infested our clothing. We could bathe once a month and all in the same water. Our cells were locked, and we had to call a guard and ask permission to go to the toilet. One of their favorite pastimes was to act as if they could not hear, or refused permission.

I dug the graves and buried several of my friends and comrades, and not one was more than 30 years old, and most in their early 20s.

When our B-24 was shot down by the Japanese, three were killed in the crash. I was flown to Ofuna for interrogation, and the remaining eight were murdered by a Japanese firing squad in April 1945.

When Congress issues a formal apology on behalf of the nation, I would appreciate it if they could inform whoever is in charge to specifically delete my name as one of the apologists.

John F. Bertrang[553]

And finally, on June 19, 2005—exactly sixty years after Jack Parker was executed—his brother, Buddy, and Buddy's two sons came to Taipei, Taiwan, for a special ceremony memorializing those who died that day. The names of the executed airmen were read. Wreaths were laid. A bagpiper played "Amazing Grace."[554]

From April 1942 to August 1945, more than ten thousand American prisoners from the Philippines died in Japanese captivity.[555]

In the Light of Eternity

And what about the ones you *have* met? Those whose stories I have so far left unfinished. What happened to them?

After failing the army physical because he was too skinny, would-be flier Bill Swink learned that the navy had no minimum weight requirements. He came home from the war, got his college degree in business, and worked as a loan officer in a bank. He met his wife, Emmy, on a blind date in college; they were married for sixty years. When Bill took her to the first squadron reunion in 1983, she asked why everyone kept calling him "Rip." So he explained about getting extra naptime during missions. The two became very active in the VPB-117 Association. Bill was secretary-treasurer for twenty-five years, and he and Emmy organized nine of the annual reunions, beginning in 1995. At the one my son Andrew and I attended in 2003, he was the first squadron member we met. That's when he told us about Carson Chalk and the Army Air Force sergeant who had just wanted to save his life. Bill died in 2008, age eighty-three.[556]

Pilot Galen Bull—whose Iowa grammar school had all eight grades in one room—came home and, like so many fellow soldiers, went back to school on the GI Bill. He earned his bachelor's degree from Kansas State Teachers College and, along the way, met and married Ivalee Kiemel. He then went on to get his master's and PhD degree in education at the University of Missouri.

In 1959, he became a professor in the natural and physical science department at San Jose State University in California. During the 1960s, he spent two years in Nigeria, West Africa, helping establish a teacher's college there.[557]

For twenty-five years after the war, he also served in the navy reserve. One of his assignments in the 1950s took him to Christmas Island (now known as Kiritimati) during early tests of the hydrogen bomb. His job was to wait on the runway with a fueled twin-engine bomber, ready to evacuate soldiers and scientists immediately if something went wrong. Fortunately, it didn't.[558]

Galen retired in 1989, after teaching at San Jose for three decades. He and Ivalee had two sons. Ivalee passed away in 2006, after sixty years of marriage.[559] Galen died in 2009.[560] Seven years later—and exactly 150 years after Galen's ancestors first broke sod outside Wellman, Iowa—the Bull family farm was sold.[561]

After E. O. Rigsbee, VPB-117's first commanding officer, gave his farewell address to the squadron on Christmas Day 1944, he reported to his new post as commanding officer of the USS *Orca*, a seaplane tender operating in the Philippines.[562] And within days, he found himself and the ship in a firefight during the invasion of Lingayen Gulf, off the coast of Luzon.

Three Japanese planes dropped down out of the cloud cover and attacked in a row. The first was hit by the *Orca*'s gunners and crashed into a nearby minesweeper, blowing the ship in half. The second plane got within five hundred yards before bursting into flames and crashing alongside the ship as its bomb exploded, drenching the ship and crew. The final attacker was hit several thousand yards away and fell harmlessly into the water.

Later the *Orca* and Rigsbee helped rescue one of his Annapolis roommates and classmates. In mid-December, McPherson Williams, head of a carrier air group on the USS *Yorktown*, had been shot down near Manila, eluded capture, and hidden in the hills with Philippine guerillas. In early February, a seaplane from the *Orca* landed near the east coast of Luzon, "right in the Jap's backyard," picking up Williams and several other evacuees. All told, the ship rescued more than a hundred servicemen after forced landings at sea or in Japanese-held territories.[563]

Rigsbee stayed with the *Orca* through the end of the war and brought the ship home to San Francisco in October 1945. Less than two months later, he was promoted to captain.[564] And early in 1946 he was named public information officer for the naval air station in Corpus Christi, Texas. It was a homecoming of sorts, nearer his own family.

While there, in August 1946 Rigsbee was awarded the Distinguished Flying Cross for his "conspicuous daring and rare judgment" on the flight from Tinian when he helped direct navy bombardments and bombed the Japanese airfield on Iwo Jima. Later that year he also received the Legion of Merit for his role as commanding officer of VPB-117 and the *Orca*.[565]

But the honor he maybe prized most came a few months after that, when the squadron he founded was presented with the Presidential Unit Citation for "extraordinary heroism in action against enemy Japanese forces." Rigsbee sent a letter to twenty officers and twenty enlisted men, "plank holders" from the original group, inviting them to the official ceremony in Washington, DC, on April 17, 1947.

A four-minute silent film of the presentation shows John Brown, assistant secretary of the navy for air, reading from the citation commending "a gallant fighting unit, complemented by skilled officers and men." Accepting the award, Rigsbee shared a three-way handshake with Roger Crowley and Harold McDonald, who wiped away a tear with his handkerchief. More than a dozen other squadron mates were on hand.[566]

As it turned out, that day would in many ways be the high-water mark of Rigsbee's career. He returned to Corpus Christi and then, a little over a year later, was named executive officer of the USS *Antietam*, an aircraft carrier docked in San Francisco. It had been built during the war and commissioned in January 1945—too late to see action in combat. And now, with postwar budget cuts, it was too expensive to keep in service. So the *Antietam* was headed for the mothball fleet.[567]

Rigsbee might have felt like he was being mothballed too. Second in command on an active warship, even in peacetime, would have been a plum position. But this was something else altogether. And sometime late in his tenure at Corpus Christi, he'd been demoted from captain back down to commander. It's not clear why, but it surely was a blow.[568] Still, in the navy you went where they sent you, and you did what you could. So he and Helen—who by now had three children, two girls and a boy—packed up and headed back to California.

Early on, his assignment got much more interesting when the *Antietam* became the floating movie set for a Hollywood film starring Gary Cooper. *Task Force* was the story of a fictional admiral who from the 1920s on advocated for and pioneered the development of aircraft carriers as a decisive weapon of war. For twenty-four days, crews and actors and a hundred tons of movie equipment roamed the ship, above and below decks, stem to stern.

The *Antietam*'s crew appeared as extras, performing their normal duties.[569] Helen and Rigsbee's children visited during the filming, and the family story said Rigsbee and Cooper got along well during the time the star was there, sharing stories and some cocktails.[570] But after Hollywood disembarked, it was back to work preparing the carrier for storage.

And not long after that, a deepening crisis began. Rigsbee became depressed, erratic. In March 1949, he began a letter to his sister Ru and her husband:

> I am more than ashamed of the way I have neglected to write to you—or to anyone—for the last two months. In December I came down with a spell of serious trouble while we were getting moved into the house—and for some unexplainable reason I have never been able to pull myself out of it. It seems I have just let everything go completely to pot, and seem to have lost my will to do anything.
>
> I have just had two days emergency leave here at home to try to get myself pulled together—but we've had quite a rainy spell and as a result we were shut up in the house most of the time and I didn't accomplish much. . . .
>
> Helen and Mom and the children are all OK, but I have surely given them a bad time with my moaning and grousing and general complaining about everything.[571]

Still, he clearly tried to keep his problems from his boss and others at work. And it seems he was at least partially successful because, on

May 2, the *Antietam*'s commanding officer, John Peterson, was relieved and Rigsbee became captain of the carrier.[572] The next day he wrote his brother, Hub,

> Here I am, two letters behind again—but I enjoyed and appreciate your letters, and all the news. Things are still hectic on the ship—and now that I am the "boss" I really have the problems.
>
> However, come eventide I'm so pooped I don't make good sense to anybody. Today I took my promotion physical and managed to pass OK (I think!).
>
> Thus far we haven't made the first preparations in our plans for the scheduled move—we keep saying we're going to start on it tomorrow, but we haven't gotten to it yet.
>
> I'm going to head for the sack, and Helen is going to take up from here. Tomorrow is another day!

Using Rigsbee's family nickname, Helen continued the story:

> Dear Hub and Myra—Ebb had to give up. I am encouraged that he got as far as he did.
>
> We have just been through the most frightening week that I have ever had. This mental depression that Ebb has been suffering got him down so badly that he began to imagine all sorts of horrible things and worked himself into such a state of tension that he just lay staring blankly into space.
>
> I was literally scared to death and called Doc Mathers to get over here fast. Hutch was scared too when he saw him, but got him up and walked him and got him to talk about what was worrying him and finally convinced him that he was imagining things and got him snapped out of it.
>
> I was sure that he was going to have to go to the hospital, but he has improved since then and both Hutch, Ebb and I are fighting to keep him going to finish this job and get his leave so that we can get him to the best darn civilian psychiatrist without getting this on his medical record. Any trace of mental

disorder on his record and Ebb would be retired at once. He knows this, and feels it would be the end of everything for him if that happened.

I am working with all my heart to bolster his pride and confidence in himself to get him through the next few weeks, so that we can get some expert help to explain what has happened and how to prevent a repetition.

Now, kids, I do not mean to frighten you but it is serious and I have told no one else about it. . . . I feel sure that we can get through this period, but pray for us and if things get bad again I will call you.

If you write, please don't let Ebb know that I have told you this and please write the most cheerful and encouraging things you can to him, as he needs it as never before.

Always,
Helen[573]

The move and the physical exam mentioned in the letter may have been linked to an expected return to the rank of captain. But it was not to be. Nine days later, in his cabin on the *Antietam*, E. O. Rigsbee Jr. took a .38-caliber revolver and shot himself in the head.

It happened around 11 a.m., and a marine stationed outside Rigsbee's cabin didn't hear the gun because of noise from the ongoing work to prepare the ship for decommissioning. Rigsbee's body was found by a steward.[574] In his desk was an unfinished letter to his brother, Hub.

His death was front-page news in San Francisco and in Texas. It was carried on the Associated Press and the United Press International newswires. There was a story in the *New York Times*. One account said he was "on the waiting list for promotion to captain."[575]

A reporter found Helen's phone number and called. She was distraught and said Rigsbee had been "greatly overworked and under great strain. . . . We both knew he needed a rest, but he could not see any prospect of leave until the ship was decommissioned."[576] But there might have been other, deeper issues as well. Rigsbee had five siblings, three sisters and two brothers. In the end, four of the six took their own lives.[577]

The navy convened a board of inquiry, which two weeks later concluded that Rigsbee's death was "in the line of duty."[578] He was buried with full military honors in Golden Gate National Cemetery.

His life, especially how it ended, can be seen as tragic. But my favorite image of Rigsbee is different. When *Task Force* premiered a few months later, its opening sequence featured a scene where Gary Cooper addresses his crew assembled on deck as he takes his leave and retires from the navy. In the shot Cooper reaches out for a microphone—and there to hand it to him is E. O. Rigsbee Jr., standing straight and tall in his dress blues, a smile on his still-handsome face.

Before joining the Blue Raiders, Commander Rigsbee's copilot, Bill Allsopp, had been born in Scotland, emigrated to Canada with his family, and met and married the love of his life, Gerri, in Michigan.[579] After Rigsbee had returned from Australia and was given command of the USS *Orca* in the Philippines, he sent a launch and brought Allsopp to the ship for dinner. It was an emotional reunion, Bill told me.[580] In VPB-117 he was named a plane commander and got his own crew. The day Tom Hyland crash-landed on Triton Reef, Bill vectored the PBM flying boat to the site, where they picked up the stranded men. Bill and his crew destroyed Japanese fighters on the ground and leveled a tunnel on the Saigon-Tourane railroad.[581]

On another mission, he was lining up for a low-level run on a munitions factory when he heard a voice say, "Turn right immediately." He did. And where he had been seconds earlier, the sky filled with antiaircraft fire. He later asked everyone in his crew whether they had sent the message to break right. None of them had. His wife always called the incident "our angel story."[582]

After V-J Day, Bill came home and earned his degree in aeronautical engineering at the University of Michigan.[583] Then he went to work at Boeing. As the USS *Antietam* was being mothballed in 1949, Rigsbee invited Bill to the decommissioning ceremony. He flew down from Seattle and was on the flight deck with all the other sailors, awaiting Rigsbee's address to the crew. When "the Skipper" didn't appear, they sent someone to Rigsbee's cabin and found that he had committed suicide.[584]

Bill became a legendary test pilot at Boeing, helped train commercial pilots for decades, and survived a 1959 crash that killed four during a test flight of an early 707 with airline pilots at the controls. Bill was not in the cockpit but in the rear of the plane.[585] When Gerri rushed to the hospital and learned he would survive, she said to Bill, "Now you're going to quit flying, right?" To which he replied, like a true test pilot, "It wasn't the airplane's fault."[586]

Bill died peacefully at the age of eighty-nine on January 2, 2008.

After succeeding Rigsbee as VPB-117's commanding officer, Harold McDonald in February 1945 was named commander of Group One in the Fleet Air Wing. There he helped develop the "pro-submarine doctrine," where squadron planes who saw enemy ships radioed their positions to American subs in the area, which then attacked. It proved to be a successful strategy, with one notable exception.[587]

The two battleships that had escaped just hours before Dan Moore's mission to Cam Ranh Bay in December 1944 had been holed up in Singapore ever since. Now an intercepted Japanese radio message ordered them to leave Singapore on February 10 and proceed directly to the port of Kobe, in Japan. VPB-117 was ordered to track them from the air. Harold McDonald took the first shift and found them just where they were expected—in fact, he got close enough to be fired on.[588] But the job of sinking the ships had been given to a task force of more than two dozen American and allied submarines stationed along the route. The only trouble was that the battleships had a head start and at top speed could go faster than the subs. So the Blue Raiders followed them from the air. Only three subs got within range to attack, and none were successful. One submarine commander was so frustrated that he came to the surface and chased them all the way to Kobe, hoping in vain to get a shot.[589]

After the war Mac was involved with Naval Intelligence and the Bureau of Personnel, taught at the Naval War College, and was executive officer of the USS *Pennington*, an aircraft carrier. His last duty was as head of Naval Intelligence for the Pacific theater.

He retired in 1960 but remained an avid fan of navy football throughout his life—having seats at Navy Stadium and attending every game for thirty years.[590] He died, at age eighty-four, in 1995.[591]

The court-martial trial of Tom Mulvihill's copilot George Parker wasn't finished until early 1946 when his conviction was overturned by the navy judge advocate general in Washington, DC—based on defense attorney Jake Dickinson's argument that Mulvihill never gave a direct order and that the right of refusal to fly with someone a pilot considered "reckless or incompetent" was "generally recognized."[592] Parker's father lost his engineering firm when his partner and his son took it over. So George ended up working in real estate, buying commercial and residential property. He also stayed in the naval reserve for another twenty years, flying in Korea.[593]

Tom Mulvihill also wanted to stay in the regular navy after the war, but his father said if he didn't come home and help manage the ranches, he'd sell them. Mulvihill reluctantly agreed and resigned his commission, after which his father told him he didn't need his help after all. Mulvihill opened a crop-dusting service and, after his father's death, helped manage the ranches and a tavern his father had owned. He also remained in the naval reserve, retiring as a captain in 1968.[594] Mulvihill became an alcoholic and was eventually hospitalized. But he dried out on his own in his seventies.[595]

Still, even many years later, he remained a polarizing figure in the squadron. In 1992, pilot Tom Hyland wrote a letter to Mulvihill's daughter, LaVelle Saier, in which he said, "All of us who were lucky enough to fly for him recognized him as the outstanding B-24 squadron commander in the Pacific. . . . 117 . . . was a bastard outfit until he took command. . . . After him, [it was] the number one outfit."[596] Sheldon Sutton echoed that sentiment in a letter to Saier: "Tom was a can-do officer [and] a fighting man. He knew what should be done in the situation that was at hand."[597] However, Art Elder called Mulvihill "a dangerous pilot."[598] And a member of Mulvihill's crew told me that "we got shot up on 35 of 50 flights," and "if it was a choice between dying and taking the safe way, he would take the dying way."[599]

So maybe we should go back to the man who flew with him the longest and maybe knew him best—at least inside the plane. At the squadron's first reunion in 1983, it turned out that Mulvihill's and Parker's hotel rooms were next to each other. Parker asked his wife, Marilyn, what he should do. She said, "Go over there, knock on his door and ask the old man if he'd like a drink." So George did, and that was that.

They only spoke one more time. Late in Mulvihill's life, when he was dying, Parker visited him in Montana. He said he wanted to set things right. And when he came back from the trip, he told Marilyn, "I don't know for sure how it was for him, but for me I felt like I said goodbye to him in a respectful way."[600]

George Parker died in 1999.

Tom Mulvihill had died four years earlier, in 1995. His headstone lists all five of his Distinguished Flying Crosses. As far as is known, he was the only PB4Y-1 commanding officer who ever tried to court-martial his own crew for refusing to fly with him.[601]

Charles Kickham, the prosecutor during George Parker's trial, went back home to Massachusetts, finished his law degree at Harvard, and opened his own practice. He served three terms as president of the Massachusetts Bar Association.[602]

Defense attorney Jake Dickinson, meanwhile, returned to Topeka. His daughter's poor spelling led him to run for the Topeka Board of Education. He eventually became head of the board during the early 1950s. As the appeals in the landmark case *Brown v. Board of Education of Topeka, Kansas* wound their way to the U.S. Supreme Court, Dickinson led the effort to integrate the Topeka schools, for which he was often criticized in his hometown. By the time the Court made its final ruling, the Topeka schools were already being integrated. Dickinson died at age sixty, in 1971.[603]

After the war, aces Jan ("Nick") Carter and Sheldon Sutton both stayed in the navy for more than twenty years. Jan retired as a captain, got his degree in civil engineering, and was public works director for the city of

Little Rock for twenty-seven years. In 1970, he was honored as National Public Works Man of the Year.[604]

Sheldon retired from the navy as a commander, worked for a time for the state of Maryland, and then spent decades as a planner and executive with the Westinghouse Corporation.[605]

In 1983, almost forty years after VPB-117 was first formed in San Diego, Jan and Sheldon decided it was time to have a Blue Raiders reunion. They made lists of squadron mates whose whereabouts they knew and asked them, in turn, to add names of others with whom they had stayed in contact. Word spread, a date was set, and reservations were made. The men put together a commemorative book with photos, letters, records and reports, and notes from friends and crewmates.

The site was New Orleans, and on the first evening waiters serving cocktails all wore navy uniforms in tribute. Those who were there remember an outpouring of tears and laughter, stories and family photos, hugs and kisses.[606]

The annual reunions continued for more than three decades. The last was held in Kansas City in 2015.[607]

Jan Carter died in 1998, age seventy-nine. I last spoke with Sheldon Sutton in March 2017. He was ninety-six years old.

Like Sheldon Sutton and Jan Carter, Art Elder served in the navy for more than twenty years after he and his decimated crew left VPB-117. Among other postings, he helped train carrier pilots and commanded an electronic intelligence squadron in Spain. He retired in 1966 and then worked with the Foreign Service, helping train pilots in Thailand and Vietnam.

After that he came home and, in 1973, enrolled as a freshman at the University of California, San Diego. After receiving his BA in anthropology, he wanted to teach. But he was told he'd have to get a PhD, and another five or six years in school didn't appeal to him. So he decided he'd rather be a handyman, and he loved it: carpentry, tiling, anything that needed doing. He said 90 percent of his clients were widows, and he only worked when he wanted to.[608]

He was a deacon in his church, having built the floor-to-ceiling wooden cross that is its focal point. He headed the congregation's food drives, donated more than forty-eight pints of blood over the years, and welcomed people on Sundays as a greeter. His wife, Lois, died in 2008. Every year, Art went to Spain for Holy Week.[609] He died in 2013.

And then there is Tom Hyland, the squadron's final ace, who really needs a book all his own—in part because, after flying and his family, books were probably the things he loved best.

After the war he stayed in the naval reserve, eventually retiring as a captain. And in 1946 he took a job as a pilot for United Airlines, for which he flew for more than three decades. He also helped found the Commercial Flight Engineers Union. He and Shirley had four children, two daughters and two sons, but divorced after sixteen years.[610]

Tom remained an unabashed patriot. His children were taught to memorize the Declaration of Independence, the preambles to the Constitution and the Bill of Rights, and the Gettysburg Address.[611] He rarely spent his pilot's salary on anything for himself. He bought junk cars at garage sales but was seemingly always ready to help finance houses or pay college tuition for his extended family.[612]

His only personal extravagance was reading. He devoured books—bought a house and filled it with them, floor to ceiling. Then he bought the house next door and filled that as well. Books were on the floor, on the shelves, in piles you had to wander through like a maze. When he died, his children took on the task of sorting them out, eventually counting more than sixty-three thousand.

He and Art Elder stayed friends for life. They started playing chess out in the Pacific, and over the years they played hundreds of times. And because they were pilots, they naturally kept score. Tom ended with four more wins than Art.

He died on December 14, 2003, on his way to have brunch with his grandchildren. At the memorial service, Art was asked to speak. All he could remember saying was "Tom was my best friend."[613]

But I also like a story Tom's grandson Max shared that day about an airline flight thirty years earlier. He and his mother were going from

Denver to New York, and his grandfather would be the pilot. So the night before, Tom asked Max and his cousins to draw maps that he could use to plot his course. They all took the job seriously and produced maps that were, Max remembered, "extensive, and utterly incomprehensible."

The next day Max and his mother were on board with the rest of the passengers, waving through the window to their aunts and uncles and cousins in the terminal, when Tom Hyland—the last to board—strode across the tarmac and up the steps to the airplane. Max recalled,

> He turned and waved to my cousins in the terminal. I could see them in response jumping up and down and waving wildly back.
> . . .
>
> But Grampa didn't get on the plane just yet. Standing at the top of the stairs there, he reached into his case and took out the maps we had drawn the night before. And he held them up—all of them—very carefully, one after the other—our drawings—and he flourished them to the crowd, smiling.
>
> He looked so happy and so proud. I could see my cousins reacting to the gesture, exhilarated, overjoyed, jumping higher than before. Then Grampa got on board. . . .
>
> I don't know if I ever believed that Grampa gave our maps to his navigator to decipher, but I do want to say this. Thank you, Grampa, for showing us the way.[614]

Despite her best efforts, Jerry Dougan's mother never did learn what happened to her son on his mission to Vietnam late in the war. But on August 14, 2015—fifty years to the day after Jerry and his crew disappeared—I got a call from David deMarrais. His older brother, Paul, had been the radioman Jerry was tutoring, and we had spoken several times. He said a genealogy researcher had just contacted him, asking for a DNA sample. David wanted to know why, and the researcher was circumspect. But she did say she sometimes worked with government groups that helped find the remains of missing soldiers. David told her about his brother's mission to Ha Tien, and she said there had been much construction going on in that area recently. But that was all she shared.[615]

So David waited for further word. And waited. All through the rest of 2015 and into the new year. We stayed in touch, and in February I offered to call the Defense POW/MIA Accounting Agency (DPAA), the group responsible for overseeing the efforts to find missing service members. Johnie Webb, the deputy director of outreach and communications, told me that "a citizen of a country in Southeast Asia" had brought a box into the DPAA office in the region. Inside the box were personal items and "some equipment" that suggested it was from a World War II aircraft. He said they didn't know whether they were from Jerry Dougan's plane, but that was one of the possibilities. And he added that very few World War II cases were still unresolved.

Webb told me the remains they received had been tested for DNA, but they had no results as yet. They were not working at the site, he said, and there was no timetable for doing so. He said he'd be happy to talk with David and might be able to share more information with him because he was a family member.[616] David did call the next day, but he didn't learn much more than I did.

He heard no more through spring and deep into summer. In some ways, the longer the silence, the more likely it seemed that they were being careful to touch all the bases before contacting the relatives of Jerry's crew. Then, in August, David deMarrais got the call.

They had found the wreckage of a World War II plane and the remains of three men.

But it was not Jerry and Paul's plane. Not their crew. Not their turn to come home.

Joe Lowder believed that he survived his plane's crash in Cam Ranh Bay and his captivity during the last weeks of the war because he was physically fit and mentally strong. When he came home, he graduated from Springfield College in Massachusetts and became a lifelong advocate of healthy living. He was a teacher and coach at the Pensacola Naval Air Station. For almost ten years from the mid-1950s to the mid-1960s, he served as an instructor in the physical fitness and survival program. He also worked with the Mercury Space Program, developing motion sickness studies for astronauts. He taught at several universities, including Auburn University in Alabama and Washington University in Saint Louis. He and Gwen had three sons. She died of cancer in 1998, as did one of their sons, Eric, in 2005. Joe lived to be eighty-four and died in 2006.[617]

Combined, crewman Gene Kern and his pilot Dan Moore would end up living more than 180 years. But for decades after Dan had his breakdown and was separated from the squadron, neither would know what had happened to the other. In the end, though, they would meet again—much better late than never.

Gene and the rest of his crew were not told why Dan had been whisked away in early April 1945 after making his broadcast about squadron morale. But after one mission with a different plane commander, they eagerly agreed to fly with Marvin Barefoot as their pilot. The patrols were mostly negative for the rest of April and May, and then, on June 2, they were processed out of the squadron.[618]

Gene's road home began in Manila, but he and his crew were stuck there for two weeks—kept across the bay in the battered remains of the American barracks on Corregidor Island. Finally they were put aboard a four-engine flying boat headed for Hawaii. For a week they were quartered in the Waikiki Beach Hotel. They gorged themselves on fresh fruit, vegetables, and milk for the first time in ten months. They weren't allowed off the grounds from 8 p.m. until 8 a.m., but they swam in the ocean, shot pool and played croquet, and gathered around two baby grand pianos on the terrace, where someone was always playing.

Then they spent ten days in the Transfer Unit waiting for a ride back to the states. Planes heading home were still full of the wounded, so they were put on a ship to San Francisco, cheering as they passed under the Golden Gate Bridge. As soon as they arrived, they were given a three-day pass, after which they could come back and pick up their papers for a thirty-day leave.

He reported back to base after the weekend and set out for what he hoped would be an important reunion. A year earlier, while training in San Diego, Gene had often spent weekends with an aunt, uncle, and cousins who lived in Los Angeles. A girl cousin liked to go horseback riding, and one weekend the stable they frequented had a hayride. That's where Gene met Pearl Syler.

They hit it off immediately, became boyfriend and girlfriend, and saw each other as often as possible. She was a nice girl, and it was a chaste, but ardent, attraction. The weekend before Gene left for the front, Pearl came to San Diego. He remained a gentleman throughout, and she wrote him several times a week when he was overseas.

While he was out in the Pacific, Pearl and her friends had moved from Los Angeles to Monterey, not far from San Francisco. So after he got his leave papers, Gene went straight to a bus station and bought a ticket.

> I got to Monterey about 4 or 5 that evening. I went to a nice hotel, rented a room, shaved, showered and dressed in my best tailor-made blues, looking good. Went down and took a taxi to the address on Pearl's letters. It was obvious that my appearance was a complete surprise and shock. The girls all remembered me, and invited me in. Pearl was not home, but was expected very soon. We sat down and visited for about 30 minutes before Pearl arrived. Now, stupid me, I did not catch the shock on her face. But there was no kiss, and not even a hug. I asked her if we could go out to dinner, so she broke the news that she was getting married the next day. She told me that she would really like me to attend her wedding.

Gene declined the invitation, took a cab back to his hotel and gathered up his things, walked to the bus station, and bought an overnight ticket to Los Angeles. While he was away, his parents had moved from Arkansas to Southern California. So his father picked him up at 10 a.m. the next morning and took him home. "I don't know why, but seeing my Mother made me feel a surge of uncontrollable emotion. I went into the bedroom and cried like a baby for two hours. I still get tears in my eyes, thinking of the relief being home again."[619]

He got a job as a machinist on the Southern Pacific railroad and stayed for ten years. It was a time of transition for the company and for

Gene. He soon knew everything about the old steam engines; he could fix anything on them and even make spare parts himself. But diesel locomotives were taking over, and Gene didn't like the smell of the fuel or the grime that went with the job.

So he left the railroad and took a giant step into the future by landing a job at Aerojet, making guided missiles. A machinist at first, in less than a year he was promoted to foreman, building Polaris missiles for atomic submarines. Later, when Aerojet had trouble meeting production goals for its Minuteman missile, the company asked Gene to become general foreman for Minuteman production, with twenty-five foremen and 350 hourly workers reporting to him. He had them back on schedule within two months.

He went on to several management and supervisory positions, helping build everything from the Apollo spacecraft to the engines for the space shuttles, before retiring in 1987.[620] And at Aerojet, as it turned out, he also found the love of his life.

He had been married twice before and had two children. Maybe his commitment to work had gotten in the way, or maybe it was just the normal ups and downs of relationships. But near the end of his time at Aerojet he met Rosie Angulo, secretary to Gene's boss. She was thirteen years younger and twice divorced herself. But the third time was a charm for them both.

They married in 1990 and a year later bought a lot in Medford, Oregon, near where Rosie had been raised. Together, they designed their dream house and built it themselves—pouring the foundation, doing the plumbing, the electronics, the roof, the walls, the ceilings, everything. Gene loved to fish, off the Oregon coast and in rivers nearby. Rosie was allergic to fish, but she helped clean and freeze the catch. They traveled to Alaska, the Carolinas, and all across the country.[621]

We first met at the squadron's reunion in the fall of 2005. Gene talked about his experiences, his crew, and his life after the war. He also told me he didn't know what had happened to Dan Moore once he left the squadron but was sure he was still alive. I said that didn't seem possible—along with my dad and many others, he had been listed as deceased at the first Blue Raiders reunion back in 1983. Several squadron members said they'd heard he'd committed suicide. But Gene was adamant: "I just know he's not dead."

So I went looking, figuring at best maybe I could find some of his children. But Gene was right. Dan was hiding in plain sight, in Phoenix.

He told me he was happy to learn that he was "no longer among the missing" and filled me in on his life after the war. On the night Japan surrendered, Hilda Moore and a friend had walked over to the White House, where President and Mrs. Harry Truman came out and waved to the celebrating crowds. But back at St. Elizabeth's the mood was more muted, because Dan's recovery was becoming a case of two steps forward, one step back.[622] A few days later Hilda phoned Dan's parents, saying he felt better than he had in months and had "the old zest" back in his voice.[623] A week later, though, she said Dan was again having intermittent periods of "confusion" and "no amount of diversion will prevent them."

But within days, Hilda wrote that the doctors said "unless something very untoward occurs, we should be on our way home 4–5 weeks from now."[624] Dan's letter a few days later said that "aside from occasional spells of trouble I have every reason to be optimistic and cheerful."[625]

By the middle of September Hilda was allowed to visit him every day. Later that week Dan was officially retired from the navy with a record of "good conduct" and a finding that his disability was "service incurred." But the navy retirement board also labeled his medical condition, which today would be considered posttraumatic stress disorder, as schizophrenia—a diagnosis that would haunt Dan, personally and professionally, for most of his life.[626]

But after all the false hopes and fresh starts, on October 3, 1945, "Lieutenant Daniel E. Moore was discharged from St. Elizabeth's Hospital and left in the company of his wife to return home."[627]

When they arrived in Bisbee, Dan went back to law school at the University of Arizona and got his degree in 1947. They started a family that would eventually include three children—daughters Jane and Maggie, then a son named Danny. And Dan opened his own law practice, doing a bit of everything—wills and estates, criminal cases, divorces. He also had wealthy clients, representing their businesses as well as their families. The work took him across the country, to Mexico and sometimes overseas. But it also ended up costing him his livelihood.

For one family, he won a large settlement in a Mexican court over their mine holdings there. For another, he handled their estate. In both cases, the children of his original clients wanted greater access to the family fortunes. One refused to pay Dan's legal fees and sued him for incompetence, citing his World War II diagnosis of "schizophrenia" as evidence. The other charged misuse of funds, because he had temporarily borrowed from the estate to pay bills. Despite the fact that Dan had long since repaid the money and that "prominent members of both bench and bar have testified to his reputation for truth, honesty and competency," he lost his case and his law license.[628]

But as devastating as that decision was, it had already been eclipsed by a far bigger blow. By then, Hilda had been battling cancer for several years. When she first heard the diagnosis, she rented a hotel room and cried for two days. But she never gave in to grief again. And for a time, she seemed to be getting better. The disease, though, was relentless. Hilda died on November 16, 1968. Within a year, heartsick and humbled, Dan left Bisbee and moved to Phoenix.

His children and friends were afraid that he might never recover from losing Hilda. But Dan kept active, and a few years later, a neighbor introduced him to Janet Nichols Selway. She had been raised on a ranch in Montana, and her first husband had died on the beach at Anzio in World War II. She'd later had two unhappy marriages before moving to Phoenix, becoming a high school teacher of the humanities, and meeting Dan. They married in 1974. Janet and Dan went to the symphony, the opera, the theater, the ballet. They traveled during the summers to Europe and across the United States. Both were active with the Trinity Episcopal Cathedral. Dan cofounded the Interfaith Coalition for Energy, which helped create a "church rate" for electricity, saving places of worship in Phoenix hundreds of thousands of dollars.

And he read, voraciously: history, the arts, science, current affairs. Late in his life, in a book titled *Origins of Mental Illness* by William Sargant, he read a description of a nervous breakdown that almost exactly mirrored his experience in the squadron. Even though it could no longer help him personally or professionally, he appealed to the navy retirement board to change his 1945 diagnosis from schizophrenia to nervous breakdown. They steadfastly refused.

Throughout, he remained close to his children. His daughter Jane Callahan-Moore is retired, after working for many years as a mental health caseworker in Chicago. Marguerite Moore Callaway is an international health-care consultant and leadership development expert. His son Dan Jr. went to college on a Reserve Officer Training Corps scholarship and became a navy pilot, eventually commanding an FA-18 fighter squadron during the 1990s. He was on assignment in the Pentagon when it was attacked on September 11, 2001.[629]

About a year after that, Dan Sr. was diagnosed with Parkinson's disease. It affected his motor skills; he needed a walker to get around. And he tired more easily. A natural-born raconteur who could tell stories for hours, his voice and his energy would sometimes falter before he could finish.[630]

In 2005, after we'd spoken on the phone and exchanged emails, I visited Dan and Janet in Phoenix. Then they and Dan Jr. made plans to attend the squadron's 2006 reunion in San Diego. The trip wouldn't be easy. The Parkinson's was progressing; by then he was wheelchair bound, and it was becoming more difficult for him to speak. But his mind was sharp, his memory clear. And he needed to reconnect with the part of his past that had been buried for decades.

Before the first morning session at the reunion, word had gotten around. The meeting had been going on for five minutes, and Art Elder was at the podium, making some routine announcements, when the side door opened. Dan Jr. pushed his father, in his wheelchair, into the room. Art stopped in mid-sentence and announced, "Attention, there's an officer on deck!" Everyone there—squadron members, wives, family members, and friends—stood and applauded.

Dan enjoyed the next two days seeing Gene and others and getting acquainted with some he'd hardly known in that earlier life. Traditionally, the last night of the reunion was more formal. Many of the men wore suits and ties; ladies were in dresses. And after dinner, there was a podium where anyone—squadron members, family members, and others—could get up and speak. I remember Farney Edwards talking about the flight with Mulvihill when he ricocheted bullets off a cliff and sank that ship. Then Dan decided that he wanted to say something.

Dan Jr. wouldn't retire from the navy until the following year, so that night he wore his dress blues as he wheeled his father to a spot facing the crowd and then stood behind him, straight and tall and proud. Even with a microphone, it was hard at times to understand what Dan was saying. But you could catch snatches and phrases: "So proud to be a part. . . . Had our hard times, but fun sometimes too. . . . A group of men I admired . . ."

Then, near the end, it became clear Dan had begun to talk about the death of his tail gunner Frank Wharton and that day off the coast of Luzon. I was sitting next to Janet, and her eyes filled. She reached under the table, grabbed my hand, and squeezed, hard. Again, it wasn't easy to make out exactly what Dan said. But it was clearly heartfelt.

When he finished, his son rolled him back to his seat at the table next to Gene Kern. I saw Gene hesitate and then turn to Dan. In an earlier life, he had always addressed him as "sir" or "Mr. Moore." And he would never have presumed to speak about anything personal. But now they were just two old men—faces maybe a foot apart, instead of fifty feet away in a plane pocked by dread and blood. And so the once-young gunner could say, as softly as his pilot spoke to him that day over the intercom, "It wasn't your fault, Dan. It wasn't your fault."

Nine years later, Gene Kern was on one of the "Honor Flights" for World War II veterans to Washington, DC. His daughter went with him, and when they arrived, they were met by his son and his nephew. By then Gene had to use a wheelchair, but he wasn't diagnosed with lung cancer until a few months later. He died, aged eighty-eight, at home on April 20, 2014. Gene is buried in the Eagle Point National Cemetery near Medford, Oregon. Rosie will lie next to him.[631]

Dan Moore had died more than three years earlier, on Christmas Eve 2010, aged ninety-three. He had told his family and his doctors that he didn't want any extraordinary measures, and when he came down with pneumonia, they honored his wish. He was buried with full military honors in the Greenwood Memorial Lawn Cemetery, one of Arizona's oldest. There was a U.S. Navy and Marine Corps honor guard and a twenty-one-gun salute. Buried next to Dan's coffin is a new set of gold navy pilot wings and the original Presidential Unit Citation ribbon that was presented to the squadron in 1947.[632]

Earlier, at the funeral service in a packed cathedral, his son spoke of Dan's life, its lessons, and his legacy. And he closed with a quote that applied not only to his father but to all the men with whom he had served and to those they left behind.

In a letter to a friend, the great Irish author Frank O'Connor wrote,

We are what we are, and within our limitations we have made our own efforts. They seem puny in the light of eternity, but they didn't at the time. And they weren't.[633]

Wide as the Water

It's a new century. Above and beyond the walls of the Manila American Cemetery, skyscrapers stand at attention. Inside the gates, though, it's always 1945. This is the largest burial ground for those who died in the Pacific theater, and most are here in name only—listed on granite walls over two stories tall, arranged in a circle. The Tablets of the Missing, they're called. More than thirty-six thousand simply swept away, lost in the flood. Wives and mothers without even a casket on which to rest a palm. Buddies who died together and were separated again, according to the alphabet. But if you know the names, here you can find Jerry Dougan's crew and Stan Sayre's and what was left of Glen Box's, and Brad Brooks's, and Joe Lowder's. More than three dozen from VPB-117—etched, if not in memory, at least in stone.

From the tablets, headstones fan out to the edge of vision, blurring into blessed silence. In the fall, after the rains, acacia trees shed blood-red leaves on bone-white crosses. Seventeen thousand.[634] One is James Taylor, radioman and top turret gunner, killed by an enemy fighter on Art Elder's final mission.[635] Another is A. B. Crofford, son of a Mississippi sharecropper, one of ten brothers, a sweet-faced tail gunner in Ralph Castleton's crew. Eighteen, he died begging to speak to his mother.[636]

And two rows away:

William T. Benn
Lieutenant (jg) USNR
Minnesota Dec 31 1944

In another generation or two, these stories will have weathered into fables, indistinct as the markers in long-ago graveyards. So while we still can, we tend the plots and trace the names.

In the beginning I knew little more about Bill Benn than what his tombstone could tell me. But it turned out his sister still lived near Minneapolis. Pat told me about their growing up, about Bill's jokes, and about that summer on the shore. She sent family photos and letters Bill wrote home from the Philippines. She also said he left a widow, June, and shared pictures of the two of them together. Snapshots from the beach in Florida, with Bill's note on the back: "The Mr. and Mrs." From San Diego, Bill and June with another couple in a convertible, gas ration stickers on the windshield. It was taken August 13, 1944—the day he left for Kaneohe. Pat and the rest of the family had been close to June, but they lost touch after the war. They knew she remarried a few years later but didn't know the name of her husband and thought maybe they had lived "somewhere out west."[637]

Later I found Harold Stang's sons, two bachelor brothers living in Jacksonville, Florida. They sent papers and clippings and some family photos. The only one they had from his time in the squadron showed Harold in his khakis, outside a tent, talking with a tall fellow wearing nothing but boots and a towel. I didn't need to see the note on the back: "Stang and Kittrell." Strange.

Harold's sons also had their father's service record, which showed he spent more than a year recovering from his injuries in the New Year's Eve crash. It left him with scars all over his legs and arms. Two fingers on one hand were permanently bent over, as if holding a golf club. He should not have continued flying but managed to keep his wings by taking physicals on days when the most junior navy doctors were on duty. He outranked and intimidated them into certifying his flight status. He flew in the Berlin airlift. He taught at the Naval War College. In the early 1960s, he finally failed a flight physical and was grounded. By then Harold had been in the service almost twenty-seven years, but he wrote his resignation letter within half an hour; if he couldn't fly, he didn't care. He died of lung cancer in 1983, and in all that time he spoke of the crash and Bill Benn only once. It was clear that he grieved for his copilot still.[638]

I heard about Bill from squadron survivors as well. When they spoke of good friends or lost comrades, his was often the first name mentioned. One story involved my dad. Bill had bought and learned to play a ukulele, and Dad always had his violin with him.[639] So they provided the entertainment in the very early days at the West of Tokyo Officers Club. One pilot remembered a night so hot that Dad played in his underwear.[640]

Then another door to Bill's past swung open—and in walked June. Visiting the World War II Memorial website, where visitors can list the names of relatives or friends who served, I typed in Bill's name and got two entries. One was from "Pat Benn, Sister." The other was from "June D. White, Wife." The *D* had to stand for Dohner, but "White" hardly narrowed the search. Yet some things are supposed to happen; in the whole country there were only three telephone listings for a June D. White, and so we met.

She told me that a year after Bill died, her parents had retired to New Mexico. She went with them and, at a church social, met an engineer named Dick White. He was a good man, and theirs was a good marriage; it lasted fifty-two years, and they raised four children, mostly in Louisiana and Colorado. A couple of years after he died, June got the urge to live near the beach again and moved to Florida, which is where I found her.

It wasn't easy at first. June had kept that part of her life locked away, not just from her family but also from herself. But she decided that she wanted to honor Bill by telling about their time together. She made notes so she could remember moments and details when we next talked. She told me that a few years after her marriage to Dick, she had thrown out all her pictures, letters, and mementoes of Bill. It was just too hard, she said. So I shared the photos Pat had sent me. In time, June laughed. And after a while the conversations turned to subjects beyond Bill and the war. We became friends.[641]

June and Pat Benn also reunited, exchanging letters and calls. After one such chat, June told me that she thought Pat wanted to know more about Bill's death—not about the accident itself but about what happened specifically to him. *How* did he die?

By chance, I knew the answer. I had seen the casualty file from the National Archives, which cited a "fracture, compound parietal bones of skull."[642] I had spoken to John Bullock, who rowed out with the navy diver the dawn after the crash, and he said the same thing in layman's terms.[643] But that only established the official cause of death. It didn't answer Pat Benn's question: *How* did he die? I had wondered the same thing, and something Harold Stang's sons told me had stuck in my head. The only time their father spoke of the crash, he said that as they came in on final approach, he told Bill to close a "vent window" in the cockpit. Maybe there wasn't time, but he didn't. If he had, Harold said, Bill might have made it. Decades later, the thought had still haunted him. But his sons had no idea what Harold was talking about.[644]

Neither did I until more than a year later. The only surviving B-24 barnstorms across the country each year, offering rides and tours to the curious. I had flown in it once, a Father's Day gift from my sons. But I hadn't seen the cockpit, and I wanted to get a good look at the pilots' "office." So this time I drove to the airport early on a Friday morning, before visitors were allowed. I explained about the book I was writing and asked whether I might just look in the cockpit, take a few pictures. They went one better: the pilot gave me a personal tour. The flight deck was cramped; we sat maybe a foot apart, surrounded by dozens of gauges and levers, beneath a greenhouse canopy of plexiglass windows. He showed me the controls, explained how they worked, and laughed about the Liberator's idiosyncrasies; of the more than fifty planes he's qualified to fly, he said, the B-24 is by far the most demanding.

At one point, talking about flying in bad weather, he showed me two small triangular windows at the bottom right and left corners of the windshield. The airflow over the plane created a vacuum in that one spot, he explained, so if, for example, rain was too heavy to see through the windshield, the pilot or copilot could open the small vent and see clearly, without the rain coming in. I asked how the window opened. He pulled a lever; the window swung inward, at a ninety-degree angle to the windshield. It was surrounded by a heavy metal frame that would have been directly in front of Bill's head, and I said out loud, without thinking, "That's how he died."[645] When the plane pitched over, Bill hit his head on that metal frame. I felt sick. This was the "vent window" in Harold Stang's story.[646] After everything else—the overlong flight, the Zero, the darkness and the squall, the aborted landings, the final approach, the sudden silence when the gas gave out, the wall of water, and the shrieking metal—after all that, Bill might still have survived if the window had been closed. And what else, then, might have been different?

The only consolation was that I knew now that Bill was dead before the plane sank. That's what I told Pat when I phoned. Did she want to know how I was sure? Yes. I explained. There was a moment, and then she said, "I'm glad I asked." All these years she had been afraid he'd drowned, trapped, gasping. Now she didn't have to picture him suffering that way.[647]

A month or so later, I got a call from a woman in Minneapolis. She said she was Pat's friend and told me that Pat had died, suddenly and alone. She had no family; the closest relative a lawyer could find was a distant cousin, fifty years younger, who'd never heard of her. The friend said she found my letters to Pat among her papers, along with a box of pictures and papers about Bill. She wanted to know whether I would like the mementoes; I called the cousin, who said he would probably have just thrown them away. So two days later a box arrived on my front step.

Inside were press clippings—a life and a time pared down to paragraphs, thin as the newsprint I held in my hand.

A photo caption from a 1935 high school track meet:

At left is Captain Bill (Big) Benn just as the hurdle cracks under the pressure of his driving legs. At the right is Bill Cunningham, who has been running second to Benn all season but has been one of Washburn's leading point getters.[648]

From a local gossip column in November 1944:

Lt. (jg) William (Bill) Benn came down on a South Pacific island to pay a surprise visit to his school and college chum Lt. William (Bill) Cunningham, Marine, in the latter's tent. The two Bills were classmates at Fuller grade school, Ramsey junior high, Washburn and the University of Minnesota, where they were affiliated with

Phi Delta Theta. Both also were track stars at Washburn and the University.[649]

Then, only months later, from his high school paper:

Latest name on the Gold Star list is that of Bill Benn, perhaps one of the most outstanding and well-liked boys ever to be grad-uated from Washburn. He was a good student here and at the University and set many track records in competition.[650]

And shortly after, from the *Chicago Tribune*:

The casualty lists wrote the end of the story.
"Lt. William (Bill) Benn, pilot of a B-24 Liberator bomber, killed in action in the Philippines . . ."
The beginning was inscribed in 1940. Young Bill Benn was a hurdler, top man on Minnesota's greatest track team, one of the first Big Ten athletes to fly a bomber. The rest of the gopher track team followed Bill into service until it became the first major team to enroll 100 percent in the armed forces.[651]

The article noted that one of his teammates was a Pearl Harbor survi-vor. Another, "one of America's most promising broad jumpers," had been captured at Corregidor.

The box also held photos, including Pat's favorite: a grinning Bill in his ensign's uniform, riding a bicycle down a street in Florida. There were his flight log and his dog tags. Then, at the bottom, faded with forty-eight stars, the flag under which he was buried in the Philippines.

And there were letters. Like the newspaper stories, they followed a familiar arc. Bill to his kid sister, from his training base in Indiana, December 30, 1942:

Last Xmas day some cadets (not me, cookie) got in trouble in Kokomo and as a result all we cadets are restricted to the base for the duration of our stay. I'm quite smitten with a beautiful gal in

town and how can I carry on my usual successful romance if they keep me on the base? I'll keep you informed as to the status of my love affair.
Love, Willy[652]

Bill to his Aunt Lois, while the squadron was at Kaneohe, on his introduction to Waikiki and the local sport:

This beach is a fine spot for surf boarding. I rented a board and paddled out about a half mile and spent the afternoon riding the big old waves. Delightful pastime.[653]

To his mother, from Leyte in December:

Dad would certainly get a kick out of seeing this country out here. It's truly beautiful. So many pretty islands. I've seen nearly all of them already.[654]

Then the telegram, now brown and brittle as a fallen leaf, delivered to Bill's parents at 8:30 p.m., January 10, 1945:

THE NAVY DEPARTMENT DEEPLY REGRETS TO INFORM YOU THAT YOUR SON LIEUTENANT (JG) WILLIAM TRAFFORD BENN WAS KILLED AS A RESULT OF PLANE ACCIDENT ON 31 DECEMBER 1945 WHILE IN THE SERVICE OF HIS COUNTRY. THE DEPARTMENT EXTENDS TO YOU ITS SINCER-EST SYMPATHY IN YOUR GREAT LOSS. NO INFOR-MATION AVAILABLE AT PRESENT IN REGARD TO DISPOSITION OF REMAINS BUT BY REASON OF EXISTING CONDITIONS BURIAL AT SEA OR IN LOCALITY OF DEATH HIGHLY PROBABLE. IF FURTHER DETAILS ARE RECEIVED YOU WILL BE INFORMED.

No one noticed that the navy got the year wrong.[655]

The box also included letters from June to Bill's family following his death. From one to Bill's aunt a few days after they received the news:

> I called Pat Williams and she was going to get in touch with Orlene and Kay. They are coming down next weekend to be with me. I am having a memorial service Sunday, January 21st in the Main Street Christian Church in Bill's memory. The girls said of course they would come. These girls I feel so close to in my hours of grief.[656]

The three "girls" were wives of squadron pilots—including Kay, my mother. It was eerie: the photo with Stang, the stories about Bill and Dad at the O Club, the note from June. The Benns might well have known my parents better than I ever did, or will. For months I'd been making a movie in my head, starring Bill and June. It had all the elements of a 1940s classic—the meeting at the canteen, courting in front of the fire, days and nights on the beach, the flyboy and his bride. In a scene I'd imagined many times, they are dancing, maybe at the Del Coronado. He is in his uniform; she is wearing pearls and a soft silk blouse. It is the night before he leaves. Bill is smiling, as usual. June rests her head on his chest. This time, though, I notice other couples in the background. And there, dimly lit but still in the shot, I recognize my mother and Dad, forever out of focus.

In the box was one last letter, from Bill to June, written Christmas Eve and received three weeks later. Actually, it was a typewritten copy made by June and mailed to Bill's parents, along with a note saying, "I shall cherish this the rest of my life."

> My dearly beloved:
> Tonight is Xmas Eve my darling and I will have to write my Christmas letter today as I shall have to fly all day tomorrow. Wouldn't you know it?
> I'm spending the day and shall spend the evening thinking and dreaming of our last two Xmas' together. The first Xmas

when Bill was a little Cadet, and how I went to church with you on Christmas Eve. . . . I resolved that night, and told you so, that I would brighten your life, make you happier, and make you mine. I resolved all that darling because I knew then, far sooner than you did, that you and I were meant for each other. . . .

Then tonight my thoughts shall stray once more to our last Xmas Eve. It was filled with laughter, gaiety, and a beautiful love for one another. Remember our preparations, the cutting out of the crepe paper "Merry Christmas," all our decorations and finally opening our presents after the folks had left. My darling, to me it was and still is a beautiful dream. . . .

Be good darling and continue to work for Bill and June during the coming year. I love you, darling, and shall for the rest of my life.

Your,
Bill[657]

I knew I had to see June.

We had talked many times but never met in person. First I told her about Pat and the box of Bill's mementoes. Then I asked whether I could visit. I said I would bring anything from the box she wanted and always keep the rest safe. So we made a date.

I recognized her right away. The tall, stunning woman I knew from the photos probably never imagined a cabbie helping her from the back seat to her walker. But there was no trace of pity in him or her. At breakfast we caught up on news about our families. She told me more about Dick White. He was quiet, steady, organized; a good father and kind husband. They lived for a time in Colorado, where the two of them loved to hike. He was buried in the small town where he grew up, in southern Illinois.

I met many of her friends in the high-rise retirement home where her top floor apartment looked out over the city. Everyone in the building seemed to know June, and vice versa. She was on committees; she visited when people were sick and helped do their shopping or write their letters. She had told me we would go to the beach that day, because it always reminded her of Bill, so late in the morning, we boarded a city bus. It took several routes and transfers to get there, and she didn't bring her walker because she said she had me to lean on.

During the rides she began to talk about how difficult it was right after Bill's death, even with people who meant well. How her single girl-friends visited and sat in virtual silence, no one knowing what to say. How her mother wanted to put away all of Bill's things and how she resisted. How friends of her father tried to sell her insurance, now that she was "on her own." I told her small stories about daily life in the squadron; she laughed when she heard about Bill and Dad at the O Club.

The last bus stopped next to her favorite beachside restaurant. We sat at a picnic table outside and ordered her usual, blackened grouper. It was a weekday; no one else around. In an envelope I gave her the program from Bill's memorial service in Kokomo, the only thing she'd asked for from his mementoes. I also gave her pictures from the box that she'd never seen, including one of her and Bill standing in front of a house in California. "Back then I still knew how to pose," she laughed. "See? One foot in front of the other." Finally, I told her the envelope contained a copy of Bill's Christmas Eve letter to her. She could read it later alone, if she liked.

Lunch came, and talk turned to Bill's crash. It seemed June had many of the same questions as Pat Benn. I asked whether she wanted me to tell her everything. She didn't interrupt, didn't ask questions, but when I was finished, she looked across at the water and said, "Thank you." Then, for the first time in any of our conversations, she cried. Quietly, "I still miss him." Another minute passed, she looked up. "I told you that the night before he left, he said he didn't want to make love. He was too sad." I nod-ded. "But I didn't want that to be his memory. So what I didn't tell you is, I talked him into it." A deep breath, hands clasped on the table. "I'm glad you did," I said. Eyes on the distance, a small smile. "So were we," she whispered.

We stood and crossed the road to the beach. June wanted to put her feet in the sand. We went a short way and sat in some chairs. I held her hand to keep her steady, and when we got back to the sidewalk, she didn't let go. We walked past seaside guest cottages. If she had enough money, she would rent one for a week or two next summer. She always felt happy by the water. We retraced our bus routes and went to dinner with some of her friends. Afterward, June walked part of the way to the curb and kissed me good-bye. We both waved until the cab turned the corner.

Boarding the airport van the next morning, I found myself next to an elderly gentleman wearing a baseball cap that proclaimed him a World War II veteran. It also had a picture of a bomber, and so I asked about his experience. He had flown B-24s over Ploesti, not in the famous raids but after. As with most of the men I'd met, there was no bluster. He answered questions and talked more about his buddies than himself. After a while he asked why I was in town, and I told him about the book I was writing. He'd never heard of the navy flying B-24s on single-plane missions. I filled him in on the basics of the squadron and shared some of what I'd learned, including about June and Bill Benn. The old pilot's chin quivered as he rubbed it with his hand. He cleared his throat and said, "People need to hear stories like that."

I had seen the same thing many times. The war got under everyone's skin, embedded like shrapnel. And it still worked its way to the surface, most often with a sudden welling in the eyes. On the first night of my first squadron reunion, someone pointed out two men sitting together at a table and told me they had been in Dad's crew. I went over and introduced myself. I'd hardly begun before they were blinking back tears. Bob Forkner, once a seventeen-year-old bow gunner, finally spoke. "Mr. Kittrell said he would get us all home. And he did."

Ever since that evening, I've lived partially in the past. In a time and place I never knew and can never forget.

On the plane home, I studied again my favorite photo of June and Bill. They are at a table in a night club, and it's a perfect tableau of the time. A fake palm tree is off to one side. A white-jacketed waiter perches in the background. It's not a paid-for picture; it's an amateur shot—they've probably asked a stranger to use their own camera. The head of someone walking by blurs the foreground. At the table are Lloyd Bloomquist, my dad's original copilot, and his wife, Verona. Next to them, looking serious and adult, are Bill's aunt Lois and her husband, Basil, who lived in Los Angeles. They must have come to San Diego to say good-bye. Bill is in his uniform, wearing a very broad grin. June has pearls around her neck and a flower behind her ear. Her left hand rests on the table. You can see her wedding ring and, on her wrist, a charm bracelet from Bill. I recognized the bracelet because June had shown it to me—the only thing he gave her that she had kept all these years.

The gulf between then and now is as wide as the water that once separated them. And yet . . .

A few years later, June told me she would have to stop our conversations. Alzheimer's was overtaking her. She died in the spring of 2017, aged ninety-six.

But I will always remember the first time we ever spoke. I had left voicemails for the three June D. Whites, explaining the project I was working on. As usual, I had no idea whether any would respond; experience told me the odds were against it. But within an hour, the phone rang. Was I the gentleman who left a message? The voice was obviously that of an older woman, so I said straightaway, "Ms. White, I'm wondering if you might be the former June Dohner of Kokomo, Indiana, who was married during World War II to a navy pilot named Bill Benn."

On the other end of the line there was a breath, and another. Time passed. Then, softly, with pauses: "He was my first husband. . . . And my dear love. . . . And we didn't have much time together."

Notes

1 Norman McLean, *A River Runs through It, and Other Stories*, 25th anniv. ed. (Chicago: University of Chicago Press, 1976), xix–xx.

2 James Gray interview, September 15, 2006.

3 Appendix 4 in Roy A. Grossnick, *Dictionary of American Naval Aviation Squadrons* (Washington, DC: Naval Historical Center, Department of the Navy, 1995), 2:729–30.

4 "Navy Patrol Bombing Squadron 117 Awarded Presidential Unit Citation," Navy News Release, May 5, 1947; *The Blue Raiders: VPB 117, United States Navy, 1944–1945* (N.p.: N.p., 1983) (a loose-leaf collection of squadron information, records, photos, and so forth, prepared for the first VPB-117 reunion in 1983; a copy is on file in the Emil Buehler Naval Aviation Library at the National Naval Aviation Museum, Naval Air Station, Pensacola, Florida).

5 Ken Nagel interview, December 2, 2005.

6 VPB-117 pilot, letter to mother, December 16, 1944.

7 At the first Blue Raiders reunion that my son Andrew and I attended in 2003, Bill Swink was the first squadron member we met. That's when he told us about Carson Chalk and the army sergeant who tried to save his life. A week later, I came home and wrote a draft of his story. After he died, I sent the finished chapter to his widow, Emmy, who made a few minor corrections and said that's how she remembered the story too. And she'd heard it more than once.

8 Elizabeth Howell, "Chuck Yeager: First Person to Break the Sound Barrier," *Spaceflight*, May 31, 2017, https://www.space.com/26204-chuck-yeager.html.

9 "John Glenn," Wikipedia, https://en.wikipedia.org/wiki/John_Glenn.

10 Edmund Goulding, dir., *The Dawn Patrol* (Burbank, CA: Warner Bros., 1938).

11 Joe Lowder interview, February 28, 2006.

12 Marc S. Gallicchio, *The Unpredictability of the Past: Memories of the Asia-Pacific War in U.S.-East Asian Relations* (Durham, NC: Duke University Press, 2007), 217.

13 Gene Kern interview, November 7, 2007.

14 "Ford Tri-Motor 5-AT," How Stuff Works, https://science.howstuffworks.com/transport/flight/classic/ford-tri-motor.htm.

15 Gene Kern, email, April 27, 2006.

16 Gene Kern, email, April 29, 2006.

17 Gene Kern interview, November 7, 2007.

18 "Gene Kern's Three-Plus Years in the Navy," written account given to the author, 2008.

19 Gene Kern interview, November 7, 2007.

20 U.S. Office of the Chief of Naval Operations and U.S. Army Air Forces, *Aircrewman's Gunnery Manual; Issued by Aviation Training Division, Office of the Chief of Naval Operations, U.S. Navy, in Collaboration with U.S. Army Air Forces* (Washington, DC: Aviation Training Division, 1944).

21 Gene Kern interview, November 7, 2007.

22 U.S. Office of the Chief of Naval Operations and U.S. Army Air Forces, *Aircrewman's Gunnery Manual*, 2.

23 Gene Kern interview, November 9, 2007.

24 Gene Kern interview, November 7, 2007.

25 Excerpt from the *Wellman Centennial, 1879–1979*, 1st ed. (Wellman, IA: Centennial Committee, 1979).

26 "List of Airliners by Maximum Takeoff Weight," Wikipedia, https://en.wikipedia .org/wiki/List_of_airliners_by_maximum_takeoff_weight.

27 "Taylorcraft Auster Aircraft History Performance and Specifications," Pilotfriend, http://www.pilotfriend.com/aircraft%20performance/Taylorcraft.htm.

28 See Ninety-Nines at www.ninety-nines.org.

29 Galen Bull interview, October 17, 2008.

30 Galen Bull interview, October 16, 2007.

31 Benjamin Hare, *Football at Military Training Centers during World War II* (Naperville, IL: North Central College, 2006).

32 Norman C. Delaney, "Corpus Christi's 'University of the Air,'" *Naval History Magazine* 27, no. 3 (May 2013): https://www.usni.org/magazines/naval-history-magazine/2013/ may/corpus-christis-university-air; www.navalaviationmuseum.org.

33 Galen Bull interview, October 16, 2007.

34 E. O. Rigsbee III, interview, March 18, 2006.

35 *Lucky Bag*, U.S. Naval Academy Yearbook, 1930.

36 "Annual Register of the United States Naval Academy. Annapolis, Md," Internet Archive, 1930, https://archive.org/details/annualregiste19291930unse, 58.

37 *Lucky Bag*, 1930, 69.

38 *Lucky Bag*, 1926, photo: "Electrical Engineering Department—Class in Radio (Juice P-Work)," United States Naval Academy, Nimitz Library, Image Number 2392.

39 *New York Times*, May 30, 1930.

40 Edward "Ned" Clarence Rigsbee, *The Rigsbee Story*, October 21, 1934.

41 E. O. Rigsbee III interview, March 18, 2006.

42 *Rigsbee USN Service Biography*, courtesy of E. O. Rigsbee III.

43 Appendix 1 in Roy A. Grossnick, *United States Naval Aviation, 1910–1995* (Washington, DC: Naval Historical Center, Department of the Navy, 1997), 414.

44 Colonel R. C. Reisinger, USMC, "The Naval Aviator in Reserve," *U.S. Naval Institute Proceedings* 60, no. 375 (May 1934): www.usni.org/magazines/proceedings/1934-05.

45 Email, library@navalaavitaiopnmuseum.org, February 11, 2016.

46 *U.S. Navy Report of the Search for Amelia Earhart, July 2–18, 1937* (College Park, MD: National Archives).

47 *Rigsbee USN Service Biography*.

48 E. O. Rigsbee III interview, March 18, 2006.

49 Thomas L. Scharf, ed., *Journal of San Diego History* 31, no. 2 (spring 1985): https:// sandiegohistory.org/journal/1985/april/index-htm-105.

50 E. O. Rigsbee III interview, March 18, 2006.

51 *Rigsbee USN Service Biography*.

52 *Rigsbee USN Service Biography*.

53 Edwin P. Hoyt, *How They Won the War in the Pacific: Nimitz and His Admirals* (Guilford, CT: Lyons Press, 2012), 272–73, 32; Clark G. Reynolds, *On the Warpath in the Pacific* (Annapolis, MD: Naval Institute Press, 2013), 248; Charles Pownall, *The Pacific War Online Encyclopedia*, http://pwencycl.kgbudge.com; Patrick Degan, *Flattop Fighting in World War II* (Jefferson, NC: McFarland, 2003), 178–79; Dan Moore, email, December 12, 2005.

54 LaVelle Saier interview, October 29, 2006.

55 John Bullock, "Crew 4," in *The Blue Raiders: VPB 117, United States Navy, 1944–1945* (N.p.: N.p., 1983).

56 Dan Moore interview, January 5, 2006.

57 Gerald Wegner interview, December 7, 2004.

58 Mel L. Shettle, *Western States*, vol. 2 of *United States Naval Air Stations of World War II* (Bowersville, GA: Schaertel, 1997).

59 Copy of Rigsbee remarks, VPB-117 Commissioning Ceremony, Rigsbee Family Papers, February 1, 1944, courtesy of E. O. Rigsbee III.

60 John Summers interview, January 11, 2005.

61 E. O. Rigsbee, letter to "Hub" Rigsbee, February 4, 1944.

62 Rod Donnelly, *A Brief History of WWII*.

63 Royce Timmons interview, June 9, 2006.

64 Sheldon Sutton interview, August 12, 2006; Royce Timmons interview, June 9, 2006.

65 Edward F. Kittrell, *Logbook*.

66 "VP-117 Mishap," U.S. Navy Patrol Squadrons, VPnavy.com/vp117_mishap.html.

67 Bill Allsopp interview, July 27, 2005.

68 George Cox interview, November 5, 2005.

69 Dean Maughn interview, September 22, 2004.

70 O'Neill Osborne interview, January 10, 2005.

71 Galen Bull interview, October 16, 2007.

72 Sheldon Sutton interview, August 12, 2006.

73 Gilbert Ragland interview, January 6, 2005; "Honoring the Planes That Helped Build San Diego," *Los Angeles Times*, December 13, 1999.

74 "Mariana Islands Campaign and the Great Turkey Shoot," World War II Database, https://ww2db.com/battle_spec.php?battle_id=10.

75 Edward F. Kittrell, *Logbook*.

76 Jim DeVine, "WW2 at Johnston Atoll," Marines @ Work, http://marinememoir.homestead.com/DeVine02.html.

77 Gene Kern, email, January 24, 2009.

78 "The 6th Bomb Group," philcrowther.com/6thBG.

79 Naval Aviation Museum Foundation, navalaviationfoundation.org; *The Blue Raiders: VPB 117, United States Navy, 1944–1945* (N.p.: N.p., 1983); "VPB-117—The Blue Raiders," Naval Aviation Museum Foundation, https://navalaviationfoundation.org/ways-to-give/national-flight-log/squadron-flight-log-entry/?id=24.

80 Gene Kern interview, November 9, 2007; Joe Papp interview, January 14, 2006; Joe Papp, "Near-Death Episode Led to Beautiful Dress for Daughter," *South Bend Tribune*, August 29, 2006.

81 Donnelly, *A Brief History of WWII*, 15–16.

82 *The Blue Raiders.*

83 Marshall Beals interviews, October 3, 2003; January 16, 2008.

84 "Navy Fliers Keep Vast Pacific Vigil," *New York Times*, December 24, 1944.

85 VPB-117, October War Diary, United States Pacific Fleet Air Force, Patrol Bombing Squadron One Hundred Seventeen (Confidential), November 1, 1944; Sheldon Sutton interview, August 12, 2006; George Cox interview, November 5, 2005.

86 VPB-117, War Diary, October 1944.

87 VPB-117, Aircraft Action Report #10, National Archives and Records Administration (hereafter NARA).

88 VPB-117, Aircraft Action Report #12, NARA.

89 O'Neill Osborne interview, September 20, 2006.

90 VPB-117, Aircraft Action Report #13, NARA.

91 Max Voelzke and J. G. Lassey in *The Blue Raiders: VPB 117, United States Navy, 1944–1945* (N.p.: N.p., 1983).

92 Bill Allsopp interview, July 27, 2005; Dean Maughn interview, September 22, 2004; J. G. Lassey, *The Blue Raiders.*

93 Samuel Eliot Morison, *Leyte, June 1944–January 1945*, Vol. 12 of *History of United States Naval Operations in World War II* (Urbana: University of Illinois Press, 2002), 130–40.

94 Donnelly, *A Brief History of WWII*; John Bullock, email, December 30, 2004.

95 Morison, *Leyte*, 350.

96 Gene Kern, note, May 5, 2004.

97 Ben Gibson, letter to P. J. Crowley, July 12, 1945.

98 Jan Carter, "Adventures of Crew 16," in *The Blue Raiders*; "Operation Te-Go: Japanese Attack on Leyte December 7, 1944," Pacific Wrecks, https://www.pacificwrecks.com/airfields/philippines/san_pablo/12-07-44/index.html.

99 Ken Nagel, "History of Crew 12," in *The Blue Raiders: VPB 117, United States Navy, 1944–1945* (N.p.: N.p., 1983).

100 Dan Moore, email, February 9, 2006.

101 Laurel Brewer interview, September 20, 2006.

102 Dan Moore, email, February 9, 2006.

103 To understand what happened that night in the launch as it headed to the *Currituck*, I spoke with all the surviving members of Commander Rigsbee's crew. The enlisted men were mostly hesitant at first. But as we spoke, they were more forthcoming. One said, "He went off his rocker there at the last." Another put it more delicately, saying, "He just got real tired." And a third crewman said simply, "Rigsbee had a nervous breakdown. Wars are like that." But the narrative of that event in this chapter comes largely from an interview with Bill Allsopp on July 27, 2005. It's important to know that I never heard Bill disparage Rigsbee in any of our conversations. And, as a later chapter in the book points out, he and Rigsbee stayed in touch for years after the war. So I have little doubt that his account is accurate and that he wished things had turned out better for "The Skipper."

104 Galen Bull interview, October 11, 2007.

105 *The Blue Raiders.*

106 James Jones, *WWII: A Chronicle of Soldiering* (Chicago: University of Chicago Press, 2014), 38, 40–42.

107 Undated letter to author, Nancy Pedretti Thompson, c. 2008.

108 Nancy Thompson interview, December 12, 2008.

109 Copy of speech from Pedretti family.

110 Bill Pedretti, letter to parents, March 18, 1943.

111 Nancy Thompson interview, December 12, 2008.

112 Bill Pedretti, letter to parents, February 13, 1943.

113 Bill Pedretti, letter to parents, July 6, 1943.

114 Kenneth Box interview, July 14, 2008.

115 Kenneth Box interview, July 12, 2010.

116 Kenneth Box interview, July 14, 2008.

117 John Summers interview, January 11, 2005.

118 "Navy Fliers Keep Vast Pacific Vigil," *New York Times*, December 24, 1944.

119 Marshall Beals interview, January 16, 2008.

120 VPB-117, Aircraft Action Report #1, NARA.

121 VPB-117, Aircraft Action Report #8, NARA.

122 Nancy Thompson, email, July 9, 2010.

123 VPB-117, Aircraft Action Report #11, NARA.

124 *The Blue Raiders: VPB 117, United States Navy, 1944–1945* (N.p.: N.p., 1983); John Summers interview, January 11, 2005; *Honolulu Advertiser*, June 11, 1945.

125 VPB-117, Aircraft Action Report #15, NARA.

126 John Summers interview, January 11, 2005.

127 VPB-117, Aircraft Action Report #15, NARA.

128 John Summers interview, January 11, 2005.

129 VPB-117, Aircraft Action Report #15, NARA.

130 John Summers interview, January 11, 2005.

131 VPB-117, Aircraft Action Report #15, NARA.

132 VPB-117, Injury Report, November 15, 1944, NARA.

133 John Summers interview, January 11, 2005.

134 *New York Times*, December 24, 1944.

135 Award ceremony photo, June 2, 1945.

136 Nancy Thompson, email, July 9, 2010.

137 Kenneth Box interview, January 14, 2008.

138 Anita Box Christy, email, January 20, 2014.

139 Kenneth Box interview, July 12, 2010.

140 Anita Box Christy, email, April 12, 2016.

141 Nancy Thompson interview, December 12, 2008.

142 Nancy Thompson interview, April 6, 2008.

143 Nancy Thompson interview, June 26, 2019.

144 Nancy Thompson interview, December 12, 2008.

145 James Jones, *WWII: A Chronicle of Soldiering* (Chicago: University of Chicago Press, 2014), 205.

146 *The Blue Raiders: VPB 117, United States Navy, 1944–1945* (N.p.: N.p., 1983).

147 Pat Benn interview, January 8, 2006.
148 *Minneapolis Tribune*, March 3, 1940.
149 Pat Benn interview, January 12, 2006.
150 Pat Benn, letter, February 21, 2006.
151 "Photographs Showing the Growth of Wold-Chamberlain Field," Minnesota Historical Society, http://www.mnhs.org/mgg/artifact/wold.
152 Pat Benn interview, January 12, 2006.
153 Application for student pilot rating and certificate, February 2, 1939.
154 Pat Benn interview, January 12, 2006.
155 Bill Benn, letter to mother, November 15, 1941.
156 Pat Benn interview, January 22, 2006.
157 "Liberty cabbage," Urban Dictionary, https://www.urbandictionary.com/define.php?term=liberty%20cabbage.
158 "The WWI Home Front: War Hysteria & the Persecution of German-Americans," History on the Net, https://www.historyonthenet.com/authentichistory/1914-1920/2-homefront/4-hysteria.
159 Richard Stang interview, February 4, 2006; Harold Stang Jr., email, March 27, 2006.
160 Richard Stang interview, February 4, 2006.
161 Harold Stang Jr., email, March 27, 2006.
162 Richard Stang interview, February 4, 2006.
163 Harold Stang service record.
164 Richard Stang interview, February 4, 2006.
165 "USS Enterprise CV-6: The Most Decorated Ship of the Second World War," http://www.cv6.org/1941/1941.htm.
166 Undated newspaper photo caption of Stang family.
167 Richard Stang interview, February 4, 2006.
168 June White interview, April 19, 2006.
169 Mel L. Shettle, *Western States*, Vol. 2 of *United States Naval Air Stations of World War II* (Bowersville, GA: Schaertel, 1997).
170 June White interview, January 19, 2006.
171 *Kokomo Tribune*, January 11, 1945.
172 June White interview, April 19, 2006.
173 Joan Mickelson, "Hollywood in World War II," *Florida's Hollywood: History and People*, November 11, 2013, joanmickelsonphd.wordpress.com/2013/11/11/Hollywood-in-world-war.
174 June White interview, April 19, 2006.
175 June White interview, April 19, 2006.
176 June White interview, April 26, 2006.
177 June White interview, April 19, 2006.
178 Harold Stang Jr., email, January 23, 2006.
179 VPB-117, October War Diary, United States Pacific Fleet Air Force, Patrol Bombing Squadron One Hundred Seventeen (Confidential), November 1, 1944; VPB-117, Aircraft Action Report #5, NARA.
180 Ralph Sanders interview, December 29, 2003.

181 Bill Benn, letter to mother, December 6, 1944.

182 June White interview, April 19, 2006.

183 "Typhoon Cobra," Wikipedia, https://en.wikipedia.org/wiki/Typhoon_Cobra.

184 Ralph Sanders interview, December 29, 2003.

185 Harold Stang Jr., email, March 27, 2006.

186 Ralph Sanders interview, December 29, 2003.

187 "Jack Sager Journal," in *The Blue Raiders*; VPB-117, Injury Report, February 9, 1945.

188 Harold Stang Jr., letter, January 23, 2006.

189 John Bullock interview, August 3, 2007.

190 Pat Benn interview, January 12, 2006.

191 June White interview, April 19, 2006.

192 Lyman K. Smith, letter to June White, undated.

193 Bill Pinney, letter to June White, undated.

194 June White interview, April 19, 2006.

195 While he was in VPB-117, Harold Boss authored a history of his experiences in World War II titled *Blue Monsters*. It was later included in *The Blue Raiders: VPB 117, United States Navy, 1944–1945* (N.p.: N.p., 1983), prepared for the squadron's first reunion in 1983.

196 Mrs. Dorothy Boss interview, January 5, 2005.

197 *Blue Monsters*, 7.

198 *Blue Monsters*, 8–9.

199 *Blue Monsters*, 10–21.

200 Mrs. Robert Massey interview, February 12, 2008.

201 Richard O'Shaughnessy interview, January 7, 2005.

202 Richard O'Shaughnessy interview, January 7, 2005; Mrs. Robert Massey interview, February 12, 2008.

203 VPB-117, Aircraft Action Report #20, NARA.

204 VPB-117, Aircraft Action Report #42, NARA.

205 Gerald "Rock" Wegner interview, December 7, 2004.

206 Richard O'Shaughnessy interview, January 7, 2005.

207 Gordon Forbes, *Goodbye to Some* (Annapolis, MD: Naval Institute Press, 1997).

208 *Blue Monsters*, 42.

209 Harold Boss obituary, Buffalo, New York, newspaper, undated; Archives, Naval Historical Center, Washington, DC.

210 "Admiral E. W. Eberle," Naval History and Heritage Command, June 11, 2015, https://www.history.navy.mil/research/histories/ship-histories/danfs/a/admiral-e-w -eberle.html.

211 "Admiral E. W. Eberle."

212 Evert Carlson obituary, *Courier-News* (Plainfield, New Jersey), May 10, 1945.

213 Mrs. Robert Massey interview, January 12, 2005; Richard O'Shaughnessy interview, January 7, 2005.

214 Gerald "Rock" Wegner interview, December 7, 2004.

215 Dorothy Boss interview, January 5, 2005.

216 Joe Papp interview, January 14, 2006.

217 Joe Papp's daughter Barbara Mansfield, email, January 8, 2009.

218 Joe Papp interview, September 30, 2009.

219 Joe Papp interview, January 14, 2006.

220 VPB-117, Aircraft Action Report #71, NARA.

221 Joe Papp, letter to Andrew Kittrell, July 22, 2009.

222 Joe Papp, email, September 30, 2009.

223 "Mechanical Accumulator," FPO, http://www.freepatentsonline.com/4046167.html.

224 Joe Papp interview, January 14, 2006.

225 Joe Papp interview, November 4, 2009.

226 Barbara Mansfield, email, July 19, 2010.

227 Patricia Renner Maguire interview, May 8, 2009.

228 John Bullock, "Crew 4," in *The Blue Raiders: VPB 117, United States Navy, 1944–1945* (N.p.: N.p., 1983).

229 VPB-117, Aircraft Action Report #16, NARA; John Bullock, email, January 23, 2007.

230 VPB-117, Aircraft Action Report #17, NARA.

231 VPB-117, Aircraft Action Report #50, NARA.

232 John Bullock interview, August 3, 2007.

233 Ken Nagel interview, March 30, 2006.

234 VPB-117, Aircraft Action Report #62, NARA.

235 Navy Cross citation, "Harold Meade McGaughey," Hall of Valor Project, https://valor.militarytimes.com/hero/6000.

236 VPB-117, Aircraft Action Report #74, NARA.

237 VPB-117, Aircraft Action Report #75, NARA.

238 VPB-117, Aircraft Action Report #85, NARA.

239 Report of Interment for Unknown X-1, Grave No. 13, Row 2, USAF Cemetery, Palawan #1, P.I.

240 Art Elder interview, October 13, 2010.

241 John Bullock, email, November 6, 2005.

242 William Loesel, Individual Deceased Personnel File, April 29, 1945.

243 Undated Henry McLemore column, McNaught Syndicate Inc.

244 William Loesel, Individual Deceased Personnel File.

245 *Fort Scott Tribune*, April 30, 1949.

246 Harold McGaughey, Individual Deceased Personnel File, April 29, 1945.

247 Brett Geneva (Fort Scott National Cemetery), interviews, August 18 and 20, 2008; "Deaths—Funerals, Group Military Rites," *Fort Scott Tribune*, April 30, 1949.

248 Patricia Renner Maguire interview, April 7, 2009.

249 Elizabeth Sutton, email, May 4, 2009.

250 LaVelle Saier interview, October 29, 2006.

251 Case of Isaac G. Parker, Ensign, U.S. Naval Reserve, May 17, 1945, Record of Proceedings of a General Court-Martial Convened at the U.S. Acorn Nineteen, Navy 3100 by the Order of Commander Aircraft, Seventh Fleet, 21 (hereafter Parker Trial Transcript).

252 Marilyn Parker interview, February 28, 2009.

253 George Parker, letter, June 1, 1945.

254 "Navy Fliers Keep Vast Pacific Vigil," *New York Times*, December 24, 1944.

255 VPB-117, Aircraft Action Report #4, NARA.

256 "Navy Fliers Keep Vast Pacific Vigil."

257 VPB-117, Aircraft Action Report #6, NARA.

258 VPB-117, Aircraft Action Report #34, NARA; James Edwards interview, March 17, 2009.

259 Parker Trial Transcript, 71–72.

260 Parker Trial Transcript, 236.

261 Parker Trial Transcript, 230.

262 Parker Trial Transcript, 13.

263 Statement of Ensign Isaac G. Parker (A1), U.S. Naval Reserve (347491), March 28, 1945, 1.

264 Parker Trial Transcript, 62–63.

265 Parker Pretrial Statement, 4.

266 Parker Pretrial Statement, 4.

267 Crew 3 rosters, Aircraft Action Reports #4, #22, #14, #34, #35, #39, #52, #60, #61, #64, #88, #89, #90, #91, #92, #93, #97, NARA.

268 VPB-117, Aircraft Action Report #88, NARA.

269 VPB-117, Aircraft Action Report #89, NARA.

270 Parker Trial Transcript, 21.

271 Dan Moore interview, May 31, 2007.

272 VPB-117, Aircraft Action Report #90, NARA.

273 VPB-117, Aircraft Action Report #91, NARA.

274 VPB-117, Aircraft Action Report #93, NARA; Parker Trial Transcript, 56–59.

275 George Parker, letter, March 14, 1945.

276 Warren Glunt, in Parker Trial Transcript, 202.

277 VPB-117, Aircraft Action Report #97, NARA.

278 Glunt, Parker Trial Transcript, 201–17.

279 George Parker, letter, June 1, 1945.

280 George Parker, letter, May 23, 1945.

281 Parker Trial Transcript, 85–86.

282 George Parker, letter, April 25, 1945.

283 Charles Kickham obituary, *Boston Globe*, January 8, 2004.

284 Topeka Public Library, email, February 14, 2009.

285 Jake Dickinson, letter, May 2, 1945.

286 Parker Trial Transcript, 22–23.

287 Parker Trial Transcript, 56–60.

288 Parker Trial Transcript, 60–63.

289 Parker Trial Transcript, 61.

290 Parker Trial Transcript, 80–81.

291 Parker Trial Transcript, 143.

292 Parker Trial Transcript, 148, 157, 163, 167, 170, 180, 188, 190, 194, 197, 200.

293 Parker Trial Transcript, 186–221.

294 Parker Trial Transcript, 248–56.

295 Parker Trial Transcript, 246–57.

296 George Parker, letter to father, June 29, 1945.

297 Jake Dickinson, letter to wife, June 1, 1945.

298 Sworn statement by Lt. Tom Perkins, USNR, witnessed by three others, plus Lt. Commander John R. Naceau.

299 Jake Dickinson, letter to wife, May 2, 1945.

300 Jake Dickinson, letter to wife, July 28, 1945.

301 Jake Dickinson, letter to wife, August 2, 1945.

302 George Parker, letters to father, June 9, 1945; July 29, 1945; July 21, 1945.

303 George Parker, letter, July 21, 1945.

304 George Parker, letter, August 15, 1945.

305 "German Strategic Bombing during World War I," Wikipedia, https://en.wikipedia .org/German_strategic_bombing_during_World_War_I.

306 "1917, June 26: First U.S. Troops Arrive in France," History.com, updated July 28, 2019, https://www.history.com/this-day-in-history/first-u-s-troops-arrive-in-france.

307 See Discover Bisbee at http://www.discoverbisbee.com.

308 Dan Moore's children (Jane Callahan-Moore, Marguerite Moore Callaway, and Dan Moore Jr.) interview, July 29, 2016.

309 Carl Zebrowski, *America in WWII Magazine*, December 2007, http://www.america inwwii.com/back-issues/december-2007.

310 "Grumman F4F Wildcat," Wikipedia, https://en.wikipedia.org/wiki/GrummanF4F Wildcat.

311 Dan Moore interview, December 3, 2005.

312 Dan Moore's children (Jane Callahan-Moore, Marguerite Moore Callaway, and Dan Moore Jr.) interview, July 29, 2016.

313 Dan Moore, email, March 30, 2006.

314 Dan Moore, email, January 5, 2006.

315 Marvin Barefoot obituary, *Tulsa World*, January 13, 2008.

316 Dan Moore, email, January 12, 2006.

317 Gene Kern, *Logbook*, November 1944.

318 VPB-117, Aircraft Action Report #25, NARA.

319 VPB-117, Aircraft Action Report #26, NARA.

320 Gene Kern, email, June 17, 2006.

321 Dan Moore, email, June 19, 2006.

322 "Ijn Hyuga: Tabular Record of Movement," Imperial Japanese Navy Page, http:// www.combinedfleet.com/hyuga.htm.

323 VPB-117, Aircraft Action Report #27, NARA.

324 Dan Moore, email, June 15, 2006.

325 Gene Kern, email, June 17, 2006; Gene Kern interview, November 9, 2007; Dan Moore, email, June 16, 2006.

326 Gene Kern interview, November 9, 2007; Frank Wharton, Individual Deceased Personnel File, December 23, 1944.

327 Dan Moore, email, June 16, 2006.

328 Gene Kern, *Logbook*.

329 VPB-117, Aircraft Action Report #58, NARA; Dan Moore, email, June 24, 2006; Roy A. Grossnick, *Dictionary of American Naval Aviation Squadrons* (Washington, DC: Naval Historical Center, Department of the Navy, 1995), 2:730–31.

330 Hilda Moore, letter, January 6, 1945.

331 Hilda Moore, letters, January 12 and 14, 1945.

332 *The Blue Raiders: VPB 117, United States Navy, 1944–1945* (N.p.: N.p., 1983).

333 Dan Moore, letter to Folsom Moore, January 17, 1945.

334 "US Army Air Forces in the South West Pacific Theatre," Wikipedia, https://en.wikipedia.org/wiki/United_States_Army_Air_Forces_in_the_South_West_Pacific_Theatre.

335 Dan Moore interview, May 31, 2007.

336 Dan Moore interview, May 31, 2007.

337 Dan Moore, email, March 20, 2009.

338 Art Elder interview, November 2, 2006.

339 Dan Moore interview, May 31, 2007.

340 "Naval Health Clinic Hawaii—a Historical Journey," Naval Health Clinic Hawaii, https://www.med.navy.mil/sites/nhch/CommandInfo/Pages/history.aspx.

341 Lance Cpl. Isis M. Ramirez, "70 Years Takes Camp Smith from Hospital to Headquarters," Marines, October 31, 2011, https://www.marforpac.marines.mil/News/News-Article-Display/Article/530521/70-years-takes-camp-smith-from-hospital-to-headquarters.

342 Dan Moore interview, May 31, 2007.

343 Dan Moore interview, August 20, 2006.

344 Dan Moore interview, August 20, 2006.

345 Folsom Moore, letter to family, June 25, 1945.

346 Dan Moore, letter to parents, June 21, 1945.

347 George Raines, chief of neuropsychiatry, U.S. Naval Hospital, Bethesda, letter to Hilda Moore, June 28, 1945.

348 Michael M. Phillips, "The Lobotomy Files: One Doctor's Legacy," *Wall Street Journal*, http://projects.wsj.com/lobotomyfiles/?ch=two.

349 Dan Moore interview, August 20, 2006.

350 News clips with Hilda Moore letter, July 23, 1945.

351 Rogues Prandoni, PhD, St. Elizabeth's Hospital, email, March 8, 2017; Glenn Frankel, "DC Neurosurgeon Pioneered 'Operation Icepick' Technique," *Washington Post*, April 7, 1980.

352 Dan Moore interview, May 31, 2007.

353 Dan Moore interview, August 20, 2006.

354 Hilda Moore, letter to Folsom and Ola Moore, July 23, 1945.

355 Hilda Moore, letter to Folsom and Ola Moore, August 1, 1945.

356 Hilda Moore, letter to Folsom and Ola Moore, August 6, 1945.

357 Folsom Moore, letter to Hilda, August 10, 1945.

358 James Salter, *Burning the Days* (New York: Vintage International, 1988), 145.

359 Commander Air Force, Pacific Fleet, Air Ops Memo, March 2, 1945.

360 Sheldon Sutton, letter to Andrew Kittrell, July 8, 2004; Roy A. Grossnick, *Dictionary of American Naval Aviation Squadrons* (Washington, DC: Naval Historical Center, Department of the Navy, 1995), 2:729–30.

361 Unless otherwise noted, all accounts are based on the manuscript "Crew 18, Creator of Legends," prepared for *The Blue Raiders: VPB 117, United States Navy, 1944–1945* (N.p.: N.p., 1983), for the first squadron reunion.

362 Alan Carter interview, January 5, 2006.

363 "Nick Carter, Master Detective," Wikipedia, https://en.wikipedia.org/wiki/Nick _Carter,_Master_Detective.

364 Alan Eichenberg, *Logbook*.

365 Joe Pistotnik interview, January 10, 2005.

366 VPB-117, Aircraft Action Report #37, NARA.

367 VPB-117, Aircraft Action Report #38, NARA.

368 VPB-117, Aircraft Action Report #71, NARA; Joe Papp interview, January 14, 2006.

369 Unless otherwise noted, all accounts are based on the manuscript "The Exciting Adventures of Crew 16," prepared for *The Blue Raiders*, for the first squadron reunion in 1983.

370 Art Elder interview, November 19, 2006; "Squadron History: VPB-54," http://www .daveswarbirds.com/blackcat/hist-54.htm.

371 "Doggy Fliers Log Many Hours in the Air," *Naval Aviation News*, August 1952.

372 VPB-117, Aircraft Action Report #76, NARA.

373 VPB-117, Aircraft Action Report #77, NARA.

374 VPB-117, Aircraft Action Report #78, NARA.

375 VPB-117, Aircraft Action Report #79, NARA.

376 Edgar Elliott, *My Story, WWII: The Big One, My Part in the Navy, December 1941– December 1945* (unpublished manuscript), 31.

377 *My Story*, 32; VPB-117 Aircraft Action Report #92, NARA.

378 *My Story*, 32.

379 *My Story*, 33; VPB-117, Aircraft Action Report #99, NARA.

380 *My Story*, 33; VPB-117, Aircraft Action Report #100, NARA.

381 *My Story*, 33; VPB-117, Aircraft Action Report #101, NARA.

382 *My Story*, 33; VPB-117, Aircraft Action Report #102, NARA.

383 *My Story*, 35; VPB-117, Aircraft Action Report #103, NARA.

384 VPB-117, Aircraft Action Report #104, NARA.

385 VPB-117, Aircraft Action Report #105, NARA.

386 *My Story*, 35.

387 VPB-117, Aircraft Action Report #123, NARA.

388 *My Story*, 37–40.

389 *My Story*, 37–42.

390 VPB-117, Aircraft Action Report #131, NARA.

391 Art Elder interview, November 19, 2010.

392 *My Story*, 41–43.

393 "The First Line: Program Broadcast to the Men and Women of Our Armed Forces Worldwide, Dramatizing Combat of U.S. Navy Blue Raiders and One of Its Planes and Crew," radio script, 1945.

394 "Military Pay Chart 1942–1946," Navy CyberSpace, https://www.navycs.com /charts/1942-military-pay-chart.html.

395 Tom Hyland, letter to mother, July 8, 1942.

396 Karen Pizarro interview, March 5, 2006.

397 "Cathedral Defeats Regis High, 19–6," *Rocky Mountain News*, November 12, 1934.

398 Karen Pizarro interview, March 5, 2006.

399 Tom Hyland obituary, *Denver Post*, December 28, 2003.

400 Karen Pizarro interview, March 5, 2006.

401 Undated letter written from Guadalcanal, 1943.

402 VPB-117, Aircraft Action Report #69, NARA.

403 VPB-117, Aircraft Action Report #70, NARA.

404 VPB-117, Aircraft Action Report #80, NARA.

405 VPB-117, Aircraft Action Report #81, NARA.

406 Dan Moore, email, October 4, 2006.

407 VPB-117, Aircraft Action Report #114, NARA; Ken Minnock interview, January 18, 2006.

408 Francis McWilliams, email, October 25, 2005; Dan Moore, email, May 4, 2007.

409 VPB-117, Aircraft Action Report #126, NARA.

410 VPB-117, Aircraft Action Reports #126, 128, 139, 140, 157, 209, NARA.

411 Francis McWilliams, email, March 25, 2006.

412 VPB-117, Aircraft Action Report #263, NARA.

413 Tom Hyland obituary, *Rocky Mountain News*, December 28, 2003.

414 *Reflections of a Lifetime*, Bill Quinn family video, 1995.

415 *Reflections of a Lifetime*.

416 *Los Angeles Times*, January 29, 2017.

417 *Reflections of a Lifetime*.

418 "Edwin Andrew Petersen," interview by Geoffrey Panos, Utah World War II Stories, PBS Utah, February 1, 2006, https://www.kued.org/sites/default/files/petersenelwin.pdf.

419 *Reflections of a Lifetime*.

420 VPB-117, Aircraft Action Report #87, NARA.

421 VPB-117, Aircraft Action Report #72, NARA.

422 David Palmer interview, October 2003.

423 *Dad's Last Flight*, Bill Quinn family video, 1995.

424 Jack Frisz (Mary's brother) speaks about Bill Quinn, Bill Quinn family video.

425 Bill Quinn interview, October 2003.

426 *Reflections of a Lifetime*.

427 *Dad's Last Flight*.

428 *Reflections of a Lifetime*.

429 *Dad's Last Flight*.

430 Kathleen Quinn interview, September 5, 2011.

431 *Dad's Last Flight*.

432 "87 and Holding," essay by Rosemary Quinn, September 2007.

433 Kathleen Quinn interview, September 5, 2011.

434 "Crumbs to Miracles," essay by Kathleen Quinn, 2007.

435 *Dad's Last Flight*.

436 Henry Robinson Luce, *The Ideas of Henry Luce*, ed. John Knox Jessup (New York: Atheneum, 1969), 203.

437 Paul deMarrais, letter to parents, undated.

438 Bud Buchheim interview, August 17, 2015.

439 Viola Dougan, letter to deMarrais family, October 4, 1945.

440 VPB-117, Aircraft Action Reports #164, 190, 194, 202, NARA.

441 Viola Dougan, letter to deMarrais family, October 4, 1945.

442 Viola Dougan obituary, *Palo Alto Times*, May 12, 1976, 21.

443 Letter to Col. G. H. Bare, Quartermaster Corps, July 18, 1948.

444 Letter from Vo Van Ho, March 2, 1950.

445 *Cleveland Plain Dealer*, March 9, 1950.

446 Report of American Graves Registration Service, March 30, 1950.

447 Cable from American Graves Registration Service to Navy, October 26, 1948.

448 Capt. Joe Vogl, memo to quartermaster general of the Army, April 14, 1950.

449 Viola Dougan, letter to Capt. Joe Vogl, June 27, 1951.

450 Report, Maj. Joe Vogl, Office of the Quartermaster General, February 13, 1952.

451 Mary Sayre (Dawson) interviews, March 17, 2006; April 29, 2009.

452 Ralph Haines interview, September 8, 2009.

453 Sally Brownlee, letter to Dorothy Vogel, July 18, 1943.

454 Mary Sayre (Dawson) interview, April 24, 2009.

455 VPB-117, Aircraft Action Report #207, NARA.

456 Sally Brownlee, letter to Dort, June 20, 1945.

457 Stan Sayre, letter to Mary Sayre, June 21, 1945.

458 See chapter "The Vacant Air."

459 John Iler interview, April 30, 2009.

460 John Iler, "Ha Tien Raid of 1945" (written account given to author in 2005); John Iler interview, August 17, 2005.

461 Roger Crowley, letter, July 7, 1945.

462 "Map of Philippine Islands with Sounding in Fathoms," from the image archives of the Historical Map & Chart Collection, Office of Coast Survey, National Ocean Services, NOAA, 1948.

463 Roger Crowley, letter, July 7, 1945.

464 VPB-117, Aircraft Action Report #215, NARA.

465 John Iler interview, April 30, 2009.

466 Mary Sayre (Dawson) interview, March 17, 2006.

467 Mary Sayre (Dawson), letter to Dorothy Brownlee, June 30, 1945.

468 "Memorial Services Held Monday for Ensign M. Brownlee," *Arcadia*, July 5, 1945.

469 Jim Brownlee interview, September 16, 2009.

470 Mary Sayre (Dawson) interview, April 27, 2009.

471 Jim Brownlee interview, September 16, 2009.

472 Ed Sayre interview, April 11, 2009.

473 Jim Brownlee interview, September 16, 2009.

474 Ed Sayre interview, April 11, 2009.

475 Mary Sayre (Dawson) interview, April 27, 2009.

476 Jim Brownlee interview, September 16, 2009.

477 Unless otherwise noted, information from this chapter came from two extended interviews with Joe Lowder, conducted by the author on February 28 and March 7, 2006; from emails and telephone interviews with his son Kevin Lowder; from an aircraft action report dated September 8, 1945; from a statement by Rudolf Stark and Joe Lowder dated September 10, 1945; and from a written account by Joe Lowder, parts of which were included in Alan C. Carey, *Above an Angry Sea: United States Navy B-24 Liberator and PB4Y-2 Privateer Operations in the Pacific: October 1944–August 1945* (Atglen, PA: Schiffer Publishing, 2001).

478 "1935 Auburn 851 SC Boattail Speedster," Mecum Auctions, https://www.mecum .com/lots/CA0816-259993/1935-auburn-851-sc-boattail-speedster.

479 VPB-117, Casualty Report, July 18, 1945.

480 Alice Dursang (Pete Hourcade's sister) interviews, March 5, 2008, and March 14, 2009.

481 Royce Timmons interview, June 9, 2006.

482 William Hagenah interview, January 30, 2003.

483 Sheldon Sutton interview, August 12, 2006.

484 Robert Forkner interview, December 8, 2004.

485 Edward F. Kittrell, *Logbook.*

486 John Bullock, email, June 5, 2007.

487 Art Elder interview, November 19, 2010.

488 Roger Crowley, Kittrell fitness report, May 15, 1945.

489 Catherine Harrison Kittrell, last will and testament, October 24, 1948.

490 Death certificate, Catherine M. Kittrell, August 26, 1949.

491 Joan McCuster letter, January 28, 2006.

492 *The Blue Raiders: VPB 117, United States Navy, 1944–1945* (N.p.: N.p., 1983).

493 Robert Faxon obituaries, unknown newspaper and *Milton Record-Transcript*, June 12, 1978.

494 Robert Faxon, letter to wife, June 19, 1945.

495 Robert Faxon, letter to wife, July 30, 1945.

496 Will Stout interview, January 5, 2005.

497 "Appendix A: Personnel Losses Including Killed in the Line of Duty," in Alan C. Carey, *Above an Angry Sea: United States Navy B-24 Liberator and PB4Y-2 Privateer Operations in the Pacific: October 1944–August 1945* (Atglen, PA: Schiffer Publishing, 2001), 137.

498 Rebecca Knowles interview, November 25, 2009.

499 Robert Faxon obituary, *Patriot-Ledger*, June 12, 1978.

500 Joe Papp interview, September 30, 2009.

501 Bob Vairo interview, December 4, 2010.

502 Dan Karjela interview, December 9, 2010.

503 Bob Vairo interview, December 4, 2010.

504 Don Golden interview, November 18, 2005.

505 *The Blue Raiders*; O'Neill Osborne interview, June 17, 2005.

506 Don Golden interview, November 21, 2005.

507 *The Blue Raiders.*

508 Don Golden interviews, November 18, 20, and 21, 2005.

509 Don Golden obituary, *Arizona Republic*, May 8, 2012.

510 "VPB-43," Wikipedia, https://en.wikipedia.org/wiki/VPB-43.
511 "Bradford M. Brooks," American Battle Monuments Commission, https://www .abmc.gov/node/497874; *The Blue Raiders.*
512 Harold Boss, "Making Aviation Legend," in *The Blue Raiders.*
513 John Bullock, email, June 5, 2007.
514 VPB-117, Aircraft Action Report #28, NARA.
515 Jack Sager's account, "December 10, 1944," in his logbook dated December 28, 1944.
516 *The Blue Raiders.*
517 Jack Sager account, "December 10, 1944."
518 Bradford Brooks, Navy Cross Citation.
519 Bud Buchheim, email, January 11, 2017.
520 Bud Buchheim, email, October 5, 2004.
521 Bud Buchheim, email, February 19, 2009.
522 Gene Kern, email, January 24, 2009.
523 Rod Donnelly interview, May 12, 2005.
524 Parker Trial Transcript, 127–28.
525 Dean Maughn interview, September 22, 2004.
526 Beth L. Bailey and David Farber, *The First Strange Place: Race and Sex in World War II Hawaii* (Baltimore: Johns Hopkins University Press, 1992), 96–106.
527 Bill Allsopp interview, July 27, 2005.
528 O'Neill Osborne interview, January 10, 2005.
529 John Iler interview, April 22, 2009.
530 Bill Allsopp interview, July 27, 2005.
531 VPB-117, Aircraft Action Report #96, NARA.
532 John Bourchier (nephew of John Bourchier) interview, August 29, 2005.
533 Marshall Beals interview, October 3, 2003.
534 Marshall Beals interview, January 16, 2008.
535 Marshall Beals obituary, *Quad City Times,* September 23, 2015.
536 Emelyn Castleton interview, October 10, 2007.
537 Gilbert Ragland, account published on lubbockonline.com, January 2, 2002.
538 Gilbert Ragland interview, January 6, 2005.
539 Ralph Castleton obituary, *Orange County Register,* December 4, 2007.
540 Gilbert Ragland interview, January 6, 2005.
541 Gilbert Ragland obituary, *Lubbock Avalanche-Journal,* March 2, 2012.
542 Gilbert Ragland, letter to Jamie, April 4, 1995.
543 Buddy Parker, *The Jack Parker Story* (unpublished manuscript), 19.
544 Jack Parker testimony, Japanese War Tribunal, February 14, 1945.
545 John Bertrang, letter to Robert White family in Parker, *The Jack Parker Story.*
546 "Kenpeitai," Wikipedia, https://en.wikipedia.org/wiki/Kenpeitai.
547 Copy of war tribunal, "Before a Military Commission Convened by the Commanding General United States Army Forces China August 10, 1946."
548 Parker, *The Jack Parker Story.*
549 John Bertrang, letter to Parker's parents, December 5, 1945, in Parker, *The Jack Parker Story.*

550 Parker, *The Jack Parker Story*.

551 Report of U.S. Military Commission, August 10, 1946.

552 Parker, *The Jack Parker Story*.

553 Terri Bertrang, interview, October 17, 2018.

554 *Taiwan News*, June 20, 2005.

555 "The Memorial of the Mind," *New York Times*, May 25, 2009.

556 Emmy Swink interview, March 3, 2017.

557 Galen Bull obituary, *Monterey Herald*, November 1, 2009.

558 Galen Bull interview, October 17, 2008.

559 Ivalee Bull obituary, *Monterey Herald*, February 18, 2006.

560 Galen Bull interview, October 17, 2008.

561 Eric Bull, email, February 23, 2017.

562 *Rigsbee USN Service Biography*.

563 *Saga of the USS Orca, AVP 49* (typewritten manuscript, 1945).

564 *Rigsbee USN Service Biography*.

565 *Standard Times News Service*, February 14, 1946.

566 Navy Department Press Release, April 17, 1947; Atlantic Video Archive, #060290, Transfer Date, April 7, 2006.

567 "USS Antietam (CV-36)," Wikipedia, https://en.wikipedia.org/wiki/USS_Antietam _(CV-36).

568 *Corpus Christi Caller*, May 14, 1949.

569 Lawrence Suid, *Sailing on the Silver Screen: Hollywood and the US Navy* (Annapolis, MD: Naval Institute Press, 1996), 86.

570 E. O. Rigsbee III interview, March 18, 2006.

571 E. O. Rigsbee, letter, unfinished and unmailed, March 6, 1949.

572 "USS Antietam," NavSource Online, www.navsource.org/archives/02/36co.htm.

573 Helen Rigsbee, letter to E. O. Rigsbee's brother Hub, March 6, 1949.

574 Henry B. Vogler, "My Experience Aboard the USS Antietam," in *History of the USS Antietam (CV/CVA/CVS-36)* (Nashville, TN: Turner Publishing Company, 2001), 31–32.

575 United Press, May 13, 1949.

576 Associated Press, May 12, 1949.

577 E. O. Rigsbee III, interviews, March 18, 2006; April 6, 2007; March 15, 2019.

578 *San Angelo Standard Times*, June 2, 1949.

579 Bill Allsopp obituary, *Seattle Times*, January 8, 2008.

580 Bill Allsopp interview, July 27, 2005.

581 VPB-117, Aircraft Action Reports #110, 111, 114, 135, 136, 150, NARA.

582 Gerri Allsopp interview, June 26, 2019.

583 Bill Allsopp obituary, *Seattle Times*, January 8, 2008.

584 Bill Allsopp interview, July 27, 2005.

585 *Seattle Times*, October 20, 1959.

586 Gerri Allsopp interview, June 26, 2019.

587 *History of Group One, Fleet Air Wing 17*, Official U.S. Navy Records, National Archives and Records Administration, 4.

588 Dan Moore, email, July 24, 2006.

589 "Ijn Hyuga: Tabular Record of Movement," Imperial Japanese Navy Page, http://www.combinedfleet.com/hyuga.htm; "Ise-Class Battleship," Wikipedia, https://en.wikipedia.org/wiki/Ise-class_battleship; Dan Moore, email, July 24, 2006.

590 Harold (Woody) McDonald interviews, April 14, 2007; September 20, 2018.

591 *Annapolis Capital*, November 26, 1995, https://annapolis.newspaperarchive.com/annapolis-capital/1995-11-26/page-44.

592 Written opinion of T. L. Glatch, Judge Advocate General of the Navy, November 18, 1945; letter to Senator Warren Magnuson, Rear Admiral G. L. Russell, Acting Judge Advocate General of the Navy, January 8, 1946.

593 Marilyn Parker interview, December 7, 2004.

594 "Thomas P Mulvihill, Jr," Find a Grave, https://www.findagrave.com/memorial/73265964/thomas-p-mulvihill.

595 LaVelle Saier interview, October 29, 2006.

596 Tom Hyland, letter to LaVelle Saier, September 28, 1992.

597 Sheldon Sutton, letter to LaVelle Saier, undated.

598 Art Elder interview, October 13, 2010.

599 James Edwards interview, January 7, 2005.

600 Marilyn Parker interviews, October 6, 2006; March 11, 2017.

601 Alan C. Carey, *Above an Angry Sea: United States Navy B-24 Liberator and PB4Y-2 Privateer Operations in the Pacific: October 1944–August 1945* (Atglen, PA: Schiffer Publishing, 2001), 40.

602 Charles Kickham obituary, *Boston Globe*, January 8, 2004.

603 *Topeka Capital Journal*, February 18, 2003.

604 Jan Carter obituary, *Arkansas Democrat Gazette*, April 28, 1998.

605 Sheldon and Nina Sutton interview, March 20, 2017.

606 Emmy Swink interview, March 3, 2017.

607 "VP-117 Reunions," U.S. Navy Patrol Squadrons, www.vpnavy.com/vp117_reunion.html.

608 Art Elder interview, November 19, 2010.

609 *LaJolla Light*, June 15, 2011.

610 Karen Pizarro interview, May 5, 2006.

611 Tom Hyland obituary, *Rocky Mountain News*, December 27, 2003.

612 Tom Hyland obituary, *Denver Post*, December 28, 2003.

613 Art Elder interview, November 19, 2010.

614 Max Pizzaro eulogy (copy given by family to the author).

615 David deMarrais interview, August 12, 2015.

616 Johnie Webb interview, February 10, 2016.

617 Joe Lowder obituary, *St. Louis Post-Dispatch*, November 30, 2006.

618 Gene Kern, *Logbook*.

619 "Gene Kern's Three Plus Years in the Navy," written account given to the author, 2006.

620 "Gene's Story from 1945 to 2013," written account given to the author, January 2, 2013.

621 Rosie Kern interview, February 23, 2017.

622 Hilda Moore, letter to Folsom and Ola Moore, August 15, 1945.

623 Folsom Moore, letter, August 19, 1945.

624 Hilda Moore, letter, October 29, 1945.

625 Dan Moore, letter, September 2, 1945.

626 Proceedings of the Naval Retirement Board, September 18, 1945.

627 St. Elizabeth's Hospital, letter to Folsom Moore, October 6, 1945.

628 "In Re Moore," Leagle.com, https://www.leagle.com/decision/infco20160727063.

629 Dan Moore's children (Jane Callahan-Moore, Marguerite Moore Callaway, and Dan Moore Jr.) interviews, July 29, 2016; March 16, 2017.

630 Dan Moore interview, December 2, 2005.

631 Rosie Kern interview, February 23, 2017.

632 Dan Moore Jr., email, January 1, 2011.

633 William Maxwell, *The Outermost Dream: Literary Sketches* (Saint Paul, MN: Graywolf Press, 1997), 149.

634 American Battle Monuments Commission, emails, April 11, 2007; October 27, 2009.

635 VPB-117, Report of Killed and Wounded, April 26, 1945.

636 VPB-117, Report of Killed and Wounded, December 13, 1944; interview, Pauline Crofford, October 2, 2009; Gilbert Ragland, letter to Jamie, April 4, 2005.

637 Pat Benn interviews, January 5 and 12, 2006; February 4, 2006.

638 Richard Stang interview, February 4, 2006; Harold Stang Jr., email, March 27, 2006.

639 Pat Benn interview, January 12, 2006.

640 John Bullock interview, May 14, 2007.

641 June White interview, April 30, 2006.

642 VPB-117, Casualty Report, February 9, 1945.

643 John Bullock interview, August 3, 2007.

644 Harold Stang Jr., email, March 27, 2006.

645 Jeff Whitesell (B-24 pilot) interview, July 20, 2007.

646 Harold Stang Jr., email, March 27, 2006.

647 Pat Benn interview, July 16, 2008.

648 *Minneapolis Journal*, May 1, 1935.

649 Undated news clipping from Minneapolis newspaper, fall 1944.

650 Washburn High School newspaper, January 18, 1945.

651 *Chicago Tribune*, May 8, 1945.

652 Bill Benn, letter to Patricia Benn, December 30, 1942.

653 Bill Benn, letter to Aunt Lois, August 31, 1944.

654 Bill Benn, letter to Mother, December 6, 1944.

655 Handwritten copy of telegram sent to Bill Benn's parents, January 10, 1945.

656 June White, letter to Bill's Aunt Lois, undated, early January 1945.

657 Bill Benn, letter to June, December 24, 1944.

Bibliography

ARCHIVES CONSULTED
National Archives and Records Administration, College Park, Maryland.
Naval History and Heritage Command, Washington Naval Yard, Washington, DC.
Emil Buehler Library, National Aviation Museum, Naval Air Station, Pensacola, Florida.

INTERVIEWS BY AUTHOR (PERSONAL AND TELEPHONE)
Allsopp, Bill. July 27, 2005.
Allsopp, Gerri. June 26, 2019.
Beals, Marshall. October 3, 2003; January 16, 2008.
Benn, Pat. January 5, 2006; January 8, 2006; January 12, 2006; January 22, 2006; February 4, 2006; July 16, 2008.
Bertrang, Terri. October 17, 2018.
Boss, Mrs. Dorothy. January 5, 2005.
Bourchier, John (nephew of John Bourchier). August 29, 2005.
Box, Kenneth. January 14, 2008; July 14, 2008; July 12, 2010.
Brewer, Laurel. September 20, 2006.
Brownlee, Jim. September 16, 2009.
Buchheim, Bud. August 17, 2015.
Bull, Galen. October 11, 2007; October 16, 2007; October 17, 2008.
Bullock, John. March 20, 2007; May 14, 2007; August 3, 2007.
Carter, Alan. January 5, 2006.
Castleton, Emelyn. October 10, 2007.
Cox, George. November 5, 2005.
Crofford, Pauline. October 2, 2009.
deMarrais, David. August 12, 2015.
Donnelly, Rod. May 12, 2005.
Dursang, Alice (Pete Hourcade's sister). March 5, 2008; March 14, 2009.
Edwards, James. January 7, 2005; March 17, 2009.
Elder, Art. October 13, 2010; November 2, 2006; November 19, 2006; November 19, 2010.
Forkner, Robert. December 8, 2004.
Geneva, Brett (Fort Scott National Cemetery). August 18, 2008; August 20, 2008.
Golden, Don. November 18, 2005; November 20, 2005; November 21, 2005.
Gray, James. September 15, 2006.
Hagenah, William. January 30, 2003.

Haines, Ralph. September 8, 2009.

Iler, John. August 17, 2005; April 22, 2009; April 30, 2009.

Karjela, Dan. December 9, 2010.

Kern, Gene. November 7, 2007; November 9, 2007.

Kern, Rosie. February 23, 2017.

Knowles, Rebecca. November 25, 2009.

Lowder, Joe. February 28, 2006; March 7, 2006.

Maguire, Patricia Renner. April 7, 2009; May 8, 2009.

Massey, Mrs. Robert. January 12, 2005; February 12, 2008.

Maughn, Dean. September 22, 2004.

McDonald, Harold (Woody). April 14, 2007; September 20, 2018.

Minnock, Ken. January 18, 2006.

Moore, Dan. December 2, 2005; December 3, 2005; January 5, 2006; August 20, 2006; May 31, 2007.

Moore, Dan (Children: Jane Callahan-Moore, Marguerite Moore Callaway, Dan Moore Jr.). July 29, 2016; March 16, 2017.

Nagel, Ken. December 2, 2005; March 30, 2006.

Osborne, O'Neill. January 10, 2005; June 17, 2005; September 20, 2006.

O'Shaughnessy, Richard. January 7, 2005.

Palmer, David. October 2003.

Papp, Joe. January 14, 2006; September 30, 2009; November 4, 2009.

Parker, Marilyn. December 7, 2004; October 6, 2006; February 28, 2009; March 11, 2017.

Pistotnik, Joe. January 10, 2005.

Pizarro, Karen. March 5, 2006; May 5, 2006.

Quinn, Bill. October 2003.

Quinn, Kathleen. September 5, 2011.

Ragland, Gilbert. January 6, 2005.

Rigsbee, E. O., III. March 18, 2006; April 6, 2007; March 15, 2019.

Saier, LaVelle. October 29, 2006.

Sanders, Ralph. December 29, 2003.

Sayre, Ed. April 11, 2009.

Sayre (Dawson), Mary. March 17, 2006; April 24, 2009; April 27, 2009; April 29, 2009.

Stang, Richard. February 4, 2006.

Stout, Will. January 5, 2005.

Summers, John. January 11, 2005.

Sutton, Nina. March 20, 2017.

Sutton, Sheldon. August 12, 2006; March 20, 2017.

Swink, Emmy. March 3, 2017.

Thompson, Nancy. April 6, 2008; December 12, 2008; June 26, 2019.

Timmons, Royce. June 9, 2006.

Vairo, Bob. December 4, 2010.

Webb, Johnie. February 10, 2016.

Wegner, Gerald. December 7, 2004.

White, June. January 19, 2006; April 19, 2006; April 26, 2006; April 30, 2006.

Whitesell, Jeff (B-24 pilot). July 20, 2007.

BOOKS AND ARTICLES

Ambrose, Stephen E. *The Wild Blue: The Men and Boys Who Flew the B-24s over Germany.* New York: Simon & Schuster, 2007.

"America in WW2—December 2007—World War II." HistoryNet. June 22, 2016. www .historynet.com/table-of-contents-december-2007-world-war-ii.htm.

"Annual Register of the United States Naval Academy. Annapolis, Md." Internet Archive. 1930. https://archive.org/details/annualregiste19291930unse.

Atkinson, Kate. *A God in Ruins.* New York: Little, Brown, 2015.

Bacon, Lloyd, dir. *Wings of the Navy.* Burbank, CA: Warner Bros., 1939.

Bailey, Beth L., and David Farber. *The First Strange Place: Race and Sex in World War II Hawaii.* Baltimore: Johns Hopkins University Press, 1992.

Ballard, Robert D., and Michael Hamilton Morgan. *Graveyards of the Pacific: From Pearl Harbor to Bikini Island.* Washington, DC: National Geographic, 2001.

Barry, Sebastian. *A Long Long Way.* Rpt. ed. New York: Penguin Books, 2005.

Bergerud, Eric M. *Fire in the Sky: The Air War in the South Pacific.* Boulder, CO: Westview Press, 2000.

Birdsall, Steve. *Log of the Liberators: An Illustrated History of the B-24.* New York: Doubleday, 1973.

The Blue Raiders: VPB 117, United States Navy, 1944–1945. N.p.: N.p., 1983.

Boss, Harold. *Blue Monsters* (included in *The Blue Raiders*).

Bradley, James. *Flyboys: A True Story of Courage.* Boston: Little, Brown, 2003.

Carey, Alan C. *Above an Angry Sea: United States Navy B-24 Liberator and PB4Y-2 Privateer Operations in the Pacific: October 1944–August 1945.* Atglen, PA: Schiffer Publishing, 2001.

———. *We Flew Alone: United States Navy B-24 Squadrons in the Pacific, February 1943– September 1944.* Atglen, PA: Schiffer Publishing, 2000.

Case of Isaac G. Parker, Ensign, U.S. Naval Reserve. May 17, 1945. Record of Proceedings of a General Court-Martial Convened at the U.S. Acorn Nineteen, Navy 3100 by the Order of Commander Aircraft, Seventh Fleet.

Costello, John. *The Pacific War, 1941–1945.* New York: Perennial, 2002.

"Current News Releases." *Current News Releases—U.S. Naval Research Laboratory.* Navy News Release, 05-05-1947: Navy Patrol Bombing Squadron 117 Awarded Presidential Unit Citation.

Degan, Patrick. *Flattop Fighting in World War II: The Battles between American and Japanese Aircraft Carriers.* Jefferson, NC: McFarland, 2003.

Delaney, Norman C. "Corpus Christi's 'University of the Air.'" *Naval History Magazine* 27, no. 3 (May 2013). https://www.usni.org/magazines/naval-history-magazine/ 2013/may/corpus-christis-university-air.

Donnelly, Rod. *A Brief History of WWII.* Memoir given to author.

Eichenberg, Alan. *Logbook.*

Elliott, Edgar. *My Story, WWII: The Big One, My Part in the Navy, December 1941– December 1945* (unpublished manuscript).

Fitts, Orvis N. *A Naval Aviator's Story World War II*. Overland Park, KS: Fowler Printing and Publishing, 1998.

Forbes, Gordon. *Goodbye to Some: A Novel*. Annapolis, MD: Naval Institute Press, 1997.

Furey, Charles. *Going Back: A Navy Airman in the Pacific War*. Annapolis, MD: Naval Institute Press, 1997.

Fussell, Paul. *The Norton Book of Modern War*. New York: W. W. Norton, 1991.

———. *Wartime: Understanding and Behavior in the Second World War*. New York: Oxford University Press, 1990.

Gallicchio, Marc S. *The Unpredictability of the Past: Memories of the Asia-Pacific War in U.S.-East Asian Relations*. Durham, NC: Duke University Press, 2007.

Goulding, Edmund, dir. *The Dawn Patrol*. Burbank, CA: Warner Bros., 1938.

Grossnick, Roy A. *Dictionary of American Naval Aviation Squadrons*. Vol. 2. Washington, DC: Naval Historical Center, Department of the Navy, 1995.

———. *United States Naval Aviation, 1910–1995*. Washington, DC: Naval Historical Center, Department of the Navy, 1997.

Hagen, Jerome T. *War in the Pacific*. Vol. 1. Honolulu: Hawaii Pacific University, 1996.

———. *War in the Pacific*. Vol. 2. Honolulu: Hawaii Pacific University, 2002.

Hare, Benjamin. *Football at Military Training Centers during World War II*. Naperville, IL: North Central College, 2006.

Heavilin, J. S., ed. *The Lucky Bag of Nineteen Hundred and Twenty Seven: The Annual of the Regiment of Midshipmen*. Annapolis, MD: United States Naval Academy, the Class of 1927, 1927.

Helprin, Mark. *A Soldier of the Great War*. New York: Harcourt, 2005.

Hersey, John. *Of Men and War*. New York: Scholastic Book Services, 1963.

Hornfischer, James D. *The Last Stand of the Tin Can Sailors*. New York: Bantam Books, 2004.

Hoyt, Edwin Palmer. *How They Won the War in the Pacific: Nimitz and His Admirals*. Guilford, CT: Lyons Press, 2012.

Hylton, Wil S. *Vanished: The Sixty-Year Search for the Missing Men of World War II*. New York: Riverhead Books, 2014.

Hynes, Samuel Lynn. *The Soldiers' Tale: Bearing Witness to Modern War*. New York: Penguin Books, 1998.

Hynes, Samuel. *Flights of Passage: Recollections of a World War II Aviator*. New York: Penguin Books, 1988.

Jones, James. *The Thin Red Line*. New York: Delta Trade Paperbacks, 1998.

———. *WWII: A Chronicle of Soldiering*. Chicago: University of Chicago Press, 2014.

Keegan, John, ed. *Atlas of the Second World War*. Ann Arbor, MI: Borders Press, 2003.

Kern, Gene. *Logbook*.

Kittrell, Edward F. *Logbook*.

Kohn, Leo J. *Flight Manual for B-24 Liberator*. Appleton, WI: Aviation Publications, 1977.

Luce, Henry Robinson. *The Ideas of Henry Luce*. Edited by John Knox Jessup. New York: Atheneum, 1969.

Maclean, Norman. *A River Runs through It, and Other Stories*. 25th anniv. ed. Chicago: University of Chicago Press, 1976.

Manchester, William. *Goodbye, Darkness: A Memoir of the Pacific War*. Boston: Back Bay Books, 2002.

Marin, Richard. *War of Our Fathers: Relics of the Pacific Battlefields*. Edison, NJ: Chartwell Books, 2001.

Maxwell, William. *The Outermost Dream: Literary Sketches*. Saint Paul, MN: Graywolf Press, 1997.

Michener, James Albert. *Tales of South Pacific*. New York: Random House, 1974.

Miller, David. *The Great Book of World War II: The Complete Story of the Weapons, the Battles, and the Fighting Men*. San Diego, CA: Thunder Bay Press, 2003.

Miller, Norman Mickey, and Hugh B. Cave. *I Took the Sky Road*. Gillette, NJ: Wildside Press, 2001.

Morison, Samuel Eliot. *History of the United States Naval Operations in World War II*. Vol. 8: *New Guinea and the Marianas, March 1944–August 1944*. Urbana: University of Illinois Press, 2002.

———. *History of the United States Naval Operations in World War II*. Vol. 12: *Leyte, June 1944–January 1945*. Urbana: University of Illinois Press, 2002.

———. *History of the United States Naval Operations in World War II*. Vol. 14: *Victory in the Pacific, 1945*. Urbana: University of Illinois Press, 2002.

"Naval Academy to Graduate 400." *New York Times*. May 30, 1930.

"Navy Patrol Bombing Squadron 117 Awarded Presidential Unit Citation." *Navy News Release*. May 5, 1947.

Ninety-Nines. "Our History." www.ninety-nines.org/our-history.htm.

O'Leary, Michael. *Consolidated B-24 Liberator*. Botley, UK: Osprey Publishing, 2002.

Parker, Buddy. *The Jack Parker Story* (unpublished manuscript).

"Pownall, Charles Alan (1887–1975)." *The Pacific War Online Encyclopedia*. http://pwencycl.kgbudge.com/P/o/Pownall_Charles_A.htm.

Rea, Robert Right, and Wesley Phillips Newton. *Wings of Gold: An Account of Naval Aviation Training in World War II*. Tuscaloosa: University of Alabama Press, 1987.

Reisinger, Col. R. C. "The Naval Aviator in Reserve." *U.S. Naval Institute Proceedings* 60, no. 375 (May 1934). www.usni.org/magazines/proceedings/1934-05.

Reynolds, Clark G. *On the Warpath in the Pacific: Admiral Jocko Clark and the Fast Carriers*. Annapolis, MD: Naval Institute Press, 2013.

Rigsbee, Edward "Ned" Clarence. *The Rigsbee Story*. 1934.

Rigsbee USN Service Biography, courtesy of E. O. Rigsbee III.

Salter, James. *Burning the Days*. New York: Vintage International, 1988.

———. *Gods of Tin: The Flying Years*. Edited by Jessica Benton and William Benton. Washington, DC: Shoemaker & Hoard, 2004.

———. *Hunters*. Washington, DC: Counterpoint, 1997.

Scearce, Phil. *Finish Forty and Home: The Untold World War II Story of B-24s in the Pacific*. Denton: University of North Texas Press, 2011.

Scharf, Thomas L., ed. *Journal of San Diego History* 31, no. 2 (spring 1985). https://sandiegohistory.org/journal/1985/april/index-htm-105.

Shettle, Mel L. *United States Naval Air Stations of World War II*. Bowersville, GA: Schaertel, 1997.

Sledge, E. B. *With the Old Breed at Peleliu and Okinawa*. New York: Presidio Press, 2007.

Smith, Douglas V. *One Hundred Years of U.S. Navy Air Power*. Annapolis, MD: Naval Institute Press, 2010.

Spencer, James. *The Pilots*. New York: G. P. Putnam's Sons, 2003.

Stevens, Paul F. *Low Level Liberators: The Story of Patrol Bombing Squadron 104 in the South Pacific during World War II*. Nashville: P. F. Stevens, 1997.

Stretch, David A., ed. *The Lucky Bag of Nineteen Hundred and Thirty: The Annual of the Regiment of Midshipmen*. Annapolis, MD: U.S. Naval Academy, Class of 1930, 1930.

Suid, Lawrence H. *Sailing on the Silver Screen: Hollywood and the US Navy*. Annapolis, MD: Naval Institute Press, 1996.

Swift, Daniel. *Bomber County: The Poetry of a Lost Pilot's War*. New York: Farrar, Straus & Giroux, 2010.

"Taylorcraft Auster Aircraft History Performance and Specifications." Pilotfriend. www .pilotfriend.com/aircraft%20performance/Taylorcraft.htm.

Terkel, Studs. *The Good War: An American Oral History of World War II*. New York: New Press, 1984.

U.S. Navy Report of the Search for Amelia Earhart, July 2–18, 1937. College Park, MD: National Archives.

U.S. Office of the Chief of Naval Operations and U.S. Army Air Forces. *Aircrewman's Gunnery Manual; Issued by Aviation Training Division, Office of the Chief of Naval Operations, U.S. Navy, in Collaboration with U.S. Army Air Forces*. Washington, DC: Aviation Training Division, 1944.

"United States Army Air Forces in the Central Pacific Area." Wikipedia. https://en.wiki-pedia.org/wiki/United_States_Army_Air_Forces_in_the_Central_Pacific_Area.

United States Naval Aviation, 1910–1980. 3rd ed. Washington, DC: Department of the Navy, 1981.

Vogler, Henry B. "My Experience Aboard the USS Antietam." In *History of the USS Antietam (CV/CVA/CVS-36)*. Nashville, TN: Turner Publishing Company, 2001.

Wakeman, Frederic. *Shore Leave*. New York: Farrar & Rinehart, 1944.

Ward, Geoffrey C., and Ken Burns. *The War: An Intimate History, 1941–1945*. New York: Alfred A. Knopf, 2007.

Wellman Centennial, 1879–1979. 1st ed. Wellman, IA: Centennial Committee, 1979.

Wharton, William. *Birdy*. New York: Vintage, 1992.

———. *A Midnight Clear*. New York: Alfred A. Knopf, 1982.

———. *Shrapnel: A Memoir*. New York: William Morrow, 2013.

Willis, Clint. *The War: Stories of Life and Death from World War II*. New York: Thunder's Mouth Press/Balliett & Fitzgerald, 1999.

Willis, Ron L., and Thomas Carmichael. *United States Navy Wings of Gold: From 1917 to the Present*. Atglen, PA: Schiffer Publishing, 1995.

Zamperini, Louis, and David Rensin. *Devil at My Heels: A Heroic Olympian's Astonishing Story of Survival as a Japanese POW*. New York: Harper Paperbacks, 2004.

Zebrowski, Carl. *America in WWII Magazine*. December 2007. http://www.americain wwii.com/back-issues/december-2007.

Acknowledgments

First and foremost, thanks to the men of VPB-117, their families, and their friends, who shared so much. Their recollections and insights, suggestions and photos, newspaper clippings and family albums, and, above all, their stories brought that time and place to life for me in ways I never could have imagined. Thanks to the organizations, institutions, and experts that helped me find and understand the facts of what happened and the context of the larger world in which those facts unfolded.

Thanks to friends and colleagues who bucked me up and urged me on. And above all, thanks to my family. They believed in me and in the book, even when I thought it could never be.

Index

About the Author

Ed Kittrell has been a working writer—first as a newspaper reporter in Chicago and then as an independent writer focusing mainly on speeches. With his two oldest sons, he compiled and published *Down Time: Great Writers on Diving*. With his youngest son, who was writing a college paper on VPB-117, he attended his first squadron reunion in 2003, which eventually led to this book.